A GOWER ANTHOLOGY

A GOWER ANTHOLOGY

Edited by David Rees

Christopher Davies
Swansea

First impression 1977
Second impression 1978

Published by
Christopher Davies (Publishers) Ltd
52 Mansel Street
Swansea SA1 1EL

*Printed in Wales by
Salesbury Press Ltd
Swansea*

ISBN 0 7154 0407 5

TO J. MANSEL THOMAS

ACKNOWLEDGEMENTS

Grateful acknowledgements are tendered to the following authors, owners of copyright, editors, and publishers who have given permission for passages to appear in this anthology.

G. Bell & Sons Ltd. for John Leland's 'Gowerland' from *The Itinerary Through Wales, c. 1536-39,* edited by L. T. Smith.

Mr. George Beynon, West Pilton, for three items, 'August Storms, 1850,' 'Mary Stenhouse, 1879,' and 'Helvetia, 1887' from *An Eye-Witness Account of Shipwrecks on the Gower Coast* by John Beynon.

A. & C. Black Ltd. for a passage on Loughor River from *Beautiful Wales* by Edward Thomas.

Mr. Leonard Clark, Literary Executor of the Andrew Young estate, for 'The Red Lady of Paviland' from *The New Poly-Olbion* by Andrew Young, published by Rupert Hart-Davis, Ltd.

Constable & Co. Ltd. for passages on Gower from *In the March and Borderland of Wales* by A. G. Bradley.

The General Committee of the Cambrian Archaeological Association for cited items from *Archaeologia Cambrensis* by G. T. Clark, George Grant Francis, E. A. Freeman, Sir Stephen R. Glynne, Sir John Lubbock (Lord Avebury), Thomas Phaer, and Clarence A. Seyler; for items from *The Lordship of Gower in the Marches of Wales* (cited as *Surveys of Gower*), edited by G. G. Francis and Charles Baker, 1861-1870 (*Arch. Camb.* supplement); and for four short items from R. H. Morris (ed.), *Parochialia* (the Gower notes in the manuscript source of this publication, NLW MS Peniarth 120, originally believed to have been written for Edward Lhuyd in the 1690s, were actually compiled by Rice Merrick, c. 1584).

Mrs. Kathleen Latimer Davies for five passages on 'Pwll-y-bloggi,' '600 Able Men,' 'Ilston Church,' 'Trinity Well Chapel,' and 'St. David's Hospital, Swansea,' all from *Pennard and West Gower* by The Rev. Latimer Davies.

Dr. Margaret Davies, Professor G. E. Mingay, and the British Agricultural History Society for extracts from 'Rhosili Open Field and Related South Wales Patterns' by Dr. Margaret Davies which appeared in *The Agricultural History Review*, Vol. IV, 1956, Part 2.

J. M. Dent & Sons Ltd., and the Trustees for the Copyrights of the late Dylan Thomas for a passage from *The Selected Letters of Dylan Thomas*, edited by Constantine FitzGibbon. Acknowledgements also to the The Poetry Collection of the Lockwood Memorial Library, State University of New York at Buffalo.

J. M. Dent & Sons Ltd. for a passage from *The Itinerary Through Wales*, by Giraldus Cambrensis (Everyman's Edition, 1908).

Mr. F. V. Emery and the Longman Group Ltd. for a passage on Gower open fields from *The World's Landscapes: Wales*. Mr. F. V. Emery and the Cambridge University Press for a passage on Gower land tenures from 'The Farming Regions of Wales,' Chapter 2, in *The Agrarian History of England and Wales, Vol. IV, 1500-1640*, edited by Joan Thirsk.

Mr. F. V. Emery, the Honourable Society of Cymmrodorion and the Bodleian Library, Oxford, for two items from 'Edward Lhuyd and some of his Glamorgan Correspondents: A View of Gower in the 1690s,' in *Transactions of the Honourable Society of Cymmrodorion*, Session 1965, Part I. These items are 1) A Letter from John Williams to Edward Lhuyd on p. 64 above; 2) a quotation from Isaac Hamon's *Description of Gower*, on p. 92.

A passage from the poem 'The Sleeping Lord' by David Jones is reprinted by permission of Faber & Faber Ltd. from the volume of the same title.

Mr. F. R. Fletcher for three passages from *Kilvert's Diary*, edited by William Plomer, and published by Jonathan Cape Ltd.

Mr. Michael Gibbs and the Editorial Committee of the Gower Society for 'The Church at Knelston' which appeared in *Gower XXI*.

Professor Gordon T. Goodman and the Editorial Committee of the Gower Society for two passages from *Plant Life in Gower*, published by the Gower Society.

The Editorial Committee of the Gower Society for an article on Gower's Own Plant, Draba Aizoides Montana, by J. A. Webb, which appeared in *Gower III*.

The Editorial Committee of the Gower Society for extracts from 'Map Making in Gower' (*Gower XXI*), and for the essays on Thomas Penrice of Kilvrough (*Gower XXIII*) and Park-le-Breos (*Gower XXV*) by David Rees.

Mr. Cyril Gwynn for his poem, 'At Penrice Castle Shoot' from *Gower Yarns*.

Robert Hale & Co. Ltd. for a short item on 'Underhill' from *Gower* by Olive Phillips.

Mr. Michael Hamburger for his poem, 'Oxwich.'

The Council of The Honourable Society of Cymmrodorion and Mr. G. M. Griffiths for 'Sir Mathew Cradock' from *The Dictionary of Welsh Biography Down to 1940*.

The Controller of H.M. Stationery Office for the Crown-copyright description of Sir Christophers Knoll and Helwick Sands from *The West Coast of England Pilot;* and for the Crown-copyright transcript of the letter from the Swansea Portreeve to the Home Office, 22 Feb. 1797, in the Public Record Office (HO 42/40).

Mr. W. T. Mainwaring-Hughes for two items from *The History of Swansea and of the Lordship of Gower,* and for two items from *History of the Port of Swansea,* both books by W. H. Jones.

Dr. E. D. Jones, the University of Wales Press, and the National Library of Wales for the poem, 'Yfory awn i Fro Wyr' from *Gwaith Lewis Glyn Cothi,* edited by E. D. Jones.

Mrs. Elizabeth Iorwerth Jones and the Editorial Committee of the Gower Society for 'Gellihir' by Dr. Iorwerth Hughes Jones which appeared in *Gower XIX*.

Mrs. Gladwyn Gwent Jones and the Editorial Committee of the Gower Society for 'Llangyfelach' by Dr. Gwent Jones which appeared in *Gower I*.

Miss Olive Jones for a passage from *The Gower Memories of William Griffiths* published by Miss Alicia Gower Jones.

Mr. George E. Long and the Editor of the *South Wales Evening Post*, Swansea, for 'The Last Days of Court Leet' which appeared in the *Evening Post* on 7 March 1957.

The Longman Group Ltd. for a short passage from *The History of Wales from the Earliest Times to the Edwardian Conquest* by Sir J. E. Lloyd, Third Edition, 1939.

Mr. R. L. T. Lucas and the Editorial Committee of the Gower Society for a slightly shortened version of 'Stouthall and the Lucas Family' which appeared in *Gower XXIII*.

A passage on the Bowens of Court House is from pp 33-36 of *Bowen's Court* by Elizabeth Bowen, Second Edition, Longmans, 1964. Reprinted by permission of Penguin Books Ltd.

Mr. Vernon Richards for his article on 'The Gower Bidding Wedding.'

Mr. Tom Ridd for extracts from 'Gabriel Powell: The Uncrowned King of Swansea,' which appeared in *Glamorgan Historian*, Vol. V, 1968, edited by Stewart Williams.

Mr. W. Cyril Rogers for a passage from 'Aber Tawy Teg Esgorfa: The Port of Swansea—A Retrospect' which appeared in *Glamorgan Historian*, Vol. V, 1968, edited by Stewart Williams.

Professor William Rees and the General Committee of the Cambrian Archaeological Association for two articles on Oystermouth and

Llandeilo Talybont from the Swansea (Lordship of Gower) *Programme* of the CAA, 1960. Professor William Rees and the Oxford University Press for a brief Quotation from *South Wales and the March 1284-1415.*

Mr. W. R. B. Robinson, the Editors of *Morgannwg,* and the Glamorgan History Society for an extract on The Free Chapel of Henllys from 'The Church in Gower Before the Reformation' in *Morgannwg: Transactions of the Glamorgan History Society,* Vol. XII.

Mr. J. G. Rutter for a passage on Paviland Cave from *Gower Caves, Part I,* by E. E. Allen and J. G. Rutter.

The President and Council of the Royal Istitution of South Wales for two passages on the Manors of Burry and Oxwich, and one passage on 'The Vice-Admiral of Gower,' from Gabriel Powell's *A Survey of the Seignories of Gower and Kilvey,* 1764. (Cited as *Survey of Gower.*)

Mr. J. Mansel Thomas and the Editorial Committee of the Gower Society for 'Phil Tanner' and 'The Gower Wassail Song' which appeared in *Gower I.*

Mrs. Eileen M. Tucker and the Editorial Committee of the Gower Society for two essays, 'Blinkers on the Moon,' and 'Winter Harvest,' and three other short passages from *Gower Gleanings* by H. M. Tucker, published by the Gower Society.

Professor J. A. Steers and the Cambridge University Press for a passage on the Gower coast from *The Coastline of England and Wales,* 1969 Edition.

The University of Wales Press for passages relating to Gower from the following publications:

John Wesley in Wales, 1739-1790. Edited with an Introduction by A. H. Williams.

Brut y Tywysogion or *The Chronicle of the Princes* (Red Book of Hergest Version). Translated by Thomas Jones.

Elizabethan Wales: The Social Scene. By G. Dyfnallt Owen.

A View of the State of Religion in the Diocese of St. David's, by Erasmus Saunders.

The Last Invasion of Britain. By Commander E. H. Stuart Jones, R.N.

Professor Glanmor Williams and the University of Wales Press for a passage on the de Breos charter to Gower from the author's *The Welsh Church from Conquest to Reformation;* the Author and the General Committee of the Cambrian Archaeological Association for a passage on the Vikings from 'The Historical Background of Gower' in the Swansea (Lordship of Gower) *Programme* of the CAA, 1960; the Author and the Editorial Committee of the Gower Society for 'The Priory at Langenydd' from *Gower III;* the Author, the Editors of *Morgannwg,* and the Glamorgan History Society for a slightly shortened version of 'Rice Mansell of Oxwich and Margam (1487-1559)' in *Morgannwg: Transactions of the Glamorgan History Society,* Vol. VI.

Professor Glanmor Williams, General Editor of *The Glamorgan County History,* Mr. T. B. Pugh, Editor, Vol. III of the series, and Mr. J. Beverley Smith, for five items on Gower history from *The Glamorgan County History, Vol. III: The Middle Ages.* Four of these items, from Chapter V, are by Mr. J. Beverley Smith and Mr. T. B. Pugh, and the fifth, from Chapter XI is by Mr. T. B. Pugh.

The Venerable Harry C. Williams, Archdeacon of Gower, for passages from the *Gower Church Magazine.*

Mrs. Gwen Watkins for the poems 'Taliesin in Gower,' 'Hunt's Bay,' and 'Ilston' by Vernon Watkins. Acknowledgements also to the Editorial Committee of the Gower Society for 'Ilston' which appeared in *Gower V.*

Mr. Stanley Younge, Assistant Librarian, Swansea Central Library, for his help during the compilation of this anthology.

The late Col. W. Llewellyn Morgan for items from *Antiquarian Survey of East Gower,* and the late Mr. E. Howard Harris for 'A Gower Fairing Song'. In these instances it has not been possible to trace the copyright-holders.

CONTENTS

IV.   PEOPLE

V.   THE LAND

Introduction: The Lordship of Gower

Throughout most of Gower the visitor often becomes aware of a remarkably powerful sense of the past, of a continuity which stretches back to the beginnings of human life.

It was at Paviland Cave, on the south-western cliffs of Gower in 1823, that Dean Buckland unearthed the first burial of Palaeolithic man to be discovered in Britain. These bones of a young man, a true representative of *Homo Sapiens,* were stained with red ochre and so the discovery, attributed initially to the Roman period, became known erroneously as The Red Lady of Paviland. Other limestone caves of south and west Gower have since given abundant evidence of both human animal occupation over many eras.

Thousands of years after the people of the Early Stone Age hunted on the plains that are now the floor of the Bristol Channel, the builders of the Megaliths came to Gower along the Western sea route from the Mediterranean. These Neolithic men were probably the first farmers to reap and to sow in Gower. They built the great tomb now known as Arthur's Stone, and the Giant's Cave near Parkmill which was first excavated in 1869. The remains of other megalithic tombs may be seen at Penmaen, at Nicholaston, and on Rhossili Down, the so-called Sweyn's houses.

Then in turn came the successive ages of bronze and iron. The Celtic tribesmen of the Iron Age, probably in the centuries immediately before and after Christ, erected many of the fortified camps which can still be seen on inland hilltops and on the coastal promontories of peninsular Gower. The fortifications found at High Pennard and at the Knave, Rhossili, are good examples of such earthworks. Other impressive earthworks, hard to date precisely, are seen at The Bulwark, Llanmadoc, and at Hardings Down, while Cil Ifor, Llanrhidian, is perhaps a true hill fort with multiple banks of defences.

Now, at the great divide between prehistory and history, came the Romans. They built a fort at Loughor, probably where their road from Neath to Carmarthen forded the Afon Llwchwr. There was a

Roman building at Oystermouth. Other tantalising Roman finds at Pengwern, Ilston, Barland, and near Southgate all point towards further, undiscovered Roman settlement in Gower. On the fringes of Empire, meanwhile, indigenous Celtic people in Gower lived on undisturbed.

This story of early man, so rich and rewarding in its legacy, is but part of the complex and sometimes mysterious past of Gower. Yet it is a story which has fired the imagination of traveller, antiquarian and poet alike, as in Vernon Watkins' 'Taliesin in Gower':

> *Rhinoceros, bear and reindeer haunt the crawling*
> *   glaciers of age*
> *Beheld in the eye of the rock, where a javelin'd*
> *   arm held stiff,*
> *Withdrawn from the vision of flying colours, reveals,*
> *   like a script on a page,*
> *The unpassing moment's arrested glory, a life locked*
> *   fast in the cliff.*

With the withdrawal of the legions from Britain in the fifth century, there followed a confused sub-Roman period, an Arthurian twilight of Saxon conquest and Celtic resurgence. It was during this period of the early Dark Ages that Christianity was established in Gower by such saints as Cadog, Illtyd, Teilo and Dewi.

These saints remain commemorated by name or dedication in such characteristic Gower churches as Llanmadoc, Ilston (Llan-Illtyd Ferwallt), Llandeilo Talybont, and Llanddewi. An inscribed stone from the fifth or sixth century survives at Llanmadoc Church, while other stones from later in the Dark Ages may be found at Llangennith, Llangyfelach, Llanrhidian and Llangiwg, the northernmost church of Gower.

Already by this period, the Welsh commote of Gwyr or Gu-hir, its name now found in the writings of Nennius, extended northwards from the coastal peninsula to the hills and moorlands between the Tawe and the Loughor. In this age of the Welsh kings we find that Gwyr's political links lay, for the most part, with south-west Wales. By the tenth century the commote was thus primarily associated with the westerly kingdom of Deheubarth, ruled from the royal residence at Dinefwr.

Another element in the confused history of Gower during this period lies in the series of Viking raids on the peninsula. These sea rovers sacked the Celtic monastery at Llangennith during the late tenth century, and such incursions were long remembered in folk memory. But the Vikings only presaged a new—and lasting—order to be imposed on Gower by their continental relatives, the Normans. With the coming of the Normans to Gower around the year 1100, the Welsh commote of Gwyr became the Norman Lordship of Gower. Moreover, these Norman conquerors inherited the regal powers of the Welsh kings whom they replaced, and so often claimed virtual royal rights, *iura regalia,* in their lordships.

From this time onwards, Gower was therefore administered from Swansea Castle, the *caput* of the Lordship. Around the first earth and timber castle overlooking the navigable curve of the lower Tawe, built in a strong strategic position to control the Lordship, sprang up a small Anglo-Norman trading community. A first charter was granted by William, Earl of Warwick, the Lord of Gower, in the twelfth century, and so began the long history of the borough of Swansea. But in these early years of Norman rule, defence against the Welsh princes to the north and west was the paramount concern of the Lords of Gower. This was the setting for the journey across Gower by Giraldus Cambrensis in 1188.

Along the western borders of the Lordship, therefore, primitive castles were built at Loughor and Llandeilo Talybont, places which guarded ancient crossing routes over the Afon Llwchwr from Deheubarth. In addition, similar earthwork castles were raised at Barland and Pennard, Penmaen and Penrice. Nevertheless, throughout the twelfth and thirteenth centuries, Gower was harried by the Welsh princes and Swansea Castle burnt on a number of occasions. But the later building of stone castles at Swansea, Loughor, Oystermouth, Pennard, Penrice and Weobley meant the final consolidation of Norman rule by about the year 1300. Yet during the great revolt of Owain Glyn Dwr, 1400-15, native Welsh forces once again swept over Gower, but for the last ime.

The new stone churches of Gower were evidence, too, of the growing ecclesiastical organisation of the area. Patronage often rested in secular hands, but some churches such as Llangyfelach and Llanddewi were held by the Bishop of St. David's, whose see included Gower until 1923. Llangennith Priory was a small Benedictine cell, an offshoot of the monastery of St. Taurin at Evreux, while the Cistercians of Neath Abbey held Gower estates at Paviland, Walterston,

Cillibion and Cwrt-y-Carnau. In addition, by the Reformation a number of Gower churches were held by the Knights of St. John, including those of Penmaen, Ilston, Port Eynon and Rhossili. The Hospitallers also held other estates in Gower, including Sanctuary in Penrice parish.

By the later Middle Ages, the bounds of Gower, now an important marcher lordship, had become firmly established. To the west, Gower was divided from the commote of Carnwyllion in the Lordship of Cydweli by the Loughor River. From the Loughor, the boundary ran along Cwm Cathan, and then over the hills beneath Penlle'r Castell, past Nantmelyn, to the Garnant, the Amman and the Llynfell. To the north lay the commotes of Is Cennen and Perfedd, part of Cantref Bychan in Ystrad Tywi.

From the Llynfell, the boundary then extended to the River Twrch, which divided Gower from the Lordship of Brecon, and so to the junction of that river with the Tawe. The eastern border of Gower with the Lordship of Glamorgan followed the Tawe. The Manor of Kilvey, east of the lower Tawe, and extending to the Glais and Crymlyn streams, was a separate appendage which was governed with Gower. These were (and remain) the historic boundaries of the Lordship of Gower and Kilvey. This is the area covered by our anthology.

Within these well-defined bounds, however, there exist enduring physical contrasts between *blaenau* and *bro,* between upland and lowland. These contrasts have substantially influenced the history of Gower and are reflected in much of the historical literature of the Lordship.

Upland Gower is composed mainly of shales and sandstones, covered by thin soils which support primarily pastoral farming on wind-swept moorlands and commons. Here the hills of Pentwyn Mawr, Mynydd-y-Gwair, Cefn Gwrhyd and their outliers rise to over 1000 feet. This upland is dissected by the deep valleys of the Dulais, the Llan, the Lliw, the Egel, and the upper and lower Clydach. Penlle'r Castell, the highest point of the Lordship of Gower, rises to 1226 feet.

In this general area Welsh customs and the Welsh language have tenaciously survived. In Welsh Gower, or Gower Wallicana, moreover, Welsh land tenures had developed into individual freeholdings by the later middle ages, and the area was but lightly administered by the Lords of Gower. Today, the Welsh chapels of Gerdinen, Baran, Gellionnen, and Gwrhyd, still isolated on the moorlands, and with splendid views over the surrounding hills, represent the continuity of the Welsh past in Gower.

To the south, peninsular Gower developed differently with the coming of the Normans. Here on the limestone plateau with its rich soil suitable for arable farming, a Norman manorial society was created early in the middle ages. Knights fees, held of Swansea Castle, were assigned by the Lords Marcher, and these fiefs were then organised internally on classic manorial lines. Open field tillage, predominated, there were both free and customary holdings, and the Old Red Sandstone hills of West Gower, never rising to much more than 600 feet, provided valuable grazing.

There were as well several important demesne manors such as Pennard, which included Lunnon, Kittle, and Park-le-Breos; and Oystermouth. One result of this enduring Norman legacy in south and west Gower was that the area became known for its fertile land.

To Camden in Tudor times, West Gower 'was more famous for its corn than its towns,' and Isaac Hamon, in the last decade of the seventeenth century, could write that 'the south part of Gowersland' was 'for the most part corn ground.' Nearly two centuries later, we find that incomparable Victorian Gowerman, C. D. Morgan, praising 'the blooming meadows and waving masses of golden grain' at Llanddewi. But the farmers of limestone Gower also kept sheep, horses and cattle from medieval to modern times. So the true mode of Gower husbandry from the Norman period to our own day remains mixed farming.

Far reaching social changes towards the end of the Middle Ages meant that open fields of lowland Gower became gradually enclosed as the manorial system waned. But there still survives a small example of open field strip farming to be seen in the Rhossili *Vile* (Field). Some manorial institutions, moreover, such as Courts Leet and Baron, survived in a few Gower manors into the early twentieth century. The tenacity of elements of this manorial system in lowland Gower, even during its general decline, is shown in the extant manorial surveys of the sixteenth and seventeenth centuries, and in the *Survey of Gower* (1764) made by Gabriel Powell. These surveys may be augmented by the beautiful Gower estate maps drawn by John Williams, surveyor to Thomas Mansel Talbot of Penrice, in the late eighteenth century.

As an integral part of this social reorganization of lowland Gower by the Normans, most of the area became English-speaking, probably through an influx of settlers from the West of England. Yet the persistence of Welsh place-names and surnames in English Gower, or Gower Anglicana, indicates the survival (and perhaps the resurgence) of Welsh elements.

The demarcation line between English and Welsh Gower lay in general along the northern boundaries of the commons of Clyne, Fairwood, Pengwern, Forest and Welsh Moor. This social, ethnic and linguistic divide has long fascinated students of Gower. Yet as William Bennett of Penrice, the seventeenth century Gower genealogist, and the later 'J. H. Pedigrees' record, the better-off families of English Gower, Welsh Gower, and Swansea alike inter-married.

Against this Anglo-Welsh background, significant historical themes have been played out in Gower in modern times. One of the most important of these was the rise of the gentry which preceded, accompanied, and followed the Acts of Union of 1536 and 1543. Of this process, Professor Glanmor Williams has written that 'uniting Gower to Morgannwg was an unnatural act; by geography, history, tradition, dialect and ecclesiastical organisation, it belonged to Deheubarth and the south-west. But the shiring of Wales offered new opportunities to ambitious families which some men within the lordship were quick to seize.'

Perhaps these changes in Gower are best symbolised by the crest of Sir Rice Mansel (1487-1559), quartered with the arms of the Penrice and Scurlage families, still proudly chiselled in the stone above the chief gateway of Oxwich Castle. This was the impressive mansion house built by this great scion of the Gower Mansel family and powerful crown officer of the Tudors. Two other ambitious notables of this period were Sir Mathew Cradock and Sir George Herbert, successively stewards to the Lords of Gower in the late fifteenth and sixteenth centuries.

Yet continuity, too, was also a feature of these developments. The Mansels, an *advenae* family, were already established in West Gower by the fourteenth century. Sir Mathew Cradock, and the junior line of the family which settled at Cheriton, were descended from Einion ap Collwyn, a Glamorgan chieftain of the early middle ages. Sir George Herbert, in his turn, was a grandson of Sir Mathew Cradock and his first wife, Alice Mansel of Oxwich. Soon, other rising Gower yeomen and farmers, some too with their family roots in later medieval Gower society, began to form a recognisable, often inter-related gentry. This new class included locally the Lucases and the Bowens, the Bennetts and the Seyses, the Dawkins and the Prices of Gellihir and Cwrt-y-Carnau.

Another important theme of Gower history after the Union was the rise of Swansea, for the town had triumphantly survived the abolition of Gower's marcher status. Trade with Bristol, Ireland and France, first established in the middle ages, continued to expand in the seventeenth and eighteenth centuries, and the town's growing merchant class propered and flourished accordingly.

There was also the extensive limestone trade from Port Eynon and Oxwich to the West Country, together with the oyster fisheries of the former village. These places had long had trading connections with North Devon, a traditional Gower sea-link to the south, and to the outside world. There is also the attendant story of the Gower smugglers, a saga which involved many villagers of south and west Gower, and a story which runs deep and long in the vivid sea-lore of the peninsular. For centuries, too, this sea-lore was nourished by the many wrecks cast on the particularly dangerous south Gower coast.

Taken together, all these complementary themes of town and country, of land and sea, and of Welsh and English-speaking people had produced an equilibrium in the life of Gower by the late eighteenth century. This was the Gower that so impressed John Wesley, Malkin and other visitors in the later eighteenth and early nineteenth centuries.

Then this equilibrium was shattered by the Industrial Revolution. Swansea now outgrew its past as market town for Gower, its role as aspiring Georgian holiday resort, and its function as a regional port. The old capital of Gower became an industrial centre with world-wide maritime and commercial links.

In this dramatic process, once largely deserted areas of upland Gower became thriving, industrial, Welsh-speaking communities, while rural Gower began a slow decline. Population fell, old customs were forgotten, the wheels of the grist mills stopped turning, and with the coming of the railways the links with North Devon withered and died. In the summer of 1876, the last Devon 'fore-and-aft-er' to enter the Port Eynon coves for Gower limestone sailed southwards from Slade's Foot. Now only the overgrown quarries remain.

Yet at the same time as these changes strengthened local Welsh traditions, the rise of Swansea, with its growing middle class, decisively broadened the town's English-speaking legacy. From this crucible sprang a new synthesis of separate English and Welsh traditions in the Lordship, and also a new awareness of Gower's past which remains commemorated in the work of such antiquarians as George Grant Francis, the Rev. J. D. Davies, Col. W. Llewellyn Morgan, and W. H. Jones. It is these traditions which the work of the Royal Institution of South Wales and the Gower Society perpetuates.

In our own time, swift social change in the wake of two world wars has blurred and even threatens the distinctive identity of both English and Welsh Gower. In upland Gower, Welsh-speaking communities are already in decline, while in the peninsula development steadily erodes differences between town and country. The Bennetts and the Bowens, the Dawkins and the Prices have disappeared as surely as the Norman lords of Gower.

What remains is the land, farming, the immemorial tillage that the Neolithic farmers first brought to Gower along the western sea route thousands of years ago.

David Rees
Swansea, September 1977

I

Prologue

1. *The Land of Gower*

Many suggestions as to the origins of the word Gower have been made from time to time . . . We are inclined to adopt the form Gohir as likely to have been the foundation of 'Gower,' an ancient British word signifying that the territory is long, outstretching, projected, which it very manifestly is as a whole, and particularly as it reaches out into the Bristol Channel. This is an attribute of the Land of Gower which must always have been noticeable, and would distinguish it from the other coastal parts of South Wales. There is only one portion of this sea-board which is similar to it in contour—Pembroke—and that also takes its name from its configuration, the Cymric *Pen-bro,* meaning the head-land or projection.

We have the satisfaction of knowing that a notable philologist, Dr. Thomas Nicholas, M.A., Ph.D., favoured this derviation, believing it to have been 'first used as a term descriptive of the country as a narrow and *long* tract, and that the ancient British pronunciation made it to be two syllables, *Go-hir*—far, out-stretching, long—at last softened into *Gwyr.'*

The earliest form in which the word has been found is used in the writings of Nennius (ninth century), where it is variously given as *Gucher, Guhir, Guher,* and *Guir* . . . the *Annales Cambriae* copies the spelling of its authorities at different times as *Goher, Gohir,* and *Goer.* It is evident that these forms could only be based upon an original denomination consisting of two elements or syllables, such as *Go-hir,* the meaning of which is so aptly descriptive of the land . . .

W. H. Jones, *A History of Swansea and of the Lordship of Gower,* 1920.

2. *Before the Normans*

There are strong indications that in the period of the Welsh kings Gwyr was a land whose political associations had normally been with Ystrad Tywi, and the wide kingdom of Deheubarth of which Ystrad

Tywi was a part, rather than with the kingdom of Morgannwg. *Pedeir Ceinc y Mabinogi* refers to an Ystrad Tywi which consisted of three cantrefs. Cantref Mawr and Cantref Bychan were certainly two of these areas; they consisted of lands dominated in the late twelfth century and thirteenth century by Welsh princes.

There is less certainty concerning the name of the third cantref. Testimony given by a jury during the legal proceedings between de Braose and the crown in 1306, stated that the third cantref consisted of the lands of Cydweli, Carnwyllion and Gower, but, significantly the cantref itself is not named. The same difficulty is found in other sources which provide lists of the administrative divisions of Wales, although in some texts the area is called Cantref Eginog. The evidence, no less than the testimony of the early-fourteenth-century jurors, must be treated with caution, particularly since it is drawn from texts ultimately derived from the western provinces of Wales. It is true that there were periods when Gwyr came within the sphere of the kings of Morgannwg. This was so at one time in the second half of the tenth century. But before the end of the tenth century Gwyr was once more associated with the westerly territories, being among the dominions of Maredudd ab Owain (d. 999), king of Deheubarth.

The evidence suggests that in the period before the coming of the Normans Gwyr was a land normally dominated by the kings of Deheubarth, who ruled in Ystrad Tywi.

J. Beverley Smith and T. B. Pugh, 'The Lordship of Gower and Kilvey in the Middle Ages,' in *Glamorgan County History,* Vol. III, 1971.

3. *Viking Raiders*

This political cohesion in the south-west was brought about to a large extent by Viking pressure. Gwyr itself, thrusting into the sea-lanes of the Bristol Channel and offering many a convenient landfall, inevitably attracted the far-from-welcome attentions of Viking raiders from the ninth century onwards. In their trail they brought death, rapine and devastation; in 986, for example, the old Celtic ecclesiastical foundation at Llangenydd was gutted by them and remained a desert for nearly a century. Furthermore, their bad example seems to have inspired Welsh chieftains to emulate them, as when Einon ap Owain ap Hywel Dda twice laid waste the plains of Gower in 970 and 977. The Scandinavians, however, did more than plunder. Older scholars undoubtedly grossly exaggerated the number of Norse names and the extent of Scandinavian settlement, but the many place-names of Norse origin found along the Welsh coast suggest that in some places these sea-rovers established fortified points or trading posts. One such may have been Swansea, a name made up of two Norse elements—the personal name Sweyn, and ey, an island. Other Norse names in the region were the Worm, Burry Holms, and the Swine houses.

> Glanmor Williams, 'The Historical Background
> of Gower,' Cambrian Archaeological
> Association *Programme,* 1960.

4. *The Coming of the Normans*

Gower had also been vested in Hywel ap Gronw, and, upon his death, had been granted by [King] Henry, like Cydweli, to a man in whom he had the fullest confidence, namely, Earl Henry of Warwick, his friend and companion, who fixed the centre of his lordship at the mouth of the Tawe and thus became the founder of Swansea. Through the influx of English settlers the southern or peninsular half of the commote soon lost its Welsh features as thoroughly as Penfro and Rhos, and the distinction was set up, which has lasted to our own day, between Welsh and English Gower. [Earl] Henry died in 1119...

> Sir J. E. Lloyd, *A History of Wales from the
> Earliest Times to the Edwardian Conquest,*
> 1939 ed.

5. *English Gower, Welsh Gower*

On the coming of the Normans a large part of Gower was divided by them into compact holdings described as vills (villae) or manors (maneria). Of these the episcopal manors were not members of the lordship, and some were demesne manors held by the Lord himself. The remaining manors were grouped with a number of free holdings not in any vill, and scattered all over Gower and held by English tenure, to form a large 'manor' called Gower Anglicana.

What remained, consisting not of manors, but of freeholdings subject to a small quit rent, was Gower Wallicana or Welsh Gower, in two groups (which counted as sub-manors) called Supraboscus and Subboscus according as they were situated in the original Uwchcoed or Iscoed . . . The holdings of Supraboscus are confined to the parishes of Llangiwg, Llangyfelach, Llandeilo Talybont, Loughor parish north of the Llan and Lliw rivers and Swansea parish. The nucleus of Subboscus was the parish of Llanrhidian Higher and part of Loughor parish south of the above mentioned rivers.

> Clarence A. Seyler, 'The Early Charters of
> Swansea and Gower,' *Archaeologia Cambrensis,*
> 1924.

6.   *A Charter to the Men of Gower*

During Edward I's reign the only other outstanding clash between the king and a marcher lord over the rights of the Church seems to have been the altercation between Edward and William de Braose, lord of Gower, in 1299. On 4 April, in response to a complaint from the bishop of Llandaff, John of Monmouth, the king set up a commission to inquire whether the lord of Gower had the right to distrain tenants of the episcopal manor of Bishopston and bring them before his court at Swansea. Braose quickly countered, on 16 April, with the submission that the king's justices who had been appointed to the commission had no right to enter his lordship to implead any case there by the king's writ. This was a dispute of long standing between Braose and the bishops of Llandaff and had flared up twice previously in the thirteenth century. Edward, determined to proceed with his policy of withdrawing church lands from marcher suzerainty, to which policy the bishops were probably a party, was undeterred by Braose's protest and ordered the commission to proceed with its work. But the quarrel was soon swallowed up in a much bigger dispute involving the lord of Gower and all the tenants of his lordship, and the delicate issue of the relationship of the lordship of Gower to the county of Carmarthen. The upshot of these disputes was a charter granted in 1306 to the men and tenants of Gower. Since the manor of Bishopston is nowhere mentioned in this important document, it may very well mean that the bishop of Llandaff had won his point.

> Glanmor Williams, *The Welsh Church from*
> *Conquest to Reformation,* 1962.

7. *Glyn Dwr in Gower*

A Welsh rising in Gower had been feared by the king's custodians of the Lordship in August 1399, shortly after the collapse of Richard II's power. In the autumn of 1401 an attack by Owain Glyn Dwr, his follower Rhys Gethin of Cwm Llanerch, and other rebels was anticipated; and Swansea castle was repaired and kept in a state of defence. There was another alarm in October 1402, when Glyn Dwr, his new son-in-law, Sir Edmund Mortimer, and their host was reported to be ravaging and burning near Brecon.

After Glyn Dwr had captured Carmarthen on July 6, 1403, he was deterred from advancing into Gower by the prophecy made by Hopkin ap Thomas ab Einon of Ynysdawy, near Clydach, that he would be taken prisoner. Swansea was still held by the king's forces in September 1403, when orders were given to levy supplies in Somerset for the provisioning of the castle and the town. When Glyn Dwr's power was at its height between 1403 and 1405, he probably controlled most of the Lordship of Gower, but we do not know when Swansea was captured. According to the *Annals of Owain Glyn Dwr,* it was not until 1406 that the men of Gower made their submission to Henry IV's lieutenants.

> J. Beverley Smith and T. B. Pugh, 'The Lordship
> of Gower and Kilvey in the Middle Ages,'
> in *Glamorgan County History,* Vol. III,
> 1971.

8. *Aftermath*

Gower: 'The two parts of the Lordship are worth £100 and no more because the Lordship in great part is destroyed by Welsh rebels.'

> Chancery records, c.1411, noted in
> William Rees, *South Wales and the*
> *March, 1284-1415,* 1924.

9. *The Act of Union*

The modern county of Glamorgan as constituted by the Act of 1536 reflected the territorial influence of Henry Somerset, earl of Worcester (d. 1549); it was formed by uniting the earl's lordship of

Gower and Kilvey with the lordship of Glamorgan and Morgannwg, which the Somerset family had administered since 1496. But for the close connection between the two lordships which had long been established by the earl of Worcester's possession of the chief local offices in Glamorgan, the lordship of Gower might well have been incorporated in the county of Carmarthen, with which it has had stronger ties before the late-medieval period. If that had been done, Gower (where Worcester was accustomed to exercise his judicial rights as marcher lord) would have been brought within the jurisdiction of Lord Ferrers as chief justice of south Wales . . . Particular care was taken in the Act of Union to safeguard the Earl of Worcester's interests . . .

> T. B. Pugh, 'The Ending of the Middle Ages,
> 1485-1536,' in *Glamorgan County History,*
> Vol. III, 1971.

II

Travellers

1. *Giraldus Crosses Gower*

Entering the province called Goer, we spent the night at the castle of Sweynsei, which in Welsh is called Abertawe, or the fall of the river Tawe into the sea.

The next morning, the people being assembled after mass and many having been induced to take the cross, an aged man of that district, named Cador, thus addressed the archbishop: 'My lord, if I now enjoyed my former strength, and the vigour of youth, no alms should ransom me; no desire of inactivity restrain me, from engaging in the laudable undertaking you preach; but since my weak age and the injuries of time deprive me of this desirable benefit (for approaching years bring with them many comforts, which those that are passed take away), if I cannot, owing to the infirmity of my body, attain a full merit, yet suffer me, by giving a tenth of all I possess, to attain a half."

Then falling down at the feet of the archbishop, he deposited in his hands, for the service of the cross, the tenth of his estate, weeping bitterly, and intreating from him the remission of one half of the enjoined penance. After a short time he returned, and thus continued: "My lord, if the will directs the action, and is itself, for the most part, considered as the act, and as I have a full and firm inclination to undertake this journey, I request a remission of the remaining part of the penance, and in addition to my former gift, I will equal the sum from the residue of my tenths." The archbishop, smiling at his devout ingenuity, embraced him with admiration . . .

Thence we proceeded towards the river Loughor, through the plains in which Howel, son of Meredyth of Brechiniog, after the decease of King Henry I, gained a signal victory over the English. Having first crossed the river Loughor, and afterwards the water called Wendraeth, we arrived at the castle of Cydweli.

Giraldus Cambrensis, *The Itinerary Through
Wales,* 1188. Everyman Edition. 1908.

2. *Gowerland*

The olde castel of Swineseye was builded or repairid by the
Normans and destroied by Lleulen prince of Wales that maryed King
Johns dowghter. And it stoode by the bisshop of S. Dauids castel that
now is there.

A iii miles from Swinsey, communely cawillid in Englisch Swansey, at the rode moth of Tawe was a castel cawllid Est Wilthlunarde,
otherwise Ostermuth, and of sum Mummess; there remaine ruines of
a castel destroied by prince Lluelin.

Swansey is a market town and chief place of Gower lande.

Moubray was lorde of Swansea and builded the old castel, and be
likelihod Ostermuth also for the defence of the hauen.

Almost in the middes of Gowerland a V miles from Swansey is the
castle of Guible[1] that longid to the Delamers.

Penrise castel standith a iii miles from Swansea in the forest of Penrise.

Lochor castel standith on the hither side of Lochor river in the
Lordship of Gower.

John Leland, from *The Itinerary in Wales*
(c. 1536-9). Edited by L. T. Smith, 1906.

3. *Camden's Gower*

All the country beyond the river *Nid* to the river Loghor the west
boundary of this country is called by us *Gower,* by the Britains and
Ninnius *Guhir,* wherein as that author says, 'the sons of Kaianus the
Scot spread themselves' till drawn out by Cuneda, British petty king.
In the reign of Henry I, Henry Earl of Warwick reduced this country
but by agreement between Thomas earl of Warwick and King Henry
II it passed to the crown. King John gave it to William de *Breos* to
hold 'by the service of one knight in lieu of all other service,' and his
posterity held it to the time of Edward II.

For then William de Breos having mortgaged this estate to several
persons, and afterwards to the prejudice of all the rest to oblige the
King made it over to Hugh Spenser, this was one of the many causes
of the inveterate hatred bore to the Spensers and of their rashly
renouncing their allegiance.

---

[1]   Weobley.

It is now divided into east and west. In the east the chief town is Sweinsey, so called by the English from the porpoises, by the Welsh *Abertaw* from the river Taw running by it. It was fortified by Henry earl of Warwick aforesaid. But much older than this is the town on the river *Loghor,* called by Antoninus *Levcarum,* by us, retaining the name intire, Loghor, where after the death of Henry I, Howell ap Meredic, coming on a sudden with his mountaineers the English cut off, many persons of distinction among them.

West *Gower,* lies below this, and by the sea insinuating itself on both sides is made a peninsula, more famous for its corn than its towns, and antiently for Kineth, whom was canonised after leading a solitary life here, of whom the reader that desires further information may consult our countryman Capgrave, who dwells largely on his miracles.

William Camden, *Brittania,* 1586.
(Gough's edition, 1789.)

4. *The Beaufort Progress*

Swansea . . .
August 15, 1684.

In the evening his Grace, having been already met and complimented by the Gentlemen of this county, was conducted by them to the Lodgings prepared for him, where he found an ample Entertainment; and he lodged that night. Upon whose entry the Town expressed their welcome by ringing of bells, firing of great guns and Chambers from ye public places of the Town and vessels in the Harbour, with bonfires.

The next morning, Aug. 16, his Grace the Duke of Beaufort, accompanied with the Earl of Worcester, Sir John Talbot, the High Sheriff . . . and the rest of the Glamorganshire Gentry, went on foot to Morning Prayer at St. Mary's Church of Swanzy, of which hereafter, where Prayers were read by the Reverend . . . which ended, his Grace, in his return, took a view of the Town and Harbour, some part of which was beautified for his reception, and ye streets strewed with fresh sand throughout his walk. Here the Shipping repeated again their Salutations by their Guns; ye Town, also, by their Chambers, and loud huzzas of the people.

Thomas Dineley, *An Account of the Progress of His Grace Henry the first Duke of Beaufort Through Wales, 1684.* Edited by Charles Baker, 1864.

5. *Wesley Preaches the Gospel*

Tuesday 31 July 1764.

An honest man at Kidwelly told us there was no difficulty in riding the sands, so we rode on. In ten minutes one overtook us who used to guide persons over them, and it was well he did, or in all probability we would have been swallowed up. The whole sands are at least ten miles over, with many streams of quicksands intermixed. But our guide was thoroughly acquainted with them and with the road on the other side. By his help, between five and six, we came well tired to Oxwich in Gower.[1]

Gower is large tract of land, bounded by Breconshire on the north-east, the sea on the south-west and rivers on the other sides. Here all the people talk English and are in general the most plain, loving people in Wales. It is therefore no wonder that they receive the word with all readiness of mind.

Knowing that they were scattered up and down, I had sent two persons on Sunday, that they might be there early on Monday and so sent notice of my coming all over the country. But they came to Oxwich scarce a quarter of an hour before me, so that the poor people had no notice at all. Nor was there any to take us in, the person with whom the preacher used to lodge there being three miles out of town.[2] After I had stayed a while in the street (for there was no public house) a poor woman gave me house-room. Having had nothing since breakfast I was very willing to eat or drink, but she simply told me she had nothing in the house but a dram of gin. However I afterwards procured a dish of tea at another house and was much refreshed. About seven I preached to a little company, and again in the morning. They were all attention, so that even for the sake of this handful of people I did not regret my labour.

John Wesley in Wales 1739-1790. Edited with an Introduction by A. H. Williams, 1971.

---

1. Wesley probably crossed the Burry estuary from Pembrey to Whiteford Point in Gower.
2. William Tucker of Horton.

6.   *The Light Fantastic*

Swansea is a very large town. (The Mackworth arms is the most frequented caravansera.) It is built at nearly the mouth of the Tovy.[1] Its chief trade is in coals, pottery and copper. It has a theatre and library, and also bathing machines. In the vicinity are many pleasant rides; that to *Mumble* castle and bay, over the hard sand at low water, is remarkably delightful. The ruins of the castle are very picturesque; This was a favourite retreat of *Oliver Cromwell.* There is a good house of entertainment here, where excellent mutton and large oysters may genreally be had.

After passing a rugged road, *Caswell* bay opens, where is the finest sandy beach I ever saw. It is frequently visited by the neighbouring mymphs and their strephons; and here, favoured by the moon's cool gleam, they trip it on the light fantastic to the shrill pipe and spirit-stirring tabor; while the gentle gliding wave murmurs in mournful accompaniment.

Henry Wigstead, *Remarks on a Tour to North and South Wales in the Year 1797,* 1800.

7.   *Mr. Talbot's Villa*

This head-land of the Mumbles forms a point of the peninsula of Gower, which extends in a long and narrow isthmus between the two great bays of Glamorganshire and Carmarthenshire; this is in general a rocky and uninteresting district, except where the sea views enliven it; yet has fancy, or some other cause of predilection, disposed Mr. Talbot to create a highly-ornamented villa, with all its luxurious appendages, at Penrice, near the extremity of this tract, where the castles of Penrice and Pennarth, built soon after the conquest, distinguish the bay of Oxwich.

The house is an elegant modern structure, and the diversities of lawn, wood and water, introduced with much taste and design, strongly contrast the asperities of the surrounding district, and surprise a stranger with a degree of refinement he could little expect in such a tract. Yet may an observer, without too critic an eye, deem the trim aspect of this park, and its smooth sheet of water, inconsonant with the rough outline of the coast and country, and censure that

---

1.   Tawe.

design which has introduced the principal approach through the fictitious fragments of a modern ruin, within sight of an ancient castle, whose ivied walls overhanding the beach, seem to frown defiance at this newly-created rival.

Still more must he wonder, that its owner should desert the noble seat of Margam, in the midst of a populous and plentiful country, to form a fairy palace in a dreary and desolate wild, far from the usual haunts of man, and near the extremity of a bleak peninsula.

Henry Skrine, *Two Successive Tours Throughout
the Whole of Wales,* 1798.

8.   *From Pwlldu Point*

From Pwlldu Point it should be the object to keep along the sea-shore as much as possible to Oxwich Point, so as to have a complete view of Oxwich Bay, with its grand shores, caverns and promontories.

Penmaen is at the feet of a mountain, one of the highest in South Wales, on which there is a huge cromlech, called in English King Arthur's Stone, and in Welsh the Stone of Sketty. The lifting of this stone into its present place is mentioned in the Welsh historical triads as one of the three arduous undertakings accomplished in the island of Britain, and still more than that, as one of the three wonderful exertions demonstrative of human power. The second was the erection of Stonehenge; and the third, the formation of a heap or pile, respecting which it cannot now be discovered what, or where it was; but some have supposed that it might have been Silbury Hill, the vast tumulus near Marlborough. This immense stone in Gower is supported by several other stones, and is a structure as similar to those already described near Dyffryn House as the nature and form of such rude monuments admit, erected nearly in the state in which they were dug from the quarry. This has also a heap of stones thrown around it . . .

A fine Gothic window is nearly all that remains of Oxwich Castle. The village is remarkably neat and pretty, and well sheltered with wood. The cottages are in the comfortable style of Glamorganshire, with neat gardens, and, what I have observed nowhere else, every cottager has either a horse or a partnership in a horse, and his little hayrick in the garden, by the side of the house. The parsonage house, built by Mr. Talbot as a testimony of respect to Mr. Collins, the present rector, is beautifully situated on the beach, at the western side of the bay. The church is situated no less advantageously; and the point of land running out into the channel at once protects the abodes of men and the works of vegetation against the destructive blasts from the Atlantic.

> Benjamin Heath Malkin, *The Scenery, Antiquities and Biography of South Wales, from materials collected during two excursions in the year 1803, 1804.*

9. Newton to Henllys

We turn towards Monk's Land, called now Monkey Land. It belonged at one time to the Knights of St. John, the monk's residence being at Sanctuary, near Penrice. A footpath through the fields leads to Newton, a fine farm house, Mr. Hughes'. This is quite an agricultural part of the country, and in the firstrate style. The traveller can be sure to recieve a genuine hospitality should he chance to pass Newton, on his way across the country to Henllys.

This Henllys is a very ancient house, once used as a court house. Many traces of its grandeur yet remians—one of the rooms nicely panelled with oak, and some old paintings. There are many strange stories respecting this old place—legends out of number. At midnight often may be seen a spectre that frightens all that chance to pass when the ghost is treading his nightly rounds. They tell you of dungeons deep and dark, sunk under the house when all is still, supposed to be of those who were sent to their cold graves uncalled for. From this house a path led to Rhossili sands, over the mountains and down its sides.

> C. D. Morgan, *Wanderings in Gower,* 1886 ed.

10. Kilvert at Ilston

Monday, 15 April 1872
From Clyro to Ilston Rectory . . . Westhorp was waiting for me at Killay Station with his new waggonette and drove me to Ilston.

Tuesday, 16 April
After breakfast we set out to drive to Llan Madoc, over high

commons, then through pretty lanes, catching glimpses of the Carmarthenshire coast, Pembrey, Burry Port, and the smoke of Llanelly, across the sands and blue water of the arm of Carmarthen Bay called the Bury River.

A sharp pull up and steep hill brought us to Llan Madoc on the brow of a windy bare hill looking out on Carmarthen Bay. Westhorp and Mrs. Westhorp went into the bare unfinished ugly barrack of a Rectory while I minded Bob and the waggonette. Presently they came out with the Vicar, Mr. Davies, who looked like a Roman priest, close shaven and shorn, dressed in seedy black, a long coat and broad shovel hat. He took us into the Churchyard, but let us find our own way into the Church which was beautifully finished and adorned but fitted up in the high ritualistic style. The Vicar said that when he came to the place the Church was meaner than the meanest hovel in the village.

The Vicar invited us to join him at his luncheon to which we added the contents of our own pcinic basket. He had a very good pie to which we did justice for we were all very hungry with the sea air. We were waited on by a tall clean old woman with a severe and full cap border who waits on Mr. Davies and is so clean that she washes the kitchen four times a day. She used to wash her master's bedroom floor as often till he caught a cold which frightened her and she desisted.

We suggested that she might be of Flemish blood which would account for her cleanliness. The idea had never occurred to Mr. Davies and he was much struck by it. The house was thoroughly untidy and bachelor-like and full of quaint odds and ends. The rigging of a boat stood in the hall for the Vicar is a great sailor and sails Carmarthen Bay in a boat built by himself. A quantity of pretty wood fretwork and carved work also stood about in the hall and the rooms, and minature bookcases and cabinets for drawing-room tables made by himself and sold for the benefit of Cheriton Church Restoration Fund. He is very clever and can turn his hand to anything. Besides which he seemed to me an uncommonly kind good fellow, a truly simple-minded, single-hearted man.

The Vicar showed us what he called his newest toy—a machine almost exactly like a sewing machine—for sawing out the pattern in his wood carving. He promised to make me a little 10/- bookcases.

We came back by another road from Cheriton, round the southern side of Cefn Bryn, past Penrice Castle and beautiful views of the coast, the sea and cliffs and Oxwich Bay with the old ruins of Penrice

Castle standing grandly up in the foreground. Between Penmayne and Kilvrough we turned off the road into some fields to visit the 'Graves of the Unknown'—'the graves of the children of the people.'

These graves consist of four chambers, each chamber formed by four rude stones from two to three feet high set on end and enclosing a square space about 3 feet square. A narrow space separates the chambers from each other and two of the chambers are on one side and two on the other of a narrow passage or gangway running the whole length of the place of burial. At either end of this gangway there is a threshold step made by a low stone set up edgewise. These graves were uncovered a few years ago and there were found in some of them skeletons sitting upright, for they were not large enough to admit a skeleton lying down.

In one of the chambers of death grew this cowslip.[1] It was a strange weird place—how old, no one could tell—and no one knew who was buried there.

No man knoweth anything about their sepulchres unto this day. The place of graves lies in a narrow green meadow shut in by lofty wooded banks and precipices of grey rock peeping through the trees. High up among the rocks on one bank is a large bone cavern.

When we reached home Louisa Sheldon came out to carry the wraps and things in from the Carriage. 'We're home in good time, are we not, Sheldon?' said Westhorp. 'Pretty well to-day, Sir,' answered the admirable Sheldon, smiling. She is a capital girl, housemaid, parlourmaid, butler, footman, valet, and the mainstay of the family. The Vicar of Sketty, Mr. Bonley, and his sister Miss Brown walked over to dine and sleep. He has for some unknown reason taken the name of Bonley, because he disliked the name of Brown. I think while I was about it I would have taken a better name than Bonley which does not seem to me a bit better than Brown. We sat up till 1 o'clock disputing about the Athanasian Creed, Bonley taking the High Church ground and Westhorp and I the liberal view. Of course we left off exactly where we began, and no one was convinced. I hate arguing.

Wednesday, 17 April

This is the cleanest coast I ever saw—no seaweed, no pebbles, hardly a shell—not a speck for miles along the shining sand, and scarcely even any scent of the sea. But the rocks were covered with

---

1. The pressed flower is inserted in the MS.

millions of barnacles, mussels, limpets, and sea snails, and there were sea anemones in the little pools among the rocks.

As we lay on the high cliff moor above Oxwich Bay sheltered by some gorse bushes there was no sound except the light surges of the sea beneath us and the sighing of the wind through the gorse and dry heather. 'They heard the voice of the Lord God walking in the garden in the cool of the day.' The white gulls were flying about among the low black rocks. Some of them sat upon the rocks round the Three Cleeves and some were floating tranquilly upon the sea, rising and falling with the waves.

When we reached home we heard there had been an accident in the coal mine at Killay. The water had burst into the pit and drowned two men and a pony. A brave fellow had volunteered to go down the pit to look after them but with characteristic recklessness he had gone with a naked light and was blown up by firedamp and fearfully burnt but not killed. They say it will be 3 weeks before the water will be sufficiently pumped out of the pit to allow of the bodies being found.

Thursday, 18 April

This morning we drove to the Mumbles, the Westhorps, Miss Brown and myself. As we went through lovely Sketty where Welby was Vicar for 14 years we stopped to look at the Church and Churchyard. The Church is nice but the lychgate is desecrated by the names of all the snobs of Swansea.

A tramway runs along the road side from Swansea to the Mumbles, upon which ply railway carriages drawn by horses.

Oystermouth Castle stands nobly upon a hill overlooking the town and bay. The lurid copper smoke hung in a dense cloud over Swansea, and the great fleet of oyster boats under the cliff was heaving in the greenest sea I ever saw. We had luncheon upon the Cliffs overlooking the white lighthouse tower upon the most seaward of the Mumbles. A shepherd was holloing and driving the sheep of the pasture furiously down a steep place into the sea, and a school of boys came running down the steep green slope, one of them playing 'Rosalie the Prairie Flower' on an accordion as he ran. A steam tug shot out of Swansea Harbour to meet a heavily laden schooner under full press of canvas in the bay, and towed her into port, and the great fleet of oyster boats which had been out dredging was coming in round the lighthouse point with every shade of white and amber sails gay in the afternoon sun as they ran each into her moorings under the shelter of the great harbour cliff. As we went along the narrow Cliff path among the gorse towards Langland and Caswell Bay, a flock of strange and beautiful black and white birds flew along the rock faces below us towards the lighthouse piping mournfully. They were I suppose a small kind of gull but they seemed to me like the spirits of the shipwrecked folk seeking and mourning for their bodies. Among the sighing of the gorse came upon a lift of the wind a faint and solemn tolling of a deep bell from seaward. It was the tolling of the buoy bell moored off the Mumbles, a solemn awful sound, for the bell seemed to be tolling for the souls of those who had gone down at sea and warning the living off their graves.

When we came down from the cliff and were going through the town to our inn a furious whirlwind of dust arose and everything was hidden in the dense white cloud. People were obliged to grope for the walls of the houses and cry out to carriages which they could hear but not see not to drive over them.

Saturday, 20 April
Left dear hospitable Ilston Rectory at 8.15 and drove to Killay Station with Mr. and Mrs. Westhorp and Henry. There I bade them all Goodbye sadly and they drove on to Swansea.

The Rev. Francis Kilvert, *Kilvert's Diary*, 1872
Edited by William Plomer.

11. *Towards the Gower Inn*

Gower is nearly twenty miles long by five or six miles in width, and has over fifty miles of sea coast, mainly rugged and often magnificent of aspect. Like Pembroke, it has nurtured two distinct races side by side for seven or eight hundred years. But the greater part of the peninsula is English; the smaller is Welsh, and lies on the north-eastern slope facing Carmarthenshire. The line between them, geographically and socially, is almost as sharp as that in Pembroke. It used to be said that when an English Gowerian was asked for the house of a Welsh neighbour just over the line, he generall replied: "I donna know; a lives somewhere in the Welsherie." Recent influences, however, have somewhat modified this remarkable cleavage, as in the case of Pembrokeshire.

But the Gower man outside the Welsherie is no more Welsh than a Devonian, though he is not like a Devonian. His voice and virtues are entirely his own, and his language, like that of South Pembrokeshire, is an English vernacular evolved in isolation. To use a convenient term, his stock, his character and his speech are Teutonic. The attitude of the Gower rustic when you touch on the matter of conversation with him is not devoid of humour. It is enough for him, of course, that he is a Gower man and not a Welshman, though he does not seem to repudiate the Cymric affinity with the same fervour of pride and prejudice that a Pembrokeshire man would. The community is of course a much smaller one, and he takes his racial aloofness merely as a fact, not as a happy dispensation of Providence as well. "We donna knaw exactly what we are, sir; some of the gentry says we're Flemings," is a stock reply, but there is beyond doubt some sort of satisfaction in belonging to this compact community of far back colonists, and even a little pride in that very mystery of origin which excites much interest "among the gentry."

A comparison between the Gower and Pembroke vernacular would have peculiar interest from the fact that they are isolated both from each other and from England. The Gower men tell you that they can detect a Pembrokian instantly. But with all their broad Teutonic speech there seemed to me an unmistakable touch of the Welsh lilt not noticeable in Pembrokeshire, and here and there a suggestively Anglo-Welsh word, such as "iss, iss" (for "yes, yes"). Till quite recently there was an old court in Swansea held twice a year, known as the court of Gower Anglicana, where the English of Gower did suit and service, and another for the Welsh, known as the court of Gower Wallica.

Gower was not included in the old lordship of Glamorgan, which stretched from the Rhymney to the Tawe, but was thrown into Glamorganshire, where the new county was formed by Henry VIII. The meaning of Gower or Gwyr has defied interpretation, and exasperated generations of Philologists. It was conquered independently soon after Fitz-Hamon's seizure of Glamorgan, the Norman undertaker in this business being Henry de Newburgh, Earl of Warwick, and it is said to have taken him eight years to drive the Welsh off the peninsula and make himself reasonably secure on it by sufficient number of castles. . . .

A branch of the powerful De Braoses, whom the reader may remember as mighty Marchers in Monmouth and elsewhere, got hold of Gower in due course, and the traditional cunning of their acquisitive stock seems to have been fully developed in the last lord. For having sold Gower off in lots to various purchasers and presumably pocketed the equivalent to cash, namely a king's favour, to one of the

Despensers, and thereby caused much bad blood and confusion of titles. Later on the lordship came to a Somerset, and is still in part the property of the Duke of Beaufort. . . .

The interior of Gower contains a delightful variety of scene: high ridges of heathery moorland, snug seats embosomed in fine timber, bosky glens through which bright trout streams prattle, and sea-coast peeps of every imaginable kind embellished not seldom by the presence of some imposing relic of border strife. There are ancient little churches, too, characteristic of a peculiar people and an isolated alien community; and always close at hand are vantage points whence you may look over wide waters to the rugged capes of Pembroke, to the bounds of Cornwall, the hills of Devon and Somerset, and to the lofty mountains of Brecon. Yet no one penetrates into further Gower save a few enlightened natives of the adjoining coast towns, who spend quiet holidays in the simple accomodation of its primitive sea coast hamlets.

When I pursued my solitary way towards Port Eynon, however, Gower had become but a summer memory to even these few adventurous folk. Wild and chill October winds were bowling over the russet uplands, rattling the bleached leaves of the exposed wayside trees, and soughing in the yellowing woodlands of the vales. It is a breezy common above Sketty, a couple of miles or so of open fern and heather, over which the road goes trailing westward, that makes one first conscious of being actually in Gower, and that of having shaken off the last trace of Swansea's remotest suburbs. Peewits and starlings in quite remarkable numbers and of surprising friendliness, had the waste to themselves as I traversed it, and dropped down the long slope into the pretty wooded dingle of Park Mill, where, together with a few other cottages, stands the more pretentious but yet modest hostelry known as the *Gower Inn*. It was erected in the last century by Mr. Penrice of Kilvrough, an old country seat above, whose woodlands contribute liberally to the arcadian charm for which the spot has some local reputation. A kindly thought for tourists or potential tourists seems to have been the motive of this former squire, for there was then no inn in Gower where any but the hardiest wayfarer might lay his head. A somewhat idyllic spot, where a bright trout stream followed closely by the road ripples through narrow meadow fringed with woods, is here. It would provoke no particular enthusiasm on the Welsh mainland, but has somewhat the charm of the unexpected in this narrow sea-girt peninsula.

For as you emerge at what would seem to be the foot of the winding gorge, it suddenly turns to the south, and shedding its foliage runs a short course to the shore, between bare hills, with the ruined castle of Pennard crowning the furthest one and overlooking the sea; and Edwardian fortress with a massive gateway, and flanking towers devoid of all ornament but the ferns with which nature decorates it. The mission and period of Pennard are obvious enough, though history is almost silent concerning it. Wastes of sandhills lie around its feet, where traces of buried buildings give great scope to the local fancy, while the view from the hill across the beautiful bay of Oxwich, with its yellow sands and its limestone cliffs, is highly inspiring. Curious bone caves, some fine rock scenery and a reputation for rare plants, give further interest to the lonely site of this really considerable fortress whose secret seems to have died with it—a rare thing enough in Wales.

A. G. Bradley, *In the March and Borderland of Wales,* 1905.

12. *Loughor River*

Leaving a hamlet near one bridge, the river runs through such a lonely land that even on stormy nights it is heard only by the groups and groves of oaks that guard the stony and tussocky pastures. Here and there, on either hand, a brook adds a murmur to its music. A throbbing flock of lapwings for ever wheels and gleams and calls over it. The royal fern basks on its edge. And there Autumn abides.

When it reaches the next village, the river is so yellow and poisonous that only in great floods dare the salmon come up. There, with two other rivers, it makes a noble estuary, and at the head of that estuary and in the village that commands it, the old and the new seem to be at strife.

On the one hand are the magnificent furnaces; the black, wet roads. On the other hand, there is the great water, bent as if it were a white arm of the sea, thrust into the land to preserve the influence of the sea.

Close to the village stands a wooded barrow and an ancient camp; and there are long, flat marshes where sea-gulls waver and mew; and a cluster of oaks so wind-worn that when a west wind comes it seems to come from them as they wave their haggish arms; and a little desolate white church[1] and white-walled graveyard, which on December

---

1. Llandeilo Talybont.

evenings will shine and seem to be the only things at one with the foamy water and the dim sky, before the storm; and when the storm comes the church is gathered up into its breast and is part of it, so that he who walks in the churchyard is certain that the gods—the gods that grow old and feeble and die—are there still, and with them all those phantoms following phantoms in a phantom land,—a gleam of spears, a murmur of arrows, a shout of victory, a fair face, a scream of torture, a song, the form of some conqueror and pursuer of English kings,—which make Welsh history, so that to read it is like walking in that place among December leaves that seem never to have lived and been emerald, and looking at the oaks in the mist, which are only hollows in the mist, while an ancient wind is ceaselessly remembering ancient things.

Edward Thomas, *Beautiful Wales,* 1905.

III

Places and Antiquities

1. *The Park Cwm Tumulus*

The Park Cwm cairn is situated on the property of my friend Mr. Vivian, in the parish of Penmaen, and in the celebrated peninsula of Gower.

In the spring of 1869 Mr. Vivian was making a new road; and for that purpose the workmen attacked a heap of stones, which stood conveniently, and the true nature of which was not then suspected. After removing a certain portion of the cairn on the north side, the men came upon some large upright stones forming a cell or chamber, and in the chamber they found portions of a skeleton. Upon this being reported to Mr. Vivian, he at once ordered that no more of the cairn should be removed, and he asked me to come down and see it explored.

The Red Lady of Paviland, and the successful researches of Col. Wood in the bone-caves along the coast, have made the peninsula of Gower extremely interesting to archaeologists.

I gladly, therefore, accepted my friend's invitation. We drove to the spot early in the morning, on Saturday, 14th August, 1869, accompanied by a party from the Cambrian Archaeological Society, under the guidance of their President, Lord Dunraven, and at once commenced operations.

The cairn is situated in a beautiful woody comb or dell, about a mile from the sea, and almost at the foot of the small cave known as Cat Hole.

It occupied an oblong area of about 60 feet in length by 50ft. in width, and was, when first noticed, about 5ft. in height . . . The direction of the cairn was north and south, the entrance, as usual, being to the south.

The entrance itself was funnel-shaped, 16 feet in length, and 12 in width at the entrance, gradually contracting to 3 feet 6 inches. The sides were neatly built of flat stones, placed on their broadside, and presenting the narrow edges externally. The walls are not perpendicular, but slope or batter outwards.

The central passage or avenue connecting the chambers is 17 feet long, with a uniform width of 3 feet. The sides were formed of ten

PLACES AND ANTIQUITES 47

large stones; but it is probable that there were originally eleven. They did not fit one another very well; but the interspaces were built up by small flat stones, arranged as in the entrance walls. The cairn itself extended some distances beyond the avenue towards the north.

At each end of this passage, and at right angles to it, are two square or somewhat oblong chambers. The first was about 3 feet in width. Where it joined the central passage was a sill-stone. The sides were each formed of two large stones; and there can, I think, be little doubt that it was originally closed by a fifth. In this chamber we found remains of three, if not of four, skeletons, and one fragment of pottery.

The second chamber is 6 feet in length, by about 2 feet 6 inches in breadth, and closely resembles the first, but is imperfectly divided into two unequal parts by two low stones. This chamber contained the remains of two skeletons.

The third chamber much resembled the second, and, like it, was imperfectly divided.

The fourth, on the contrary, like the first, had no division; it had been somewhat disturbed, as was also the case with the second, by the roots of an ash.

At each end of the central passage was a long sillstone. The large stones forming the central passage and side chambers were very irregular in height; and we saw no sign of any covering slabs. The interspaces were filled up with stones and earth—the latter probably arising from decomposed leaves, etc., and quite unlike the natural soil of the cwm, both in colour and character.

In all cases the large stones were placed with their flatter sides inwards. On the outside they were very irregular; none of them were at all worked.

The upper part of the cairn had been removed long ago, and the upper parts of the large stones had been long exposed.

It also appeared to me that the tumulus had been opened at some previous period, although Mr. Vivian did not feel satisfied upon this point. The bones were much broken, and in no regular arrangement. There appeared to be at least twenty skeletons. The bones were very tender; and the skulls, unfortunately, were crushed into small fragments. The teeth, as usual, were ground flat, and showed no trace of decay.

The only bones of other animals were a tooth, I believe, of a deer, found in the space on the east side . . . and a few pig's teeth, which occurred in the entrance. Close to [a] sillstone . . . we found some fragments of pottery; but throughout the mound we met with no

ornament or implement of any kind, no trace of metal, nor a sigle bit
of worked flint.

Sir John Lubbock (Lord Avebury), *Archaeologia
Cambrensis,* 1871.

2. *Hunt's Bay*

Hurled, hollow darkness, hungry caves
Where the eye, bending, magnifies
The Sea-world, all the imagined graves
Of voices where a tree-log lies:
The centre is never attained;
All is deception, broken-grained.

I have been among broken things,
Picked up the fragile lace
Of a sea-shell through which the wings
Of a gull in a clear blue space
Could be seen, then lost:
By a wave of the sea it was tossed.

Black, tousled weeds,
Bundles of foam, bottles,
Oil, shivering seeds,
Urchins, razorshells, cuttles,
And clouds combed like fleece:
The roar of the sea was peace.

I have walked this beach alone,
I have startled with my praying
The cloven tongue of stone
And seen the white foam straying
Where raven, rock and air
Rock in a dead man's care.

The winds are mad about this time,
Mad the storm's outrageous drum.
Man himself a witless mime
Because the equinoctials come
To snap the needle of his fate,
Tempting his eternal state.

Yet, whether he go or come,
Tossed to the Furies, lost in foam,
Struck by destruction's beak or dumb
Steel, the spirit finds its home,
The raging moon has lost
All conflict with that ghost.

Between the carcase of the tree
And life's imponderable seed,
The mammoth sea-log and the sea
Clutching it with mounting greed,
The creature's truthful husk
Casts out the pagan dusk.

Touch you may and touch you can,
White and strange, the drifting wood,
But never touch the severed man
Torn from history for good,
Nailing to splints and spars
Night, and the turning stars.

Vernon Watkins, *Cypress and Acacia,* 1959.

3. *Paviland Cave*

The cavern is somewhat difficult to locate without a little knowledge of the precipitous and broken coastline between Port Eynon
and the western extremity of Gower. Its position is on the cliff-face
facing seawards at a distance of about 1¼ miles east of Mewslade Bay
and 2 miles west of Port-Eynon. Previously known as Goat's Hole, it
received its present name from the nearby farm of Paviland, although it is situated just outside the boundaries of that property.
    The easiest method of approach is from the Swansea-Rhossili road
at Pilton Green, which involves a walk of nearly 1½ miles . . . The entrance to the cave is on a cliff as Yellow Top (although the O.S. 6″
sheet applies this name to a crag a little to the east) and faces the sea at
a height of about 30 feet above the present high-water mark. Inside,
the cave measures about 15 feet in width and extends inwards for 70
feet. On the right of the entrance is a "chimney" leading to a secon-
dary opening on the cliff at a higher level; and further in, on the left, is
another chimney.

The first recorded exploration of Goat's Hole was undertaken by two brothers named Davies in 1822. Later in the same year Mr. L. W. Dillwyn and Miss Talbot of Penrice carried out further investigations and unearthed a large collection of teeth and bones and traces of occupation during the Roman period.

Dr. Buckland, hearing of these discoveries, came to Gower and made a more thorough examination of the cave, finding amongst other material, part of a human skeleton stained with red ochre—the famous Red Lady of Paviland. Excavations of a lesser nature were undertaken by Mr. Vivian in 1909 and Messrs. Chambers and Morgan in 1911; but it was not until 1912 that a complete and exhaustive study of the cave and its contents was made: this was under the able leadership of Prof. W. J. Sollas and the results described in a lengthy essay were of extreme importance.

Although the skeleton of the Red Lady was regarded by Buckland and other authorities as of Romano-British date, Sollas showed that, in all probability, the remains belonged to a Cro-Magnon man, the first representative of *Homo sapiens* and the successor of *Homo Neandertalensis*. Other Gower caves have revealed artefacts of Palaeolithic date but only in Paviland have human remains of this period been exhumed.

During excavation Sollas found over 3,600 flakes and fragments of worked flint and chert, of which 700-800 were implements. Besides this large number, several hundreds had been discovered on previous occasions. Owing to the absence of stratification in the deposits, the various industries represented by the implements had to be established typologically. The principal industries recognised by the Abbe Breuil were Mousterian, Middle and Upper Aurignacian and Proto-Solutrean.

In addition to the vast quantity of stone implements, the excavators found fragments of worked bone and ivory, including the perforated teeth of the Reindeer and Wolf. Especially remarkable was the discovery by Sollas of an ovoid piece of ivory, pierced and probably used as a pendant. This had been fabricated from a growth produced by a wound in the pulp cavity of a tusk belonging to a mammoth. The object fitted perfectly into a deformed tusk discovered by Buckland, thus proving that the article had been manufactured on the site. Other material included bone awls, pieces of rubbed bone, a fragmentary ivory ring, several ivory rods and three bone spatulae of uncertain use.

Valuable remains from Paviland are in the Royal Institution of

South Wales and other discoveries are in the National Museum of Wales, Cardiff, and the university Museum , Oxford. At present the cave shows unmistakable signs of careful excavation. Even the smallest and most remote crevices and pockets have been examined, although, during a scrutiny of the loose material on the floor of the cave, we unearthed a waste fragment of flint possessing the deep, white patination typical of Paviland implements . . .

E. E. Allen and J. G. Rutter, *Gower Caves,*
Part I, 1946.

4. *Arthur's Stone*

As to ye Stones . . . they are to be seen upon a jutting attye North-West of Keven-bryn ye most noted hill in Gower. They are put together by labor enough but no great art into a Pile, and theire fashion or posture is this. There is a vast unwrought stone (probably abt 20 tun weight) supported by 6 or 7 others yt are not above 4 foot high, & these are set in a Circle some on end; and some edgwise of ye Lapis Molaris for kind wch is ye natural stone of ye mountain. The Great one is much diminished (of wt it has bin) in bulk; as haveing 5 tun or more (by report) broke off it to make millstones; so yt I guess ye stone originally to have bin bewteen 25 and 30 tun in weight. The carriadge, rearing and placeing of this master rock is plainly an effort of humane industry & art; but ye pullys and leavers, ye force & skill by wch twas don are not so easily imagind. The Comon people call it Arthur's Stone, by a lift of vulgar imagination attributing to yt Here an extravagant size and strength. In my conceit tis some signal boundary.

The Rev. John Williams, Rector of Cheriton,
to Edward Lhuyd, 30 November 1693, in
F. V. Emery, *Edward Lhuyd and some of his*
Glamorgan correspondents: A View of Gower
in the 1690s, 1965.

5. *Burry Holms*

The island called in English the Holm, in Gowerland, in the west part of Gowerland, beyond Swansea, lies between Swansea town and Kidwelly town, Swansea on the northside, and the town of St. David's on the west, forty miles off, and is half a mile long, and about quarter broad, and the Severn sea surrounds the said island.

William of Worcester, *Itinerary,* 1478, from
James Nasmyth's ed. 1778.

6. *Bishopston Valley*

Bishopston Valley and the adjoining sea-cliffs at Pwlldu are ideal places in which to see how some of the commonest Gower habitats are inter-related. The Valley itself, like others in Gower, has a very characteristic shape. Walking along one of the foot-paths or lanes through farming land, nothing but gently undulating countryside can be seen all around, until the lane opens out on to the steep Valley side and one is suddenly confronted by an enormous jagged cleft in the land surface.

Its harsh outlines are softened by a curiously random mixture of woodland, scrub, heath and grassland forming a complex pattern. There seems to be no obvious reason for this mosaic of contrasting plant cover. Here and there, outcrops and screes of pale limestone break through the skin of vegetation, emphasising its precarious foothold on the sloping rocks and suggesting a line of enquiry into the origin of the varied pattern.

Down below, in the sheltered Valley the air is still, for the strong winds and salt laden gales which buffet and scorch the vegetation on the cliff terraces of Pwll-du Head, seldom more than ruffle the tree tops of the Valley floor. And yet, despite this the plant cover on the exposed sea-cliffs at the Head is remarkably similar to that of the sheltered Valley, for there too, fragments of heath are mixed with patches of grass and scrub in a meaningless jumble—only the woodland is absent. Yellow rockrose and gorse, purple knapweed, bell heather and thyme, pale blue scabious and speedwell, all these are there too, and hundreds more, giving scent and colour to both sea-cliffs and Valley slopes. By contrast, the flat cliff top at the Head has a monotonous cover of short grass, bramble and bracken.

Why should it be so different from the cliff and Valley slopes, and why indeed should they themselves support such a jumbled variety of plant-communities? Is it possible to understand the factors which have been at work to create such diversity? The answers are not far to seek for the forces which moulded the existing vegetation are still operating. However stable the present pattern may appear, there is a continual struggle for living space, resulting in a slow but unceasing change in the mosaic of plant cover. Nearly all the successive stages in the evolution of the vegetation throughout the centuries are still there, spread out in space, for the curious to attempt to link together.

Gordon T. Goodman, *Plant Life in Gower,* 1962.

7. *Underhill*

From Underhill the waters of Oxwich marches, cleared of much of their summer vegetation, gleam ice-cold and still in the winter air: wild duck, an occasional snipe disturbed, a lonely gull and a coot on the quiet water, and always the dry rustle of the rushes. No more the busy movement of the warblers, nor the yellow of the flags. The lichen-covered, skeleton trees show more clearly, grey-green and dead. Then the pale sun of winter colours the marshes and there is life again.

Olive Phillips, *Gower,* 1956.

8. *Monkton Wood*

. . . the said Jurors say that the tenants of the demesne tenements of the said manor do claim liberty to cut furze and fern for their use upon a parcel of waste ground called Monkton Wood by ancient meres and bounds well known, lying on ye Common called Cefn Bryn and on the south side of the said Manor, as a right which time out of mind hath been used and enjoyed by the Tenants of the said demesne Tenements without any interruption . . .

Survey of Walterston and Cillibion, 1689, in
Baker and Francis, *Surveys of Gower,*
1870.

9. *Sanctuary*

There is within the said circuit one message and tenement of lands called Sanctuary, being by estimation 45 acres lying in itself, having the highway that leadeth from Penrice Church to Porteynon moor on the east part, the Lord's Land in the hands of David Bennett called Miller's moor of the south part, the Lord's land called Brinsill on the West Part, and the free lands of Gryffyth Bowen on ye north, the which said messuage and tenement John Bennett holdeth of the ye manor of West Millwood, being parcel of the late dissolved Priory of St. John of Jerusalem in England . . .

Survey of the Manor of Penrice, 1632, in
Baker and Francis, *Surveys of Gower,*
1870.

10. *Port Eynon, 1833*

Port-Eynon (Porth-Einon), a parish, in the union and hundred of Swansea, county of Glamorgan, South Wales, 15 miles (w.s.w.) from Swansea; containing 380 inhabitants. It is situated on the Bristol Channel, and is inclosed and in a good state of cultivation; the village, which occupies a pleasant situation on the west, forms an agreeable feature in the picturesque scenery with which the environs abound.

There is an extensive oyster-fishery on the coast, which, with the exportation of its produce, affords a lucrative employment during the season to a large proportion of the inhabitants. There are from fifteen to twenty vessels, varying in burthen from thirty to sixty tons, engaged in this and the limestone trade, the oysters, when obtained in sufficient quantity, being shipped off to Bristol. The parish abounds with limestone, which is procured in large quantities for exportation, and also for the supply of the neighbouring districts; on that which is exported a toll of two-pence per ton, called "cliffage," is paid to the lord of the manor, and frequently amounts to £40 per month.

The living is a rectory, rated in the king's books at £9. 5. 10., and in the patronage of the Crown; present net income, £121, with a glebe-house. The church is dedicated to St. Cadocus. A National day school, containing 50 children, is supported partly by an annual donation of £10 from C. R. M. Talbot, Esq., and partly by payments from the parents, the master instructing 10 poor children gratuitously. Mr. Talbot gave the ground for the erection of the school, which was completed in 1817, at an expense of £67 2., of which £40 was a bequest of Frances Gibbs, in 1794, remaining in the hands of the churchwardens and overseers, and the residue was made up by subscriptions. A Sunday school for 60 persons, also, is maintained by voluntary contributions. Mr. John Clement, in 1784, left the sum of £14. 9. 6d., directing the interest to be laid out in bread for distribution on Christmas-day, among the poor receiving parochial relief.

Samuel Lewis, Topographical Dictionary of Wales, 1833.

11. *Port Eynon Quay*

The cliffs overlooking the quay bear witness to the thousands of tons of stone that were quarried in the old days. Every quarryman had his own *quar*, a fact which accounts for the bewildering multiplicity of channels and isolated troughs cut in the rock, which one sees on every hand. He possessed also his horse and *butt*, whereby the stone was conveyed down the tortuous tracks to the quay. His women-folk invariably took charge of the transport of the stone. They, too, had their rules. Unlike the men, they worked to suit the tides, as the whole cargo had to be piled on the quay in such a position that the vessels could berth alongside for leading; it was considered a good day's work to average twelve *butts* per tide.

The quarrymen received eighteen pence per ton, which covered drilling, blasting and transporting the stone to the foreshore. Of this sum, a tithe was payable to the lord of the manor as *cliffage*. A bailiff had been appointed in each manor since the 17th century to collect *cliffage, keelage,* and customs charges on exported animals. Each ship that berthed on the foreshore was charged four pence *Keelage*. Twelve pence per annum was demanded from locally-owned vessels. The customs charge on horses was twopence, on hogs a halfpenny, and on sheep a farthing.

During the winter, when the men-folk were employed in the oyster fishery, the women set out for the cliffs with their *pick*, hook and rope to cut gorse which was used as fodder for the horses. The prickly bundles were carried home and bruised with heavy wooden clubs before being fed to the animals. When the grass was very sparse in the winter, this was the only food available, but the horses, nevertheless, throve upon it. The bruising process was known as *pounding vurse*.

Apart from the expert trade, limestone was quarried and burnt for local use. Before the days of superphosphate, lime was used extensively for promoting fertility and for *sweetening* the land. The *culm*, or small coal, used for igniting the kilns was bought by the local smacks from Swansea or Port Talbot. In Port-eynon parish alone, dotted along the cliffs westward of the bay, there are seven or eight kilns in various stages of dilapidation.

The quayside, where a hundred years ago a dozen or more Devon craft might be seen loading limestone, is now devoid of shipping, and is being gradually silted up. Many a quarryman's cot has crumbled away, and the common land where he grazed his horse has been enclosed and added to the adjacent farms. The *quars* on the clifftops, where strong arms wielded the heavy sledgehammers, are now overrun with bramble and gorse; but their harsh outlines are being mellowed by time. Many of the tracks where Uncle John Eynon's *Fly Dragon* and Isaac Champion's *Bowler*, together with a string of other horses, tugged and strained at the clumsy *butts*, are now obliterated. These disappearing landmarks are reminiscent of an era when Porteynon was a village of some consequence in the Peninsula, and when its prosperity depended on more hazardous and exciting activities than it does today.

H. M. Tucker, *Gower Gleanings,* 1951.

12. *Oxwich*

Wide windscape; the sand moulded
As waves are, into mounds,
But higher, scalloped, rounded
To hold the heat in craters
Walled against winds.
So too birch and ash bend,
Succumb to lichen, salt,
Early stunting, decay;
Brambles crawl, lying low
To save their sparse blue berries,
Intruders here, though prolific
Farther back where the tall trees huddle
And the wind's way ends
Up against rock and the rainy hillside.

Long seascape, interlocked
With various land.
Fresh water comes down to brine
From loam through marshland to gravel
And with the lushest warbling
Of Blackbird, thrush in warm leaves

Mingles a curlew's fluting
And, windblown, an oystercatcher's;
On shallow banks the footprints,
The detritus of herons, of gulls.

Discount the castles above,
Hidden, and foreign here
As campers who drink a morning
Too bitter-sweet for comfort
Though wind and rain hold back,
A jungle of weeds exhales
Earthy richness beyond the dunes.
Guests at a dangerous marriage
Daily solemnized, broken,
They walk abeyance, close
To whirlpools, to sheer cliffs,
And will not return when the fox
Leanly lopes over ice.

Michael Hamburger, *Travelling,* 1969.

13. *Burry Head*

We must look at all the nooks and corners of Gower, so we visit
Burry, where the Burry stream has its source. It is a fine spring
bursting out of the limestone rocks and rolling down the sweet vale to
Cheriton. It is the finest stream in Gower, and is celebrated for its
golden trout. The traveller cannot fail to notice the noble old elm tree
bridging the mountain rill at the top of the Burry. It lies across from
bank to bank, affording a good footway for the traveller, and
luxuriates grandly, like a "tree planted by the waters." A rocky lane
leads from here to Llangennith, or up to the main road. Through this
old bye-way the waters in winter come raging down.

Here superstition gives us ghosts and goblins, and few venture
through the lonely place in the dark hour of night. Sometimes may be
seen strange and terrible sights—huge black dogs like calves, or
monsters with flaming eyes and fiery breath, and again they see large
balls of fire leaping over the hedges and sweeping through the gorse-
covered fields. The peasantry, when gazing with horror at the (to
them) supernatural spectre, believe it to be the king of evil, the

monarch of the burning lake, and hasten with terrified hearts away. To tell them it is but a vapour, the *ignus fatuus* or Will o' the Wisp, is in vain. So firm a hold has superstition on their senses, that they will not believe it to be anything but agents from that gloomy land where the enemy of the human race holds his empire.

We stray back again the way we came, pass Llanddewi, and on by Scurlage Castle. There is no trace of a castle here now. If there ever was a castle here it has mouldered to decay, for not one stone can be seen upon another . . .

C. D. Morgan, *Wanderings in Gower,* 1886 ed.

14.   *On the Worm's Head*

I often go down in the mornings to the furthest point of Gower—the village of Rhossili—and stay there until evening. The bay is the wildest, bleakest, and barrenest I know—four or five miles of yellow coldness going away into the distance of the sea. And the Worm, a seaworm of rock pointing into the channel, is the very promontory of depression. Nothing lives on it but gulls and rats, the millionth generation of the winged and tailed families that screamed in the air and ran through the grass when the first sea thudded on the Rhossili beach. There is one table of rock on the Worm's back that is covered with long yellow grass, and, walking on it, one feeling like something out of the Tales of Mystery & Imagination treading, for a terrible eternity, on the long hair of rats. Going over that grass is one of the strangest experiences; it gives under one's feet; it makes little sucking noises, & smells—and this to me is the most grisly smell in the world—like the fur of rabbits after rain.

When the tide comes in, the reef of needle rocks that leads to the base of the Worm is covered under water. I was trapped on the Worm once. I had gone on it early in the afternoon with a book and a bag of food, and, going to the very, very end, had slept in the sun, with the gulls crying mad over me. And when I woke the sun was going down. I ran over the rocks, over the abominable grass, and on to the ridge overlooking the little reef. The tide had come in. I stayed on that Worm from dusk till midnight, sitting on the top grass, frightened to go further in because of the rats and because of the things I am ashamed to be frightened of. Then the tips of the reef began to poke out of the water, and, perilously, I climbed along them on to the shore, with an 18 mile walk in front of me. It was a dark, entirely silent, entirely empty road. I saw everything on that walk—from snails, lizards, glow-worms & hares to diaphanous young ladies in white who vanished as I approached them,

> Dylan Thomas to Pamela Hansford Johnson.
> October 1933, from *The Selected Letters*
> *of Dylan Thomas,* 1966.

15. *The Three Cleeves*

Whitsun Monday, 10 June 1878

Fine morning. Price drove me to the station to catch the 9.50 train for Three Cocks en route for Llechryd and Killey to stay with the Westhorps at Ilston Rectory. Reached Killey at 3.30, but there was no one to meet me, my letter not having reached Westhorp. Walked over to Ilston Rectory, 4 miles, over the fine high common through the screaming of peewits and a strong wind blowing from the sea. Found Mrs. Westhorp alone in the house and had tea with her on the lawn. Westhorp, Ilston and Miss Huband had driven to Killey to meet me by a later train. I brought a 2 gallon stoneware jar to get it filled with sea water for Miss Newton's acquarium. Westhorp affected to think it contained wine or brandy and water for my private refreshment and called it my 'flask.'

Whitsun Tuesday, 11 June

Barnaby Bright, but the weather wild, cold and wet and stormy. Walked with Westhorp to Penmaen. We went down to the Three Cleeves (Cliffs) Bay through the fox-gloves and the fern, among which white fantail pigeons were walking. The fern and foxgloves clothe the hillside down to the sandhills. The storm at Penmaen high on the hill looking seaward was tremendous. We sat on the rocks as the tide came in and watched the wild grey sea and the waves breaking white with foam and the surf dashing high against the black cliffs and falling back in showers of spray while a solitary deserted boat with a bare mast rode tossing at anchor in the bay.

Thursday, 13 June

A lovely day. Paddled with Ilston in the Ilston river and got out his iron harp for him. A lovely walk with Westhorp through the cwms to Park Mill and then up the Green Cwm to 'The Groves' and the great bone cavern, where Westhorp could not see even 'the outline of a female.'

Friday, 14 June
Paddled with Ilston in the river. Walked with Westhorp down the Bishopstone Valley to Pwll Dhu bay. Bathed in the Cove, while Wethorp lay on the rocks.

Saturday, 15 June
Beynon filled the 2-gallon 'flask' for me with sea water last night at Three Cleeves Bay. Left Ilston with regret after a happy time at 9.30. Reached Kinnersley 2.30.

The Rev. Francis Kilvert, *Kilvert's Diary,* 1878.
Edited by William Plomer.

16. *Blue Pool Bay*

This bay derives its name from a circular pool, about 15 feet in diameter, but now of no great depth, formed by nature in the rocks, and just about high water mark, so that the sea washes into it during spring tides. Twenty years ago its depth was about 15 feet, and it was supposed to be unfathomable; it is now quite shallow, and nearly filled up with sand, which has drifted into this bay very much of late.

About half way between Blue Pool and the Arch, or as it is sometimes called, the 'Three Chimnies', a remarkable discovery of gold doubloons and moidores was made by John Richard and Honora his wife, about 100 years ago. They had been drawing for fish, with the net used for that purpose in these parts, and were resting on the rocks after their work, when the old man observed some glittering yellow substance in a crevice of the rock on which they were sitting; his curiosity being excited, he picked it out, and discovered it to be a large piece of gold; both then proceeded to search the place more closely, and it is said that these two people found at that time a large number of these coins.

Whether any were met with by other parties I have not been able to learn; but the fact seems to have been well known; and about forty years ago, two men, Thomas Hullin and William Taylor, went with their quarrymen's bills purposely to search this spot, to see if they could find any, and strange to say, they had not been long at work before they came upon several more of these coins sticking in the crevices of the rocks, and as bright as the day they came out of the mint. After a while others joined them, and the rocks were blasted with gunpowder, and it is said some few were found in this way.

But at this point of the proceedings, the Lord of the Manor (the late Major Penrice, of Kilvrough) interfered and stopped them, and I have never heard that any were found since.

The Rev. J. D. Davies, *A History of West Gower,* Vol. III, 1885.

17. *Highway*

Highway was the great emporium, and many are the strange stories associated with this old farm. In the thick darkness of night the peasantry of Gower used to assemble here, mounted on their horses, and also well armed. In the large room a good feast was always prepared at a certain hour, and the pure unadulterated spirit from the vintage of France went briskly round. After being well primed they sallied forth their work—each had straps fastened to his saddle which held the ankers of cognac—down through the valleys, and over the rocks to the landing place; little cared those desperadoes for the then weak power of the law. Into Pwlldu bay the French luggers used to come—discharge their cargoes and away. Under the stables, in the rick yard, and all about Highway cellars were made to receive those contraband goods. Many are the midnight carousals that have taken place here—the old walls have often shock with the noisy revelry. We easily picture the scenes—we fancy we see the old, oak table spread with the good things of the earth, and the huge bowl full of genuine Geneva, crowning the board.

C. D. Morgan, *Wanderings in Gower,* 1886 ed.

18. *The Pengwern Hoard*

Mr. Dods, writing from Park, March 23rd, 1826, described this find. "The coins were found, 1823, at Pengwern Farm, adjoining Llethrid in the parish of Ilston, amongst the loose stones and rubbish of a limestone quarry close to a kiln. They were dispersed through a space scarcely exceeding 18 or 20 feet square, and in general lay within 12 in. of the surface, over most part of which a slight turf has formed since the removal of the rubbish. No vessel, or fragments of any were found near the spot, though sought for. They were all *denares* of the Emperors or Empresses from Nero to Marcus Aurelius, inclusive, those of Trajan being by far the most numerous. Probably more than 200 were picked up in all, of which Mr. Lucas, of Stout Hall, I believe next to myself, obtained the greater part; some are still in the houses of the adjoining cottages. I had originally as many as 130 or 140."

Pengwern, as the name denotes, is an elevated spot overlooking a wet moor; a narrow valley runs down from it to the sea.

In a further letter he says that "the series is as follows: Emperors Nero, Vespasian, Titus, Domitian, Nerva, Trajan, Hadrian, Antoninus Pius, Macus Aurelius. Empresses Platina, Sabina, Faustina, senior and junior."

The earlier coins, with the exception of one Vitellius, are described by him to be much worn, and one which he thinks may be an Otho has the inscription too much defaced to be legible. About both the Faustinas he has some doubts, but the coins of a later date are mostly in a good state of preservation.

"The reverses, though in general of a commonplace sort, in a few instances present some interest; among the Trajans there is the 'Dacia Capta'; among the Hadrians, Egypt with her sistrum, and Africa with her scorpion; and in one of the Antoninus, Romulus and Remus are apparently figured sucking the wolf. The most singular reverse, as it seems to me, is a diademed head, the obverse being Trajan."

> Col. W. Ll. Morgan, *Antiquarian Survey of
> East Gower*, 1899.

19.   *Park-le-Breos*

The Normans left behind them in Gower their castles and churches which to some extent still dominate the landscape. But perhaps one of the most tantalising vestiges of the feudal order in Gower is Park-le-Breos, the great deer park which was probably created in the thirteenth century by the de Breos Lords of Gower whose name it still bears. In 1203 King John gave Gower to William de Breos, and already by 1230 there is a documentary reference to *"silva de Bruiz."*

Park-le-Breos was part of the Lord's manorial complex which was centred on the demesne manor castle of Pennard, for with this manor were associated the Knights Fees of Lunnon and Kittle. From the demesne of the Fee of Lunnon lying to the west of Llethrid Cwm and Green Cwm, and probably still covered in the early middle ages by the primeval woodland, was staked out a large park of 500 acres. The area included two deeply wooded valleys, and with the deer park was probably built the Lord's hunting lodge at Park-le-Breos House. Tooth Cave, Cathole, and Giant's Grave with their prehistoric remains, all hear evidence to the great antiquity of the Green Cwm area.

To the Norman Lords of the early Middle Ages, parks and forests had a special significance. "In the forest are the secret places of the kings," wrote one medieval chronicler, "there they can for a little while breathe in the grace of natural liberty." The chase also provided good training for war, and great landlords naturally wanted a reliable supply of fresh meat for the winter months. In such carefully constructed deer parks as Park-le-Breos, red, fallow and roe deer were hunted with due ceremony. But the animals were otherwise strictly protected by the laws of *venison,* just as the forest was protected by the laws of *vert.* Glades were also built, and carefully planted with oaks.

The folk memory of the ancient Park, with its undertones of forest lore, the world of Tolkien, remains commemorated in the names of Park Place, Park Cwm, Park Woods and Park Mill. The main entrance lay past the Park Mill—still in use—and then along Park Cwm and so westwards above a shallow valley leading to Park-le-Breos House with its splendid vistas over the woods. From the Park's central glade, today marked by Green Cwm Cottage, two steeply wooded cwms led to the main hunting slopes on the west of the Park. The first cwm ends near Longoaks, the second, or Lodge Cwm, climbs to the ruins of Lodge farm on the boundary of the Park with Walterston Manor. Here at Lodge was probably an ancient hunting box.

Place name evidence gives only part of the story of Park-le-Breos. Medieval deer parks were usually surrounded by a continuous earth bank capped by a fence or pale, which was often reinforced—as at Park-le-Breos—by a wall and an inside ditch to prevent escaping deer. Later, when disparking occurred, the Park wall remained. Even today, some five hundred years after disparking, the boundary line of Park-le-Breos can be seen quite clearly along most of its four mile circumference. At Park Mill the boundary appears as the line of the old road to Northhill Farm and South Gower, a line running south of the modern highway which slices through the ancient parkland to Penmaen. From Northhill Farm, the Park wall then ran across the eastern flank of Cefn Bryn to Longoaks Farm, with some traces of old walling and a ditch visible as one approaches Longoaks.

After Longoaks, on the gently sloping parkland above the Green Cwm, the boundary curves north-west, and then north-eastwards to Lodge and Llethrid, the northern limit of the Park. Here the continuous line of the Park wall may be seen at its clearest as it separates the old enclosed demesne of Walterston and Cillibion Manors from the irregular fileds carved out of the disparked land. On large-scale Ordnance Survey maps and air photographs the boundaries of Park-le-Breos stand out quite distinctly.

The size and scale of Park-le-Breos still surprise. Yet this hunting ground of the Lords of Gower may have had a relatively short life. We know that in 1317, William de Breos III, the last of the Gower de Breoses, granted to William his huntsman—remembered in Hunt's Farm and Hunt's Bay—full liberty "to take all manner of venison, foxes, hares and rabbits" in the sand burrows of Pennard.

The grant may indicate that de Breos was no longer interested in his manorial estates at Pennard. And that in any case, besanding of the demesnes here, which lay between the Castle and the bridge, today's stepping stones, had reduced the value of the Manor, By 1331 the Lordship of Gower had passed to the Mowbrays whose interests lay mostly in the north of England. After that date, Gower ceased to be ruled by a resident Marcher Lord.

Other factors, some local, some not, may have hastened the decline of Park-le-Breos. The Mowbray succession was followed in mid-century by the Black Death, by rural depopoulation, and an associated agricultural crisis. Feudal dues began to yield to cash rents, open arable fields began to be gradually enclosed, and whatever the precise cause, the revenues of the Lordship of Gower declined by half during the last thirty years of the fourteenth century. Then, in 1400, came the great revolt of Owain Glyn Dwr, which affected Gower, and which probably accelerated these profound social and economic changes. Throughout this latter period, then, manorial and medieval institutions generally were in decline in Gower, and with them declined Park-le-Breos.

Finally, the Wars of the Roses signalled the passing of the old medieval aristocratic society, and the rise of new, aspiring families of gentry such as the Gower Mansels and the better-known dynasty founded by William Herbert, Earl of Pembroke, Lord of Gower, 1468-9. By 1450, in all probability, Park-le-Breos had been disparked, its open spaces let and parcelled out into fields and closes, its

woods and glades allotted for grazing.
Yet the old deer park continued to fascinate. In the 1580s, Rice Merrick, the Glamorgan chorographer, recorded that in Penmaen parish stood 'an ancient lodge house call'd Park y Price . . . sometimes emparked with a wall and pale but long time past disparked . . .' Over half a century later, the Cromwellion Survey of Gower (1650) recorded, under Pennard, that 'Park le Bruce' contained about 500 acres and had 'a longetime been disparked and divided into 3 partes which are farmed out to severall tenants . . .' The Survey noted that the Park had been divided into the three farms of Longoaks, Park Price, and Llethrid, each farm let by the Lord of Gower at an annual rent of £36 13. 4d. Evidently the Earl of Worcester was an early conservationist, for his tenants covenanted that they were 'not to cutt down or trapp any oake, ash or elme."

The walls of the deer park probably continued to stand into the eighteenth century. In a manorial survey of the Manor of Walterston and Cillibion in December 1689, the jurors testified that the bounds of the Manor extended from Cefn Bryn, 'along the Park wall or ditch to a tenement of lands called the Lodge' and 'from thence along as the said parke wall or ditch leadeth to another tenement' called Llethrid. Eight years later in July 1697, in his 'Description of Gower,' Isaac Hamon, Steward of the Manor of Bishopston, wrote to Edward Lluyd that 'the walles are up in some places . . . there is much wild and woody ground.' Hamon went on to record, citing the Cromwellian survey, that the area 'hath been disparked about 250 years, according to ye survey of Gower.'

Since Isaac Hamon's time the walls and ditch of Park-le-Breos have disappeared, but the area still retains something of its mystery. From the Somersets, Hereditary Lords of Gower after 1492, the Park-le-Breos estate passed to a branch of the Vivian family in the nineteenth century. Then, in the summer of 1938, Admiral Walker-Heneage-Vivian led the great shoot on the estate, driving up Lodge Cwm towards Cillibion, surrounded by scores of guns, beaters and retainers.

Following the Admiral's death in 1952, the estate was sold to the tenants, and the woods to the Forestry Commission. But as in the early seventeenth century, the old Park still remains divided the three farms of Long-oaks, Llethrid and Park-le-Breos. Appropriately enough, Park-le-Breos house has become a trekking centre. The ancient parkland above the Green Cwm now sports corn and cabbages, while other enclosed fields have relapsed from arable into pasture.

The deer have long since left and now only foxes roam the still thickly-wooded cwms of Park-le-Breos.

David Rees, *Gower XXV,* 1974.

20.   *Carn Llwyd*

On this wild and desolate moor, on Mynnydd y Gwrhyd mountain, 1½ miles from [Llangiwg] church and a few yards to the left of the road running due north from thence, not far from Llwyn y Pryfed farm, there are now evident remains of a circle, 67 ft. in diameter, enclosing the remains of a carn. There are five well defined stones on one side and three on the other, besides several just showing above the surface, making in this (outer) circle fifteen stones in all; and there are also seven holes from which stones have been taken at some recent date. The largest stone is 3ft. 3in. long, 11in. above the ground and 6in. thick; all the others are much smaller.

The circle is also defined by a slight bank of earth except for a distance of twenty;five feet, where it has been destroyed. A stone (2ft. 6in. by 8in. by 1ft.) eleven feet inside this circle, is probably the remains of an inner circle, there being also slight traces of an earth bank.

In the middle is a hole apparently the site of a cist-vaen, which has plainly been but recently (1893) destroyed.

It was described in Rees' *Beauties of England and Wales,* 1819, thus: "Three concentric circles of flat stones placed like those at Carn Llechart and about the same size. The diameter of the largest circle is about twenty yards; the inner circles are separated from this and from each other by a space of about five feet. In the centre is a cistvaen vulgarly called the altar, which is quite perfect. Several of the upright stones have been removed and the areas between the circles have been nearly filled up by large pebbles from the adjacent common."

The present appearance is such that we may consider that account as then correct, though the circle is now virtually destroyed, and its very existence is almost unknown to local antiquaries.

Col. W. Ll. Morgan, *Antiquarian Survey of East Gower,* 1899.

21. *Pwll-y-Bloggi*

This is one of the few Welsh place names in Pennard parish. The word is derived from *pwll*—the resort or lurking place of the *bleige* or *bleiddgi* (corrupted into *bloggi*) the wolf dog. It is a name of great antiquity. According to the *Annales of Wichcomb* (1136), packs of wolves descended into Gower, and devoured the bodies of a large number of men slain in battle between the Normans and the Welsh, when 516 were killed, and their bodies devoured, April 15, 1136. Among them was Richard Fitzgilbert, earl of Hertford, afterwards buried in Gloucester Cathedral.

The Rev. Latimer Davies, *Pennard and West Gower*, 1928.

22. *Barland Common*

Barland, wild and black as it is, awakens stirring mementoes of the past. On this old green more than half a century ago, the sons of Gower used to meet as "soldiers"—then ready to protect their homes from the fangs of the foreign foemen.

On this moorland they used to drill. The Dogs of War were loose, and Europe in dire convulsions. Napoleon was shaking the mighty from their pinnacles, and the echoing of his voice made nations tremble. England called to her bravest—nor called in vain; the eagle of France swoop'd aloft, and no one knew the moment it would pounce on its prey. Welshmen responded to the cry of their country, and Gowerians buckled on their swords—it was no fancied alarm, the the thunderstorm brooded over the world, and England waited the bursting of the lightning's flash. The hills and vallies of Gower sent forth their sons, hardy and brave, ready to meet the foe. In the hour of danger—in the days long past—Gowerians could have shouted the motto of Napier—Ready! aye, Ready!

Some were tried and proved true—some followed Wellington in his glory-crowned career—others shared Nelson's danger on the deep, and some also bled at Waterloo. More than fifty years ago Gower sent out her children first and foremost. They were then deemed worthy to defend their own Peninsula. The late Thomas Mansel Talbot, Esq., formed a company of Rifles (Rangers) and felt so proud of his men—all his tenantry—that they were taken to England to be reviewed, where they were highly commented on their efficiency. There was also the Local Militia, of which the late Mr. Voss, of Swansea, was captain, and who took an active interest in the corps, being most zealous in his duties as officer; and, again, there were the Fencibles, and Volunteers—it was thought essential to arm for real service in those days. The terrible Bonaparte was a lion, whose march was death.

With an open line of coast this Peninsula offers so many favourable landing places—a hundred thousand men could disembark in Rhossily or Oxwich Bay in a very short time—the whole of the produce of Gowerland would be a happy supply, and a landing effected undisturbed, would enable any foe to take up a position, and from which they could not be dislodged without considereable cost.

C. D. Morgan, *Wanderings in Gower,* 1886 ed.

23.   *The Battery*

The Battery, built of selected limestone, whose foundations are laid in the solid rock, skirts and surrounds the Mumbles lighthouse on its southern side. It was completed in 1860 at a cost to the War Department of £10,000. The erection of the battery for the protection of the roadstead and shipping was brought about the persistent exertions of Col. Geo. Grant Francis. It was not the first battery at the Mumbles, for four-18-pounders were previously (about 1804) mounted on the extremity of the main headland; and in the seventeenth century there was a battery overlooking the bay at the Dunns.

At the [Swansea Harbour] Trustees' meeting, 10 Sept. 1861, the chairman (Mr. Starling Benson) said he had been informed by very competent authority that whenever the guns in the Mumbles battery were fired off, every pane of glass in the lighthouse would be blown out, but there was one consolation; the guns were not likely to be fired except in case of war. The suggestion was not borne out, however, and the guns have frequently been fired for long-range practice.

W. H. Jones, *History of the Port of Swansea,* 1922.

24.   *Dervill's Well*

The ancient bounds and meres of the said Manor is and time out of mind hath been as followeth: Beginning at the fall of the water of the river of Bury into the great river of Loughor, and as the same river of Burry leadeth into a well called Dervill's well, and from Dervill's well southward to a place called the old fort on Llanmadoc Down, and from thence eastward . . .

Survey of Landimore, 1598, in Baker and
Francis, *Surveys of Gower,* 1870.

25. Neuadd Wen

. . . *In Kilgerwen*[1] *standeth an ancient house called neadd wen as fame remaineth built by Sir Rys ap Thomas Kt for a lodge when he came to that parts to hunt* . . .

Rice Merrick, c. 1584.

---

1. Caegurwen. The old house stood near the junction of the Amman and the Garnant rivers, at the most northerly reaches of the Lordship.

IV

People

1. *The Son of Juanus*

AD VECTI FILIUS

JGVANI HIC JACIT

*(The stone) of Advectus (?), son of
. . . Juanus. He lies here.*

Inscribed stone in Llanmadoc Church, 5th-
early 6th century AD.

2. *Prince Llywelyn at Llangiwg*

1217

And thereupon he led his host to Gower over the Black Mountain, where many of his sumpters were lost. And then he encamped at Llangiwg. After Reginald de Breos had seen the ravage that Llywelyn was inflicting upon his territory, he took six ordained knights along with him and he came to surrender himself to Llywelyn at his pleasure, and he surrendered the castle of Seinhenydd [Swansea] to him. And that Llywelyn entrusted to the keeping of Rhys Grug.

And after having stayed there a few days, he led his troops towards Dyfed against the Flemings . . .

> *Brut y Tywysogion or The Chronicle of the Princes*
> (Red Book of Hergest Version), translated by
> Thomas Jones, 1955.

3. *Henry de Gower*

Bishop of St. David's: 1328-1347

Henry De Gower, the eminent building prelate of St. David's in Wales, may justly be compared with his almost contemporary brother, William of Wykeham, Bishop of Winchester, in England. Both were men of original genius, cultivated taste, great wealth, ample opportunity, and large performance.

He was, there are good reasons for believing, a native of Swansea, the chief town of the Lordship Marcher of Gower, whence he took his cognomen, and which forms the south-western extremity of the county of Glamorgan. In earlier times this district was claimed for Carmarthenshire in Deheubarth . . .

No record of his parentage or early training remains, but as we know that he became a canon of St. David's in 1314, and may thereupon presume him to have been twenty-one years of age, it may be averred with some degree of confidence that he was born *circa* 1293.[1]

Bishop Godwin informs us that he was educated at Merton College, Oxford, whence according to the Register of Canterbury, he took the degree of LL.D. It is generally allowed that he held the office of Chancellor of Oxford, a circumstance which has probably led to his being sometimes described as Lord Chancellor of England, a position he certainly did not occupy.

There are records to show that in 1324 he was appointed Archdeacon of St. David's, an office of active importance; and further, that on the 21st of April, 1328, he reached his crowning dignity as Bishop of that see, the temporalities of which were, as usual, restored to him by the Crown in May of the following year.

As early as 1332 his especial interest in Swansea was shown by the founding and erecting in St. Mary Street of that town an Hospital for the aged and decayed priests and laymen of his vast diocese.

In that work of piety and true charity he was liberally aided by the great folk of the district, but especially by Alinora, the eldest daughter and coheir of the last William de Breos . . .

> George Grant Francis, 'A Brief Memoir
> of Henry de Gower,' *Archaeologia
> Cambrensis,* 1876.

4. *Lewis Glyn Cothi in Gower*

Yfory awn I Fro Wyr
Nid aethom yno neithiwr;
Doe hwyliaw, da wehelyth
Trenydd; a pheunydd; a phyth

---

1. Henry de Gower was probably born c. 1278.

Heddyw'dd af, Sion ap Dafydd,
Heno i'w dai yn y dydd.
Impyn yw'n mhob pen i wyr
A'i gred ieuanc hyd awyr!
A gwinllan yn llawn dail
Ym Mawd lle mae ei adail

Gwaith Lewis Glyn Cothi, ed. E. D. Jones,
1953.

5. Sir Hugh Johnys of Landimore

Pray for the sowle of Sir Hugh Johnys, knight, and Dame Mawde his wife. Which Sir Hugh was made knight at the Holy Sepulchre of Oure Lord Jhesu Crist in the city of Jerusalem the 14th day of August the yere of our Lord Gode 1441. And the said Sir Hugh had conynuyd in the werris[1] their long time before, by the space of five years, that is to sey against the Turkis and Sarsyns[2] in the partis of Troy. Grecie and Turkey under John, that time Emprowre of Constatynenople. And aftir that was knight marchall of France under John, duke of Somerset, by the space of five yere. And in likewise aftyr that was knight marchall of Ingland under the good John duke of Norfolke. Which John gyave unto hym the manor of Landymor to hym and to his heyres for evermore. Appon whose soulis Jhesu have mercy.

—Monumental brass, St. Mary's Church,
Swansea.

6. William Herbert

In view of the strength of Lancastrian resistance in south-west Wales, it was essential for Edward IV to put Gower in safe hands, and on February 12, 1462, the king committed the custody of the lordship during the young duke of Norfolk's minority to the most prominent Yorkist supporter in Wales, William, Lord Herbert. John, duke of Norfolk, was given seisin of his lands in March, 1465, but Herbert remained in control of Gower, presumably as the duke's tenant. He was able to exploit the lordship more effectively than the fifteenth century Mowbrays had done . . .

1. Wars.
2. Saracens.

The fourth and last Mowbray, duke of Norfolk, was not a man of much intellect. Obstinate and capable of fits of violent rage, Duke John III (d. 1476) had to be managed by his amiable duchess, Elizabeth Talbot, or by his council. Edward IV in 1469 believed that Norfolk was under the thumb of one of his councillors, Sir William Brandon, and his influence was apparently still paramount in the Duke's household in 1475. Norfolk was anxious to extend his territorial influence in East Anglia, the region where he was most powerful, and in return for Thomas Charles's two manors the duke was induced to convey his lordships of Chepstow and Gower to Lord Herbert. This transaction, which was carried out by the Court of Common Pleas in the autumn of 1468, was subsequently confirmed by the king on May 3, 1469. The political struggles of the wars of the roses had enabled an ambitious and grasping Welsh squire to become one of the chief marcher lords and during Edward IV's first reigh he established the Herberts of Raglan as the dominant family in south Wales.

> J. Beverley Smith and T. B. Pugh, 'The Lordship
> of Gower and Kilvey in the Middle Ages,'
> in *Glamorgan County History*, Vol. III.

7. *Charles Somerset*

Following the marriage of Charles Somerset and Elizabeth Herbert in 1492, the hereditary lordship of Gower remained with the Somerset family. Sir Charles was styled Baron Herbert, in the right of his wife in 1504, and created Earl of Worcester in 1514. A direct descendant was made Duke of Beaufort in 1682:

After the death of William, earl of Huntingdon (d. 1490), the succession to his estates was disputed between his daughter Elizabeth and her uncle, Sir Walter Herbert. This quarrel, which was not settled until 1505, led to the disappearance of the Herbert family from its recently-acquired place among the small group of English earls. Although the crown was at first prepared to recognise Elizabeth Herbert as Countess of Huntingdon, this earldom was soon allowed to lapse. Henry VII aimed to reduce the number of powerful magnate families, and moreover, as Elizabeth Herbert never succeeded in gaining possession of a large part of her father's lands, she did not have the resources necessary to support the rank of countess.

It was probably to further her own interests in her litigation with her uncle that Elizabeth Herbert decided to marry the king's kinsman, Sir Charles Somerset, and her marriage took place in the king's presence on June 2, 1492. As the illegitimate son of Henry Beaufort (d. 1464), third Duke of Somerset, he was a second cousin to Henry VII. Marriage with a bastard involved disparagement for an heiress of high rank, but to establish her claims securely Elizabeth Herbert needed to have the king's goodwill. Arbitration in her dispute with Sir Walter was still awaited in September 1491, and it was probably as a result of her marriage that Elizabeth managed to retain the greater part of the Herbert inheritance in Wales, including the Lordship of Gower and Kilvey, but Sir Walter remained in occupation of Raglan castle, the lordship of Chepstow and Tidenham, and a few manors belonging to the late earl.

> J. Beverley Smith and T. B. Pugh, 'The Lordship of
> Gower and Kilvey in the Middle Ages,' in
> *Glamorgan County History,* Vol, III.

8. *Sir Mathew Cradock*

Sir Mathew Cradock (1468?-1531), royal official in South Wales. Descended from Einion ap Collwyn, he was the son of Richard ap Gwilim ap Evan ap Cradock Vreichfras, and Jennet Horton of Cantelupeston (Candleston) castle near Newton, Glam. In his official capacity he is said to have wielded tremendous power in South Wales. On his tombstone he is described as deputy to Charles, earl of Worcester, in the county of "Glamorgan and Morg.", as chancellor of the same, and steward of "Gower and Kilvei." He is believed to have been steward of Gower in 1491 and 1497. A Matthew Cradok was appointed constable for life of the castle of Kayre Filli and Kenfike in South Wales, 6 March 1485-6 (*Cal. Pat. Rolls,* 1 H. VII), and in July 1491 a Matthew Cradok or Cradoke, with others, is granted a commission to seek assistance for the king for his French wars in the lordships of Cardiff, Glamorgan, Morgannok, Gower, Ilande, Vske and Carlyon (*Cal. Pat. Rolls,* 6 H. VII). The contemporary Welsh bard Iorwerth Fynglwyd composed two poems referring to sir Matthew, one when he was imprisoned by him at Swansea, and another seeking to be reconciled to him (Lewis and Jones, *Mynegai*). He was twice m. — first to Alice, daughter of Philip Mansel of Oxwich Castle, and second to Katherine Gordon, widow of Perkin Warbeck. By his first wife he had a daughter Margaret, who m. Richard Herbert of Ewyas, Herefords., and became the mother of William Herbert, who was created earl of Pembroke in 1551. He died between 14 June and 16 Aug. 1531, and was buried at Swansea.

G. M. Griffiths, *The Dictionary of Welsh Biography down to 1940*, 1959.

9. *Sir Rice Mansel*

Of all the old families of Gower, the Mansels were the most talented and the most famous. The most successful scion of the Gower Mansels was Rice Mansel, born at Oxwich Castle in 1487. His father, Jenkin Mansel, was an ardent Lancastrian and may well have marched with Henry Tudor and Sir Rhys ap Tomas to Bosworth Field in 1485:

Jenkin Mansel's eldest son, Rice (or Rhys) was born on St. Paul's Day (25 January) 1487. An old, but not altogether reliable, source claims that the boy's name was given to him as a tribute to a Welshman "who was acquainted with the name Rhys and was such a Welshman as was not ashamed of the same name but bare it himself." This was unquestionably a reference to Jenkin Mansel's influential patron, Sir Rhys ap Tomos. The same source even went so far as to claim that it was the formidable knight of Dynevor who himself christened the child.

As a youngster, Rice Mansel seems to have been placed in the care of Sir Matthew Cradock, who was connected with the Mansel family by marriage, having married Jenkin Mansel's sister, Alice. Cradock was one of the leading personages in South Wales at this time, and it may well have been be he who gave Rice Mansel a good start in life . . . In 1509 we find Rice Mansel acting as Cradock's deputy in charge of two ships, the *Anthony Cradock* and the *Mary Cradock,* and as captain of the latter. A few years later, Mansel was captain of a ship called *Mathew Cradock* after his uncle and mentor. In 1510 Sir Mathew Cradock, as Rice's guardian, delivered up to his young charge his family estates.

This may well have been a preliminary to his marriage, which took place in the the following year. His wife was Eleanor, daughter of James Bassett, Esquire, of Beaupre. The Bassetts were a family with whom the sixteenth-century Mansels were to be closely linked. Eleanor Bassett was the first of three wives whom Rice Mansel married. This first marriage did not last long. Eleanor must have died in, or just before, the year 1520, when she is referred to as "late wife" of Rice Mansel.

Between the years 1513 and 1526, however, there is very little record of Rice Mansel's activities. We find trace of him only in service with the earl of Worcester in Flanders in 1517 and in a few legal deeds of no great consequence signed by him. Yet by 1526 he had been granted a knighthood, for in a lease dated 30 November 1526 he is described, for the first time in any surviving document, as Rice Mansel, knight. We do not know why he had been made a knight, but his subsequent services to the Crown suggest that during these years he had been gaining considerable experience in war and administration.

He had certainly been acquiring experience of another kind. During these years he had been married a second and third time. In 1520, soon after the death of his first wife, he had married Anne Brydges, by whom he had two daughters. In 1527 he married Cecily, daughter of John Daubridgecourt of Solihull. His third wife had influential contacts with royalty in the person of the Princess Mary, daughter of Henry VIII and Katherine of Aragon. Some years later, Princess Mary was to write to Thomas Cromwell seeking his favour for Rice Mansel, because Mansel had "married one of my gentlewomen whom, for her long and acceptable service to me done, I much esteem and honour". The marriage contract between Sir Rice and his third wife, Cecily, still survives. Dated 19 June 1527, it provided for the settlement on Cecily by her husband of lands to the clear value of £40 a year.

In the 1530s Mansel was to see a great deal of military service in Ireland . . . Whether in response to his wife's anxious solicitude, or simply because his work in Ireland was done, Mansel was allowed to return home about the end of 1535 or early in 1536. This episode of successful military service in Ireland could well have been an important turning-point in his career. Possibly he had done well out of it financially. Certainly he had drawn himself to favourable notice by the king and his ministers.

From 1536 onwards we find him being increasingly employed in positions of trust and authority. In 1536 he became Chamberlain of Chester. He was also a member of the Council of the Marches, was placed on the commission of the peace in more than one county, and was pricked as sheriff of Glamorgan. He was held in readiness for service against the northern rebels of the Pilgrimage of Grace, but never seems actually to have taken the field against them. In 1538, too, he and George Mathew were commissioned to take charge of a delicate and potentially dangerous enquiry into the accusation against one of the powerful Herbert clan of having stolen a ship.

But perhaps the most valuable reward for his services in Ireland and elsewhere came after the dissolution of the monasteries, when Rice Mansel was allowed first to lease, and later to purchase, the site and the greater part of the lands of Margam Abbey. Margam, a Cistercian convent, was one of the largest, best known, and most desirable houses in South Wales... It meant abandoning as the headquarters of the family Oxwich Castle on which Rice Mansel had already spent a considerable amount of money in converting it from a medieval castle into a more comfortable and gracious fortified Tudor manor-house, as is attested by the handsome stone panel with his carved initials on it on the now-crumbling gatehouse of that once handsome building...

In November 1553, Mansel was appointed to the offices of Chamberlain and Chancellor of South Wales and the counties of Carmarthenshire and Cardiganshire. He became the steward of many royal manors and lordships and custodian of royal castles. He now had succeeded to a position of very great importance in his own region. This kind of authority had been held earlier in the century by Sir Rhys ap Tomas, and when Sir Rhys's grandson had been passed over in favour of Lord Ferrers the slight had led, in 1529-31, to some of the most serious riots in the history of sixteenth-century Wales. Being appointed to these offices had helped make the Devereux family the most influential in south-west Wales. The same positions had now made Rice Mansel the biggest man in the royal administration in South Wales...

Glanmor Williams, 'Rice Mansell of Oxwich and
Margam (1487-1559),' *Morgannwg,* Vol. VI, 1962.

10. *600 Able Men*

During the reign of Elizabeth the country seems to have been in a constant dread of a Spanish invasion. A muster, taken September 1572, procured 600 able men from Gower. The accoutrements of the men supplied were: Corsellettes, 200; Pikes, 200; Swords, 19 score; Daggers, 7 score; Harquebuses, 14 score; Flaxes and twos, boxes, 16;

Blanche morions, 32; Captains for the leading of 300 [men]; Nicholas
Herbert, George Mansel . . .

The Rev. Latimer Davies, *Pennard and West
Gower,* 1928.

11. *Gower Surnames*

1583-1687

Pennard.—Ace; Alester; Austin; Bowen; Bydder; Bynon; Button;
Batcocke; Clement; Cradocke; Dauid; Domer; Dawkins; Franklen;
Flemmings; Griffith; Gamon; Gronow; Hemmings; Hoskings;
Hopkin; Harry; Jones; John; Knayth; Llowarch; Lucas; Morgan;
Mansell; Price; Parry; Rees; Richard; Smith; Sutton; Steven;
Thomas; Taylor; Walker; Webb; Watkins.
Gosse (Lunon).

1584

Penmaen.—Creek.
Ilston.—Bowen; Daniell; Lucas; Knayth; Price.

1632

Nicholaston.—Benet; Bowen; Button; Chauke; Donne; David;
Franklen; Gamon; Howell; Hopkins; Jenkin; Kneath; Longe; Lia;
Lukas; Langley; Phillips; Russell; Richard; Smith; Sadge; Sprote;;
Sussex; Stephen; Tailor; Vosse; Williams.

1665

Reynoldston.—Bassett; Bowen; Bennett; Davies; France; Gwyne;
Grove; Hullins; Huges; Jenkin; Jones; Lucas; Lamphey; Meyricke;
Mansel; Phillip; Rogers; Seyse; Sussex; Johns (later).

1538

Knelston.—Hearne; Austine; Bennett; Bowen; Bidder; Clement;
Davies; David; Eynon; Edwin; France; Gibb; Grove; Jones; Long;
Lucas; Morgan; Maunsell; Morice; Thomas.

1632

Penrice.—Ace; Beaven; Bennett; Bowen and Bowenne; Button;
Chalke; Curtes; Dawkins; Gibb; Grove; Gamon; Hodge; Hoskin;
Harry; J. ap Jevan; Knayth; Lucas; Lewis; Lunday; Lawrence; Mayo;

Mansell; Pigge; Prissen; Parret; Perkins; Ponner; Russell; Rees; Stephens; Sweard; Somley; Turbeville; Tailour; Vowle; Vaughan; Westland.

1689

Walterston.—Bennett; Bower; Bynon; Colin; Dox; David; Gwyn; Jones; Lucas; Lewis; Lloyd; Lyson; Long; Matthews; Treharne; Tale; Philip; Price; Royland; Walter.

Col. W. Ll. Morgan, *Antiquarian Survey of East Gower*, 1899.

12. William Bennet of Sanctuary

Near this place lyeth interred the body of William Bennet, of Sanctuary, Gent., who departed this life 24th June, 1698.
Also Priscilla, his wife daughter of Rowland Dawkin of Killuorough, Esq., who died April ye 30th, 1685.
And in memory of Rowland Bennet, Gent., son of ye above Wm. & Priscilla Bennet, who died Jan. 11th, 1714, in ye 32 year of his age.
Sarah the widow of Rowland Bennet Gent, D'ter of Manasseh Matthews, Gent, a sure friend, a good neighbour & a charitable Benefactress to the poor of this parish and of Pennard, dyed April 23, 1735, Aged 67, and underneath lies buried. She gave thirty pounds.
This monument was erected by his widow Mrs. Sarah Bennet 1728.

—*In Penrice Church.*

13. Joseph Pryce of Gellihir, d. 1785

Quod Mori Potuit
All that was mortal in Joseph Pryce Esqr late of Gellihyr in this Parish whose amiable qualities Endear'd him to all his friends: Religious without hypocrisy, humble without meanness, charitable without ostentation, humane, hospitable, an affectionate husband and indulgent Father, a Sincere friend, impartial Magistrate. His life exem-

plary, his death happy; unfeigned Piety accompanied him thro every scene to the last moment of his life; supported him with assurance of hope, the source of Peace and Earnest of Blissful Immortality.

Memorial Tablet, south wall of Ilston Church.

14.   *The Rev. Watkin Knight*

The following record of Mr. Knight is from a mural tablet to his memory in the Chancel of Llanmadoc Church:

Underneath
Lie the remains of
W. L. Knight, Clark,
Who died January 2nd, 1795. Aged 74.
Having been 22 years Rector of this Parish.

He married a Miss Cuny, of Ilston, and was of the family of the the Knights, of Tythegston, Glamorganshire.

Arms: Three pellets gu., within a bordure engr. az., on a canton of the second, a spur or.

Crest: Over a ducal coronet, an eagle displ., or,

Motto: "Gloria clacar habet."

The old people relate, that he was an enormously fat man, and that on his death, the coffin containing his body had to be taken through one of the bedroom windows, and lowered to the ground by ropes.

The Rev. J. D. Davies, *A History of West Gower,* Vol. II, 1879.

15.   *Gabriel Powell*

Throughout successive decades of the eighteenth century, Gabriel Powell, Steward to the Duke of Beaufort, Lord of Gower, Recorder of the Corporation of Swansea, and compiler of the Survey of Gower (1764) *exercised virtually autocratic powers in Swansea.*

Gabriel Powell, the second son of Gabriel Powell of Pennant and Swansea, was born in 1710. A qualified lawyer, Gabriel Powell first gained legal experience and acquired expertise in guardianship of the

Duke of Beaufort's ancient rights and prerogatives in the employ of his father, who for many years managed the estates of the Lord of the Seignory of Gower. It was, too, his father's influence with, and possible control over, the Corporation of Swansea that secured young Gabriel his admittance as a burgess of the borough and on the very same day, shortly after his twenty-first birthday, his election to the ranks of the aldermen. By 1740, however, such was Gabriel Powell's standing and pre-eminence in the borough that he himself secured his appointment to the remunerative office of portreeve, and, five years later, to that of recorder and solicitor to the Corporation: an office he was to hold until his death in the year 1789.

To understand how this tall, austere, irascible, old man came to "rule" over the borough of Swansea, one must examine the powers and authority which he exercised in his dual capacity as recorder and steward and see how far these powers impinge on the autonomy of the Corporation as it was constituted in those decades before 1835 when, with the passing of the Municipal Corporation Act, it finally secured its full and complete independence of the Duke of Beaufort and his officials.

In the late eighteenth century the term "municipal corporation" can be used only as a collective designation for a multitude of local authorities each nominally responsible for municipal administration in a certain area. But there was no general law as to the constitution, function, or powers of a borough corporation. Each had its own set of charters, and each set at some time or other had been modified, legally or illegally, to suit local circumstances. Borough constitutions, therefore, were generally so exceedingly varied in detail as to preclude summary description except with regard to some of their most prominent features. Gradation in status between one corporation and another was consequently the most distinctive feature of the unreformed corporations.

At the top of the scale stood those authorities which enjoyed the privilege of appointing and controlling their own borough magistracy: lower down the scale stood the majority of the corporations—a heterogeneous collection of quasi-municipal authorities or "manorial boroughs" as Sidney and Beatrice Webb described them, exhibiting every form of constitutional structure, but all falling short of complete judicial and administrative autonomy: and all, in some way or other, connected with the manorial jurisdiction from which they had sprung. Swansea was a classic example of such a manorial borough.

In the late eighteenth century its governing body—the portreeve, steward, twelve aldermen, an idefinite number of burgesses, together with a recorder, two common attorneys, and several minor officials—testified to its highly developed municipal structure; while the powers exercised by the steward over the election of these various corporate officials, together with his control over the burgesses in Common Hall, were sufficient to ensure its ancillary or subservient status to the lord of the borough.

The outstanding feature of the system of electing corporate officials in the late eighteenth century was the omnipotence of the steward who always had the last word in the appointments to office. Thus, in the annual election of the portreeve (the chief corporate officer), the aldermen on Michaelmas Eve selected four of their number by ballot and on the following day, in conjunction with the burgesses in Common Hall, chose two out of the four to be returned to the steward, who nominated one of them to the office. Similarly, in the election of aldermen it was the steward who selected one of the two burgesses presented to him for this office. In the case of the minor corporate officials, lists of prospective candidates were compiled by the burgesses and aldermen in Common Hall, but the actual appointments, nevertheless, were made by the steward. Thus could the steward, both directly and indirectly, influence the whole hierarchy of the Corporation; and the extent of his influence was far greater than a mere enumeration of his rights and powers might suggest . . .

The steward then, in his control of the election of corporate officials, his dominance of the burgesses in their meetings in Common Hall, and his presidency of the Leet Court, was virtually omnipotent; but it must not be forgotten that his pre-eminence was due entirely to his position as steward to the Duke of Beaufort as Lord of the Seignory of Gower.

> Tom Ridd, 'Gabriel Powell: The Uncrowned
> King of Swansea' in *Glamorgan Historian,*
> Vol. V, 1968.

16.   *David and Jane*

Here resteth the Body of David, the sonne of David the sonne of Richard the sonne of Nicholas the sonne of Rys the sonne of Leison the son of Rys the sonne of Morgan Ychan the sonne of Morgan the sonne of Cradocke the sonne of Iustin ap Gwrgan Sometime Lord of

Glamorgan interred in the 21st day of August in the year of our blessed redemption 1623. In this bit of earth likewise reposeth the body of Iane his wife deceased the 23 of Febr 1631 whome God consorts in sacred rites and love.
Death, cannot separate marrow from the dove.

—*In Penmaen Church.*

17.   The Apostle of Gower

In 1814 Lady Barham, daughter of Pitt's First Lord of the Admiralty at the time of Trafalgar, came to live at Fairyhill in the parish of Reynoldston. During the next nine years she established six dissenting chapels in Gower. But this programme of evangelising the peninsula was not without its human problems, as William Griffiths (1788-1861), later known as 'The Apostle of Gower,' discovered:

In the course of the second three months [in Gower] a new door opened in connection with Lady Barham's operations. A young man—Phillip Gwyn—who was schoolmaster under Lady Barham at Trinity Chapel, Cheriton, became ill and I was requested to take his place for a month that he might try a change of air; which I did. He never recovered his strength and died in less than twelve months. I continued for more than three years teaching Lady Barham's School in that place, preaching there once or twice every Sabbath and itinerating on week evenings over the whole country as circumstances suited. I had no separate Church at that little Chapel, but laboured in Conjunction with the ministers and Church at Bethesda Chapel [Burry Green] which was then supplied by ministers of the Countess of Huntingdon's connexion, sent in rotation.

Being so near to that place, I was not allowed to have free scope in the ministry while I was at Trinity Chapel. Great fears were felt and sometimes manifested not in a very Christian-like spirit, that frequent meetings held at this Chapel were injurious to the cause at Bethesda. So high did this feeling grow that at last her Ladyship was prevailed upon to use her authority to stop ministry on the Sabbath day, with the exception of once every other Sabbath afternoon.

This step, originating in jealousy, did not increase attendance of members at Bethesda, but produced the contrary effect and made my situation rather painful. I had much to do to please all parties, endeavouring to keep a conscience void of offence towards God and man, by not slackening in my public labours in preaching the Gospel to the people around me, yet not giving offence to the proud minister who then supplied Bethesda Chapel.

A new Sabbath School was opened in private houses, from house to house, in the neighbourhood of Cillibion and the central parts of the country which I then attended and where I preached on Sunday evenings in surrounding villages.

In March, 1821, a new day school was opened at Pilton Green on the south west of Gower, under the patronage of Lady Barham, to which I was removed. The school at Trinity was given up but I continued to visit the old place once a fortnight on a weekday, and once a month on the Sabbath to preach and to catechise the former scholars. In the summer of the same year a spot of ground was obtained at Pilton Green to build a Chapel for school and preaching. There Immanuel Chapel was built and opened in three months. The school rapidly increased and a large congregation attended the preaching. In the following winter a new Christian Society was formed of converts from the world who had never before made a profession of the Gospel, 14 in number.

Here I was in a new field at a considerable distance from all other Chapels of Lady Barham. Although I consented, reluctantly at first, to this removal and was quite alone for nearly a year with no religious person to help in school or prayer meeting, I became much attached to this place. The children and people were attached to this place. The children and people were attached to me and I to them and for a while we went on happily.

I made it my work to preach alternately in all the surrounding villages on week evenings. I had plenty employment between school and preaching and my soul found frequent enlargement and spiritual pleasure in it.

The Gower Memories of William Griffiths, 1957.

18. *David Waters' Law*

We follow the road towards Cheriton, through the beautiful and poetical named place, Frog Lane. Here a certain law had its origin—it is called "David Waters' law" by the Gowerians, although I think it is the ruling law of the land—a law more adhered to than any other; but to explain it, I must relate the particulars:—During the war with France, many years ago, the peasantry of the country were often terrified by the cry of "The French have landed!" and it appears that a couple of wags ran through Llanmadoc shouting this dreadful news. Away, pellmell, they fly, the whole of the villagers running for life; but this David Waters had sworn to stand fast and die for his birthplace should the whole host of savage Frenchmen assail his home; but now poor David forgot his heroism, and he was not the last in the scampering race. His son, a boy of about sixteen or less, fell into a large bramble bush and cried out, "O Father, help I! help I!" but David had no time, and he answered, "Can't, boy, can't! Every man for himself now!" and to this day, in Gower, they say when they see a selfish man, "Ah! 'tis David Waters' law with him."

We admire the clean white-washed cottages skirting the road, and we soon come to the Britannia Inn. The host and hostess are the kindest people imaginable, and if the traveller feels fatigued he may safely enter this clean little Inn, and be sufficed with delicious ham and eggs by the obliging landlady, and furnished with a soft bed for the night if required, home-brewed ale, of course, to wash down the dust . . .

C. D. Morgan, *Wanderings in Gower*, 1886 ed.

19. *The Westhorps*

Wednesday, 16 October 1878

All six of us, Mr. and Mrs. Westhorp, Ilston, Hettie, sweet Annie Mitchell and myself drove in the waggonette with Tattersal of Oystermouth and went down to Langland Bay, where we had luncheon among the rocks, the ladies drinking wine out of shells as the cup had been forgotten. Ilston and I took off our shoes and socks and paddled in the sea. The water was grey, cold and nasty. Then the dear girls helped me to gather some of the beautiful seaweeds among the rocks. A very happy day, made happier by sweet Annie Mitchell and her lovely innocent trustful blue eyes.

Thursday, 17 October

After breakfast Hettie and Carrie set the Langland Bay seaweeds for me beautifully in paper. They turned out to be lovely specimens. Then we walked down the Cwms to Three Cleeves Bay. The morning was perfectly glorious, a brilliant cloudless blue sky, a tender blue haze hung over the green and golden woods like a gauzy veil, and the gossamers shot and twinkled into green and gold in the grass which in the shade of the woods was still hoary with the night's frost. Mrs. Richardson and her cousin Miss Vansittart rode from Sketty to lucheon. After luncheon I played croquet with the girls.

Friday, 18 October
St. Luke's Day. This week has indeed been the summer of St. Luke. Five of us drove in the waggonette to Oxwich Bay through Penrice Park, stopping at the empty house to see the pictures. We had a merry windy luncheon on the bank near the Churchyard gate, and great fun and famous laughing. An E. wind was blowing fresh and strong, the sea was rolling in grey and yeasty, and in a splendid sunburst the white seagulls were running and feeding on the yellow sands. A wild merry happy day.

Saturday, 19 October
I parted sadly from all my dear kind friends and looked my last into sweet Carrie Mitchell's lovely blue eyes. The morning was gloomy and rainy. The weather seemed to have broken up with our pleasant party. Westhorp drove me into Swansea for the 11 o'clock train . . .

The Rev. Francis Kilvert, *Kilvert's Diary,*
1878, Edited by William Plomer.

20.   *The Dixes*

In 1950, there passed away at Stavel-Hagar, Harriet Dix, the last link with the weaving industry at Llanrhidian and the last of that ilk in the village. Weaving ceased there about 1904 when Richard Dix dismantled his looms and left the parish, but his father Joseph Dix, remained in occupation of the farm. A hundred years ago, Joseph brought his bride from Cheriton, took over from his father, and for many years plied his craft at Stavel-Hagar. His looms were driven by a water wheel, water being taken from the river at a point near the church stile, and conveyed through a long leat to the mill. His wife Mary dyed the yarn, and as more colours became available, so did the number of spools on Joseph's loom increase. By the close of the century, quilts and bedspreads woven by Richard Dix reached a high standard of perfection, while at Cheriton and Stembridge, the

Tanners were turning out shining examples of the weaving art, but early in the 20th century weaving in West Gower ceased altogether.

H. M. Tucker, *Gower Gleanings,* 1951.

21. *The Glamorgan Rangers*

The Gower Contingent

The formation of a troop of Yeomanry in Gower by Mr. Ernest Helme, of Hillend, having had a fairly good start, and its first fortnight's regular training having taken place at Margam, in May last; it might interest many of the present inhabitants to learn something of the soldiering of their grandfathers in these parts rather more than one hundred years ago.

From the materials at my disposal, I gather that the forces raised in the County of Glamorgan for home defence, from 1798 to 1802, consisted of Yeomanry, Volunteer Cavalry, Infantry, and the Sea Fencibles; and it seems that they were all represented in Gower by small detachments, the supreme command being vested in Lieut. Col. Thomas Mansel Talbot, of Margam Park and Penrice Castle; at any rate he is distinctly stated to have been the commanding officer of the Glamorgan Rangers, as will be seen from the commission of one of the captains of the regiment.

The following is a fragment of an old song, once upon a time well known, and very popular in Gower, and composed in honour of the Glamorgan Rangers. My informant, Mr. John Chalk, of Cheriton Glebe, who has often heard his father sing it, could, unfortunately, only remember the first two verses; the tune was a march, this he recollects very well, and has given me the music:

> Colonel Talbot leads the van,
>   Bless the County, skilful man.
> 'Twas he that formed the wondrous plan,
>   Of the old Glamorgan Rangers.

> Captain Gordon, bold and free,
>   A better man could never be,
> We'll follow him o'er land and sea,
>   Say the old Glamorgan Rangers.

The Sea Fencibles were dressed in blue, and armed only with pikes and cutlasses. They had their head-quarters at Porteynon, their drilling ground being on the adjoining burrows, on a spot called the "bowling green", but very unlike one now. The late Rev. Wm. Melland, Rector of Porteynon, informed me that two very aged inhabitants of that parish told him that they remembered seeing the pikemen go through their drills, and "minded" their being inspected by a mounted officer in a cocked hat, who galloped his horse up to the pikes to see if they would keep their ground. He proceeds to say, "in those days of oyster dredging and drilling money came in easily, and was spent foolishly, few laying anything by for old age."

There was a drilling ground at Barland, in the Parish of Bishopston, but whether for the Cavalry or Infantry I cannot say with certainty.

In those stirring times, when a French invasion was expected, the excitement in all parts of the country, especially on the sea coast, was very great; and Gower being particularly exposed in this respect, the inhabitants were continually on the alert day and night; occasionally there were false alarms which caused a stampede to Swansea, the fuguitives leaving everything behind, except what they could carry away on horseback, there being no other mode of conveyance at that time.

Beacons, by order of the Government, were kept ready for lighting on Cefn Bryn, Oystermouth, and all along the coast of England; and it was on the night of Feb. 2nd, 1804, that the watchman at Hone Castle, fired his beacon by mistake, and roused all the coast of Northumberland. According to an old survey of the Manor of Weobley, dated 1630, it appears that the duty of watching and guarding the beacon on Cefn Bryn was one of the duties of that Manor. This beacon was no doubt on the spot, still called the "Beacons", on the end of Cefn Bryn, overlooking the parish and village of Penmaen.

In 1798, the year of the great Irish rebellion, when there was much talk and many fears of a French landing, Mr. Thomas Gordon, of Llwyn-y-bwch, in the parish of Llanrhidian, was appointed Captain of a company of the "Glamorgan Rangers". His commission, of which the following is a copy, was taken by me from the original in the possession of his grandson, Mr. Thomas G. Gordon, and preserved at Llwyn-y-Bwch.

"George the Third, by the Grace of God, King of Great Britain,

France, and Ireland, Defender of the Faith, etc. To our Trusty and Well-Beloved Thomas Gordon, Esq., Greeting: We reposing especial Trust and Confidence in your Loyalty, Courage, and good Conduct, do, by these presents, constitute and appoint you to be Captain of a Company in the Glamorgan Rangers, Commanded by our Trusty and Well-Beloved Lieutenant Colonel Thomas Mansel Talbot, but not to take Rank in Our Army except during the time of the said Corps being called out into actual Service.

You are therefore to take the said Company into your Care and Charge, and duly to exercise as well the Officers as Soldiers thereof in Arms, and to use your best endeavours to keep them in Good Order and Discipline; and we do hereby Command them to obey you as their Captain— and you are to observe and follow such Orders and Directions from Time to Time as you shall receive from us, of any other your Superior Officer, according to the Rules and Discipline of War, in pursuance of the Trust reposed in you.

Given at Our Court of Saint James's the Twenty-ninth Day of November, 1798, In the Thirty-ninth Year of our Reign.

By His Majesty's Command,
Portland.

Entered with the Secretary at War,
M. Lewis,
En'd with the Com's'rs,
General of Musters,
Wm. Woodman.

Thomas Gordon, Esq., Captain
of Glamorgan Rangers."

It would appear from the fact of Mr. Thomas Gordon being styled in his Commission as Captain of a company, that the Glamorgan Rangers was an Infantry regiment; had it been a cavalry one, I conclude the word troop would have been used.

The Rev. J. D. Davies, *The Gower Church Magazine,* July 1902.

22. *Phil Tanner*

The silent moorland between Rhossili and Llangennith has few songbirds. On a calm day the soaring paean of the skylark is often the only sound of life. But there was a time when the lark had a rival on these Downs. Long before one reached the little white-washed cottage above Hillend the strains of another songster might be heard; it was old Phil Tanner, singing to himself, all on his own since his wife died in 1921. His singing was one of the less known delights of Gower; many a traveller has been cheered by it and has returned home with a memory of an unexpected open-air concert on the hillside. The villagers were long accustomed to hearing his robust treble:

> Piping down the valleys wild
> Piping songs of pleasant glee.

He was the blackbird at the bottom of their garden, though, indeed, his little home at Barreston was a good quarter of an hour's walk away, down past the church, over Coity Green and "upalong."

But few Llangennians have heard his voice in the last ten years; their loss has been Penmaen's gain, for it is in the Eventide Home on the side of the Bryn that Phil is singing away the rest of his days.

The Tanners of "Llangenny" have more than one claim to fame. For generations they were weavers in the two mills that were then standing between Coity Green and College Farm. It was their boast that the sheep they reared helped to feed and clothe the family: that they could handle every process from the fleece to the finished cloth. In the village there are still blankets, counterpanes, shawls, which must have been made by the Tanners. In their early days Llangennith, with its four public-houses, used to be regarded as a wild place, the Tipperary of Gower, where the menfolk, true sons of Anak, tall and muscular, had little respect for the law. It was said that they used to stake even their fields on their cock-fighting, quoit-playing and gambling games, and that it was a thoroughly unhealthy spot for strangers. That was a hundred years ago—and visitors are now very welcome! But the Tanners, with their passion for singing, must have been even then bringing a little sweetness and light into the life of the village.

Phil Tanner, himself, is now in his 87th year. He was born on February 16th, 1862, and, the youngest of six brothers, decided not to follow the rest of the family into weaving, but to become a farm-labourer and sing in the fields. All his brothers, however, could "crack a note," as he puts it. He learned his songs from his father and grandfather, and picked up new ballads as soon as reached the neighbouring villages. His repertoire of Gower songs and Victorian ballads was at one time almost inexhaustible; but after 86 years his modest claim is "I'd have to pull myself together to find thirty of 'em now, boy." For over two generations he was a treasured guest at any "do" in Gower; sooner or later someone would be sure to say, "Phil, let's have a song!"—and the rest of the evening would be his.

He remembers most fondly the jolly, carefree atmosphere of the "beading wedding," the custom known also in the North Country as "bidden wedding" and "bridewain," which was practised in Gower until about 1905. Wedding celebrations have become pinched with the times; but in the old days they were no unwelcome formalities with a bare minimum of guests: festivities would begin weeks before, brewing utensils would be borrowed from an obliging publican, and the home-brewed would be available to the village a whole fortnight before the wedding day—always a Thursday—when the fun would reach its climax.

The fiddler, with white-beribboned fiddle, would escort the procession to the church and back again, and, after the "wedding supper," would supply the music for dancing in the kitchen or barn. It was from one of these fiddlers, old Tom Lloyd, known as "Morriston Tom," although he lived in Mumbles, that Phil Tanner picked up many tunes, including the well-known Gower Reel, the accompaniment to the four-handed reel that the Gower boys and maids used to perform with much gusto. Old Phil later supplanted the fiddler and, for a long time, accompanied the dances himself. The Gower Reel has disappeared, but Phil can still set one's feet tapping with the infectious lilt of the tune—and his breath control is something to be marvelled at. Just as irresistible is the chorus of the "Gower Wassail Song."

His art is the art of the true folk-singer: the simple telling of a story is the main object of his song, not the exploitation of a tune or a display of virtuosity, and to hear him even now singing "The Banks of Sweet Dundee," "Fair Phoebe and the dark-eyed sailor," or "Young Henry Martin," is to appreciate what a true artist he is in his way. He clears his throat, makes sure of the key, tilts his head back a little, then gives himself, without self-consciousness of mannerism, to the telling of the tale. His handsome grey-bearded face, with its contented cheeks, twinkling eyes, straight nose and almost unlined forehead, reflects the changing moods of the old song, while his hands, pipe in one and "baca" in the other, gently point the rhythm. Very occasionally his voice is a thought disobedient to the tune, but his memory, for each song has at least a dozen verses, is always faultless and his diction distinct. It is hard to believe that his last tooth fell out nine years ago!

He is still singing at Penmaen—"I couldn't go to bed without it," not only to himself but also to his fellow-pensioners at the Home, in the concerts which they hold there twice a week. It is good to know that he is still able to look out on his beloved Gower fields, as he stands, a tall and impressive figure, on the terrace of the "Institution"—that restful, well-appointed and above all very human Eventide Home. Long may it keep him in good happy voice!

J. Mansel Thomas, *Gower I*, 1948.

23. *At Penrice Castle Shoot*

'Twas while returning after the sport,
 That one of the gents so they say,
Asked Tom Davies if he could report,
 The extent of his bag for the day.

Now Tom you know was a bit of a wag,
 A joke he could never resist,
And when he was asked to account for "the bag,"
 He started off something like this:

"Five hundred pheasants and fifteen hares,
 Seven woodcocks we rose in the Boxes,"
Eighteen pigeons, ducks five pairs,
 Ten rabbits, and two foxes."

"Two foxes!" said the gent in surprise,
 "What next will you tell me pray?
I've got a pair of very good eyes,
 But I've seen no foxes to-day."

"You have," said Tom. "I haven't," said he,
  They argued it might and main,
Till poor old Tom now shaking with glee,
  At last set out to explain.

"Excuse me, sir, for my bit of fun,
  But foxes I know you've seen,
That's old Sam Fox and Ivor his son,
  Two beaters from Oxwich Green."

Cyril Gwynn, *Gower Yarns,* 1928.

24. *Petty Officer Edgar Evans*

To the Glory of God
and in memory of
Edgar Evans
1st Class Petty Officer, R.N., and a native of this Parish, who
perished on the 17th February 1912, when returning from the South
Pole with the Southern Party of the British Antarctic Expedition
under the command of Captain Robert Falcon Scott, C.V.O., R.N.

'To seek, to strive, to find and not to yield.'

Erected by Lois Evans.

—*In Rhossili Church.*

25. *The Sleeping Lord*

And is his bed wide
        is his bed deep on the folded strata
is his bed long
        where is his bed and
        where has he lain him
from north of Llanfair-ym-Muallt

(a name of double gladius-piercings)[1]
south to the carboniferous vaultings of Gwyr[2]
(where in the sea-slope chamber
they shovelled aside the shards & breccia
the domestic litter and man-squalor
of gnawed marrowbones and hearth-ash
with utile shovels fashioned of clavicle bones
of warm-felled great fauna.
Donated the life-signa:
the crocked viatic meal
the flint-worked ivory agalma
the sacral sea-shell trinkets
posited with care the vivific amulets
of gleam-white rodded ivory
and, with oxide of iron
ochred life-red the cerements
of the strong limbs
of the young nobilis
the first of the sleepers of
Pritenia, pars dextralis, O! aeons & aeons
before we were insular'd.) . . .

David Jones, *The Sleeping Lord*, 1974.

---

1. Llanfair-ym-Muallt: "Mary's church in Buellt." The town now called Builth Wells. It was between Llanfair and Llanganten that the Lord Llywelyn Prince of Wales was killed in 1282. Hence my reference to a *double* piercing in that any place-name with marian associations necessarily recalls the passage in the gospel of the gladius that would pierce the heart of the God-bearer. Pronounce: Llan-veir-um-mee-allt.—D.J.
2. Gwyr: The Gower Peninsula: pronounce approximately goo-eer. It was in Gwyr that human remains, ritually buried, were discovered of a young man of the Palaeolithic period, so many, many millenniums prior to Britain becoming an island.—D.J.

V

The Land

1. *The Natural Divisions of Gower*

The South pt of Gowerland (being Swanzey hundd) being in length from Swanzey to Worms head about 12 miles is for the most corn ground with store of limestones, & limestone cleeves, wherein are many great holes or Caves, here are also divers places from Mumble rode westward divers harbours & Creekes where they doe transport much limestones, & other goods &c along this coast there are these sort of fish taken or to be taken (viz) Salmon, hering, suen, cod, mackrell, plais, millet, sole, flooke, flawnders, Thornback, Skate, Whiting, Turbut, hawk, Congger-eeles, bowman, bream, and of Shellfish, Crabs, Lobster, musles, cockles, oysters,&c. And in Oxwich sands there is a strange sort of shellfish called harofish, here are these sorts of sea hearbes, as scurvie grasse, Sampire & lavar of Rock herbs, Cetrack, maiden hair, walrue, & in the pishes of Bishopston, Pennard, & Oystermouth there is plenty of Juniper & some buckthorn.

Of field hearbs (especially in the said 3 pishes) .Argimony, wild carret, mulleyn, Dandelyon, Pelamountain, mallows, Burdock, Tutsan, Eybright, Bettony, Elecampane, Foxfingers, yellow & blue Kay-roses, Rames or Ramsey, Centry, Yarrow, Adders tongue, vervain, St. Johns wort, Cancker wort, Devilles bit, Ragwort, mugwort, Breakstone-paley, Larks bill, plantane, Pimpnell, Fumitory, Burnet, Botchwort of hearbs in some waterie places, as water cresses, Rosa solis, Lungwort, Liver wort

The midle pt of Gowersland from Swanzey in ye East to Whiteford in the west which is abt 9 miles in length, & about 2 miles in breadth (through the Country) is more cold than the rest & it is full of woods, coale veynes, moores & wet grounds, yet there are many considerable tenemts or pt of them, that is good ground for corn & hay

The Northern pt of Swanzey hundd is good land for corn &c with woods & coale veynes (see the discription of Loughor & Llandilo talybont in pticular)

The higher pt of Gower or Blaen Gwyr, which is Llangevelach & Llanguick, is a mountainy countrey, yet there are many pcells & tenemts of Cornlands, with plain ground amongst them

The Corn & grain that growes in all pts of Gowersland & thereabts are wheat, barley, Ry, oates white & gray, pease, & fitches, & in divers pts of Swanzey hundd there are much Clover grasses & seede especially at & near Bpstown.

> Isaac Hamon, 'Description of Gower,' 1697, in
> F. V. Emery, *Edward Lhuyd and some of his Glamorgan Correspondents: A view of Gower in the 1690s,* 1965.

2. *Flowers of the Limestone*

Nowhere is the limestone rock better exposed than along the South Gower Coast from Mumbles Head to Worm's head, a strip of limestone cliff broken only by the dunes at Penmaen, Nicholaston and Oxwich. It is along this coast that some of the outstanding plants of Gower are to be found, species which are perhaps common enough along the cliffs but which may be very rare in the rest of the British Isles.

Noteable among these are the 'Isle of Man cabbage' (*Rhynchosinapis monensis*) at Three Cliffs Bay; rock whitebeam (*Sorbus rupicola*) from Crawley Cliff; and yellow whitlow grass (*Draba aizoides*) which though common enough at Pennard Cliffs and many sites further west, is found nowhere else in Britain. Along the beautiful stretch of coastline between Port Eynon Point and Worm's Head occur three plants of considerable rarity and interest, small rest harrow (*Ononis reclinata*), an inconspicuous annual of cliff ledges; spiked speedwell (*Veronicae spicata* ssp. *hybrida*) and goldilocks (*Aster linosyris* or *Crinitaria linosyris*). Other rare species found here are rock hutchinsia (*Hornungia petraea*) and hoary rockrose (*Helianthemum canum*). In May these cliffs are bright with the yellow flowers of spring cinquefoil (*Potentilla tabernaemontani*), and with patches of spring squill (*Scilla verna*) forming a delicate blue sheen over the turf. Closer to the sea, often catching blown spray grow clumps of golden samphire (*Inula crithmoides*) and feathery sea asparagus (*Asparagus officinalis* ssp. *prostratus*).

The presence of this group of twelve cliff plants which are rare or unusual in the rest of Britain raises the obvious question—why are they in Gower? Geographical distribution problems of this sort are always extremely interesting even in our commonest British plants. Nearly all of the twelve species requires a calcium rich soil of a high mineral nutrient content. Another interesting fact is that none of them tolerate shading by bushes or trees and require an open type of situation fairly free from competition with other species. Some obtain this by growing in rock crevices or in very thin stony soils. Others grow on unstable cliff-ledge soils which are continually slipping down the cliff slopes.

In certain rare instances, the soil is kept fairly open by the activities of small mammals, rabbits and even sheep. In addition to these requirements, many of the twelve demand the mild oceanic weather such as is found in Gower and these species are common in open, limy or fertile situations all along the Atlantic seaboard of the southern half of Europe or around the coastline of the Mediterranean. In Gower these plants are towards the northern edge of their geographical range and it is a curious fact, not yet fully explained, that this often increases their lime demands, which makes their confinement to very calcereous soils in Gower all the more rigorous . . .

All the evidence so far collected suggests that these species are relics of a former British flora which flourished all over these Islands about 10,000 years ago, having invaded this country from Europe.

Gordon T. Goodman, *Plant Life in Gower*, 1962.

3. *Draba Aizoides Montana*

A Short History of the Yellow Alpine Whitlow Grass

I trust that, among the many activities of the Gower Society, the study of the Flora of Gower, and the preservation of rare plants may be included, and therefore it may be appropriate to include in this number a short note on Gower's own plant, a plant which is (at least in its varietal form though not as a species) is peculiar or endemic to Gower. Even the species is not found elsewhere in Britain, though, as its name "Alpine" implies, it exists in the mountain ranges of Central Europe.

In Gower, it occurs on parts (for obvious reasons not particularly specified) of the south coast, mainly, though not entirely on limestone cliffs, on at least two of which it may fairly be described as abundant.

It possesses a root which is found very deep in the crevices of the rocks so that, fortunately, it would require a cold chisel to dislodge large specimens. Above the foot is a semi-woody branched stem, each branch ending in a tuft of short stiff somewhat hairy leaves, each ending in a bristly point. The plant belongs to the Cruciferne (Wallflower or Cabbage Family) and the bright yellow flowers, which in an advanced season may appear as early as the first week of March, present the typical cruciferous form—four *free* petals in the shape of a cross. It is necessary to stress the word *free,* for there are other families of plants which have four petals. The fruit which is set by the end of April is a short pod-like structure (it is not a true "pod") ending in a short point.

The species appears to have been observed by Lucas on the limestone rocks of Worm's Head as early as 1795, but it was not until 1842 that Gutch described it as occurring on Pennard Castle (it still does in small quantity). Fortunately perhaps the floras still give "Pennard Castle and rocks near," as if this were its sole habitat, which is far from being the case.

It does not occur east of Pwlldu Head, nor on the limestone cliffs of north west Gower.

As recently as 1929 Druce ("Comital Flora of the British Isles") describes our plant as a definite endemic (peculiar) variety under the name *montana* which means that Glamorgan, like Brecon, possesses at least one plant variety not found elsewhere on earth.

I have said that the plant is mainly a calcicole (Limestone-loving), but its occurence on the Old Red Sandstone pudding-stone of Pennard Castle implies that it is at least tolerant of other situations than limestone, though as a matter of experiment, I can avouch that it will not grow on Millstone or Pennant grit. Occasionally small plants may be seen on sand under limestone rocks, but they do not persist.

Attempts have been made to prove that the plant was first brought in by the Romans, or the Normans, because of its presence on Pennard Castle, but in answer to this, three objections may be maintained: (1) Pennard Castle is not a Norman but a later castle, I believe; (2) it occurs frequently in purely natural habitats even as far remote as Worm's Head; (3) if the Gower form is endemic it *cannot* have been introduced since the variety *montana* does not occur elsewhere.

J. A. Webb, *Gower III,* 1950.

4. *The Bounds of Gower*

... We say that ye circuit and general bounds and members of this Lordship do extend to the river Twrch, on the confines of the county of Brecon on the north-east, and so downward the river of Tawe parteth or divideth this Lordship from Kilvey on the east side, and so as the river leadeth about Swanzey bordereth upon the sea coast to Mumbles, and from Mumbles to Worm's Head the sea being on the south, and from Worm's Head the ocean sea beneath, on it to the Holmes and Broughton, and so turneth about again where Loughor and Burry's water fall into the sea on the north-west, and so up along the river of Loughor parteth it from the county of Carmarthen, then as far as Bridge end [Talybont], and so to Cathan water, and on the northside to Cogowen [Cae Gurwen] the river of Amman doth divide it from the mountains of Carmarthenshire, and so about again till Twrch divide it from Brecknockshire ...

Survey of Gower Anglicana, 1583, in Baker
and Francis, *Surveys of Gower,* 1870.

5. *The Language of Open Fields*

Medieval records contain the unmistakable language of open fields. In Gower, a grant of three-quarters of a virgate of land was made at Penmaen in 1320, 22½ acres in all but split into six different parcels varying in size from 1 to 9 acres. They were located by naming the fields in which they lay: in Stedfurlong, South Field, East Field, Buttsacre and Footland. At Llanmadoc, also in Gower, in 1308 the husbandman had shares in the open fields totalling 63 acres, while 52 acres of demesne in the fields were let to them. A plan of 1740 showed these fields close to the village, strips of intermixed ownership still lying within them and called 'landshare pieces'. They were demarcated one from the other by turf balks, one farmer holding three pieces in Ladys Park, a piece in East Fields, another in Bush Park, and two pieces in Field. Nowadays the pattern can be picked out in the narrow furlong fields that represent bundles of strips or pieces. Where demesne land was thrown together from the open fields, and it was usually the first to be consolidated, larger farms and enclosures were created, hence the biggest rectilinear fields of 10 acres and more.

F. V. Emery, *The World's Landscapes: Wales,*
1969.

6. *Common of Pasture*

. . . We say, the commons and wastes commonly called Rhossili
Down, Cefn Bryn, Broad Moor[1], and Ryer's Down, Graig Fawr and
other and certain commons of the Lord within this Lordship,
whereon as well as on Carn Goch, freeholders and their tenants have
had free common of pasture time out of mind with all kinds of cattle
sans number at all times of the year, the certainty of the quantity, or
contents we know not; and we say that therein all the tenants and
inhabitants of several manors which be members of this Lordship, do
inter-common, by what title we know not certainly . . .
. . . we say that for all commons of any Lordship as Llanrhidian
Marsh, Llanmadoc Down, and any other in any manor, now or at
any time holden, or as member of this Lordship, the lord and tenants
of this Lordship may enter common, and have done time out of mind,
without contradiction, as we know, without let or interruption . . .

Survey of Gower Anglicana, 1583, in
Baker and Francis, *Surveys of Gower,*
1870.

7. *Mill Stone*

The Old Red Sandstone of the West Gower hills was known locally
as 'Millstone':
. . . upon Rhossili Down, Cefn Bryn, and Ryer's Down certain
stones, whereof mill stones are and have been made . . .

Survey of Gower Anglicana, 1583, in Baker
and Francis, *Surveys of Gower,* 1870.

8. *Some Gower Manors, 1650*

The Manor of Vernhill [Fernhill] held by the heirs of Morgan
Vaughan, Owen Perkins, and Richard Bydder by one knight's fee,
and six swallow tailed arrows yearly or 6d.
The Manor of Kilvrough held by George Bowen and Rowland
Dawkins Esqrs by one knight's fee.
The Manor of Landimore and Rhossili held by the heirs of the Earl
of Pembroke by one knight's fee, a pair of golden spurs or 20s per
annum.
Half Weobley held by the said heirs by half a knight's fee.

1. The common to the immediate south-west of Cillibion.

A parcel of meadow ground lying at a place called Wernllath in the Parish of Bishopston held by Robert Wibborne in Grand Sergeantry and is to pay a bow and an holbeart.

Survey of Gower 1650, in Baker and
Francis, *Surveys of Gower,* 1870.

9. *Llangennith Tithe Terrier, 1720*

A terrier of all and singular, the houses, buildings, tythes, dues, and profits whatsoever of and belonging to the Vicarage of Llangennith, in the County of Glamorgan and Diocese of St. David's, made the 20th day of December, in the year of our Lord 1720.

N.B.: Notice was given by the Clerks of the Parish on the 11th of this instant, that all the Parishioners should meet to sign the terrier, so that the absence of one or more of them is owing to their own neglect.

Imprimis: A Vicarage House, containing three rooms upon a floor; and a stable. A garden containing about a quarter of an acre. Item. There is due at the feast of Easter, yearly for offerings from every married couple Three Pence; from every widower or widow one penny half penny, from every single person above the age of sixteen years one half penny; from every convenanted servant man sixpence and from every servant maid fourpence.

Item. There is due at every Feast of Easter for every Stone Colt foald in the said Parish, Two Pence, and for every mare Colt one Penny.

Item. There is likewise due at the feast of Easter for every sheep sold between sheering time and Michaelmas ensuing a penny, and between Michaelmas and Easter following, or till the sheering time, two pence.

Item. There is due for every calf reared a half penny, for every calf killed or sold Three pence. But if the owner kills a calf for the use of his own family, then the three pence is disputable &c.

Item. There is due at the said Feast of Easter from every person exercising or possessing and Trade at any time four pence.

Item. There is due from every mill in the said Parish six shillings and eight pence to be paid at Easter. The College Mill is disputable.

Item. Hay, Clover, &c pay tithe in Grass Cocks. Item wool pay Tithe on the day of sheering the sheep.

Item. There is due Adjustment money, the sum of one shilling and eight pence in the pound, according to the value of any Tenement or tenements or part thereof, which is depastured by barren cattle of the owner or pastured by cattle of other persons.

Item. There is due for every calf cow, one shilling or six pounds of dry rind cheese, which may be sold at or adjudged by honest persons to be worth a shilling.

N.B. Whether a cow of the first calving should pay equal with other cows is disputable.

Item. There is due from every farrow cow (that is a cow not having calved that year) the sum of six pence, or three pounds of dry rind cheese, which is valued at six pence.

Item. Lambs pay Tithe, and of grasing on one or more tenements belonging to the family, or inhabitants of one house, to be tithed together, the head of the family, his substitute, may take up five, and the Vicar is to chose one, and so on according to the usual practice of under five, the Vicar may book them till the ensuing year, or conclude them for so many half pence. If there be only the number five, the Vicar takes a lamb, half a Lamb; if six 9c., but under ten, the Vicar takes a lamb, and allows so many wanting of ten, at the ensuing year's Tithe.

N.B. To book down the number of odd Lambs, as well under five, as above five, and less than ten, was the continued practice of the Rev. Mr. Portrey for near fifty years &c., and for whatsoever Lambs are sold, the Vicar is to be satisfied.

Item. Pigs pay Tithe when fit to live from their dame.

Item. Eggs pay Tithe, two for every Hen, and three for every Cock.

Item. There is due at Easter for Registering of burials, six shillings and 8d.

Item. Flax, Hemp, Apples, Hops, Geese, &c., pay Tithe, and the Tithe in kind are payable of all other titheable matters and things whatsoever within the said Parish.

Witness our hands the day and year above written,

RICHARD FRANCE
JOHN ROGERS
GEO. JENKINS   DAVID PRUDDERO
WILLIAM ROBERT   Vicar.
RICHARD GORTON
JOHN SUSSEX
RICHARD WILLIAMS
THOS. FRANCE
NICHOLAS HULLIN
GEORGE TAYLOR   The Rev. J. D. Davies,
                        A History of West Gower, Vol. III, 1885.

10. *The Seven Mills*

. . . upon Burry . . . 7 grist mills builded within a mile space . . .

Rice Merrick, c. 1584.

11. *West Gower Grist Mills*

The largest stream of water in West Gower is the Burry stream, which rises at Burry Head and flows north, entering the sea at Cheriton. It is not surprising, therefore, that seven of the thirteen grist mills which worked at various times should be found on this stream. Alas, today only one mill is in operation in West Gower—Mr. Willis's Lower mill at Llanrhidian. The Upper Mill at Llanrhidian was abandoned about a century ago, while Thomas Aubrey's mill at Cheriton, and the Stone mill at Kytle, which was the Custom mill for Landimore manor, were in ruins long before that.

Contemporary 18th century literature and art show the water mill to be as much part of a rural community as the local inn or Post Office is today. In the Georgian period, all thirteen mills flourished in West Gower, and it was not until late in the 19th century that the decline set in. The old mills at Cheriton and Kytle finished, not because of economic changes, but probably because these ancient structures had fallen into dilapidation brought about by the ravages of time. Local tradition relates that a century and a half ago the miller at Upper mill in Llanrhidian was apprehended for the crime of sheep-stealing. He was convicted on the evidence of a witness who hid inside the mill-wheel after dark and saw the miller dressing carcases.

Pitton mill, one of the last to be built in West Gower, was never a custom mill, and was not equipped for grinding flour, but it provided most of the barley and oat meal for the parish. It was worked by the Taylor family for generations until it ceased operations about 1890. In contrast, Penrice mill, which closed down about the same time, seems to have been occupied in turn by representatives of most of the tenantry of the manor. At Penrice, the highway dips sharply down to the mill and rises steeply again after crossing the bridge over the stream. In the old days, the miller kept a horse ready-harnessed for hitching to customers' carts or slide cars, to give them an extra pull up the steep slope from the mill. For this service he charged one penny. Ever since, the hill leading from the mill to Penrice Home farm, has been known as Penny Hitch.

Three mills which drew their water from the Burry stream, Western mill, Stembridge mill and Higher mill (the latter known in the 18th century as Hentlis mill) carried on till about the turn of the century. Stackpool mill, also on the Burry stream, worked until 1914. This mill was known locally as *Stoppers mill* and was formerly the Custom mill for Reynoldston manor. College mill and Lower mill, both at Llangennith, survived till a few years after the first world war. The Lower mill ended its days in the occupation of Phil Tanner. Middle mill, the last mill to work on the Burry stream, was forced to close down in 1942 owing to wartime restrictions.

H. M. Tucker, *Gower Gleanings,* 1951.

12.   *Burry Alias Stembridge*

Thomas Mansel Talbot, Esq., Infant, holds the Manor of Stembridge, otherwise Burry, which is situated in the Parish of Llangennith, and consists of about Seven Freehold Tenants, and several Tenants holding in Demesne.

Gabriel Powell, *Survey of Gower,* 1764.

13.   *Oxwich Manor*

Thomas Mansel Talbot, Esq., Infant, holds the Manor of Oxwich by fealty Suit of Court and Heriot. This Manor comprehends the whole Parish of Oxwich, and consists of freehold Tenants who hold their lands in Common Soccage and several Tenements held in Demesne. The Lord holds a Leet and Baron Court for this Manor, Porteynon, and Pitton also Pilton twice a year at May and Michaelmas, and this Manor and Porteynon bordering upon the sea, the Lord claims Wreck de Mer, and all Wastes within the same. But all Royalties which lye in grant belong to the Lord of the Seigniory.

Gabriel Powell, *Survey of Gower,* 1764.

14. *Llanmadoc Suit Roll, 1802*

November 4th, 1802

FREEHOLDERS

THOMAS MANSELL TALBOT, ESQ.
JOHN, EARL ASHBURNHAM.
JOHN HOLLAND.
JOHN LUCAS, ESQ.
JOHN LLEWELLIN, ESQ.
HENRY GRIFFITH.
MRS. ANNE WILLIAMS.
SAMUEL DAVIES, CLERK.
HENRY GORTON, gent.
JOHN ROWLAND.
THOMAS REES in right of his wife
JOHN GRIFFITH.
JOHN WALTER.
EDWARD ARTHUR.
HENRY GORTON

LEASEHOLDERS

JOHN JONES.
JOHN EVANS.
DAVID JENKINS. JOHN POWELL.
DAVIS LEWIS.
DANIEL EVAN.
ELIZABETH MATTHEWS, widow.
WILLIAM HOWELL.
GEORGE HOLLAND.
NOBLE CHAMPION.
GEORGE AND ANNE JENKINS.
MARY BOWEN AND ELIZABETH WATER.
WILLIAM LEWIS.
GEORGE THOMAS.
THOMAS REES.
WILLIAM HUGH.
GEORGE HOLLAND, JUN.

The foregoing list was copied by me from the Old Minute Book of the Court Leet and Court Baron of the Manor of Llanmadock. These Courts appear to have been held for many years at the dwelling-house of Mr. George Holland, of Cwm Ivy. The oldest entry in the said book is of a Court held in 1801.

Manor of Llanmadoc: The Court Leet and View of Frank Pledge of our Sovereign Lord the King and Court Baron of Sir John Aubrey, Baronet, the Lord of the said Manor, holden for the said Manor at the dwelling-house of Mr. George Holland, sen., in the Parish of Llanmadock, within the said Manor, on Wednesday ye 4th day of November in forty first year of the reign of our Sovereign Lord George the third, King of the United kingdoms of Great Britain and Ireland and in the year of Our Lord one thousand eight hundred and one, before Richard Mumford, Gent., steward there.

Leet and Homage Jury

JOHN GRIFFITH, Gent.
THOMAS REES
WILLIAM LEWIS
JOHN EVAN
WILLIAM HOWELL
JOHN POWELL

SWORN

GEORGE JENKIN
NOBL. CHAMPION
DAVID LEWIS
HENRY HOWELL
JOHN BUTTON
JOHN JAMES

The business transacted at these Courts was the presenting the deaths of tenants within the Manor, the right of ways, repairing of roads, wreck of sea, constables, strayer sheep, fences and gates, land share marks, and the judging of heriots on the decease of tenants.

On the death of the incumbent of this Parish a Heriot of ten shillings is claimed by the Lord of the Manor, whose residence in ancient times was probably the house which now goes by the name of the Mansion House. It is a very old building and not at all unlikely to have been in former times the Lord of the Manor's chief dwelling within his fee. All the timber in this old edifice is of oak which according to a tradition preserved in the parish is said to have been cut on Whiteford Sker. It is now in a somewhat decayed state, and much of the original building gone, which in its day was doubtless on a par with other dwellings, of the then resident gentry, and would have been considered a fine place.

The Rev. J. D. Davies, *A History of West Gower*,
Vol. II, 1879.

15. *Barley, Oats, Clover*

Old men in Glamorgan were used to say, that by mowing clover twice every summer, it lasted in the soil three or four years; and by grazing it, it would continue five or six years. However, it is said that its hoving quality brought it into disrepute, and its culture was discontinued for some years. The recollection of its former productiveness procured it a second trial, and the sowing of it alone in autumn, continued till the year 1716, when the great frost of that winter destroyed it on Mr. Lucas's farm at Stouthall. Mr. Lucas was deemed one of the first agriculturists of his time: not willing to forego his clover crop for a whole year, he made an experiment to sow it with barley in the spring: it of course succeeded; his neighbours followed the example; and from that time to the present, clover is generally sown with spring crops, barley, oats, and sometimes with beans. About 1720 wheat came to be sown by a few on clover ley of two years standing; the clover being grazed the first year, and two crops of hay taken the second year.

Walter Davies, *A General View of the Agriculture
and Domestic Economy of South Wales*,
Vol. I, 1815.

16. *Copyhold to Leasehold*

The mixed farms in Gower were mainly customary holdings of 15-22 acres, in varying degrees of consolidation in the common fields. Freeholders were larger, up to sixty acres, but it is hard to be precise because of rapid changes taking place throughout our period. These changes saw copyholders or customary tenants becoming tenants-at-will and leaseholders by deed, not "by the rod"; their services becoming money payments; and large fines imposed upon alienation or succession.

The freeholders were strongly placed, whatever their origins. As socage tenants with token rents, they profited from rising prices, and were eager to enlarge their property. They played a leading part in enclosing the common fields in south Wales, about 90 per cent of which were enclosed by 1640. But their extinction was not uniform: common fields seem to have survived longer in the more westerly parts of the coastal plain, although in Pembrokeshire itself one finds all the many stages of rearrangement.

F. V. Emery, 'The Farming Regions of Wales,'
in *The Agrarian History of England and
Wales, Vol. IV, 1500 to 1640,* 1967.

17.   *Gower Enclosures*

The manors of the Gower peninsula provided several examples of small open fields until the nineteenth century, but with the exception of Rhossili Vile all are now enclosed. Occasionally the balk which separated two strips can still be found, topped with a wire fence, e.g. Broad Acre, south of Pyle Cross at Bishopston. The extensive common pastures of Gower have resisted enclosures to a remarkable degree, and Port Eynon Moor, enclosed in the early seventeenth century, is the only considerable common which has been converted to hedged arable fields and meadows in recent centuries. Boundaries of commons and rights of grazing and of quarrying (of limestone on cliff commons and millstones on sandstone commons like Cefn Bryn and Rhosili Down) were always clearly defined in manorial surveys.

The tithe map and award of 1844 for Ilston parish show "Llithered" (Llethrid) Meadow between Pengwern Common and the stream which drains Welsh Moor and drops underground in the limestones of Park-le-Breos Cwm, south of Llethrid. The outer shares in Llethrid Meadow were enclosed by the early nineteenth century, but two groups of unfenced strips (described as landshares) lay within them. The strips varied from half to one and a half acres in the northern to two and a half to seven acres in the central block of strips. Llethrid Meadow may well have been the remnant of a lammas meadow similar to the Lord's Meadow granted to the burgesses of Swansea by the de Breos charter of 1305-6 . . .

In the north of Gower there are more examples of arable strip fields and scattered holdings. From medieval times onwards the beasts of the northern farmers had access not only to Cefn Bryn and other large hill commons, but also to the vast salt marshes which fringe the south side of the Burry River estuary. In 1847 Llanrhidian village, and Leason west of it, were flanked by small groups of unfenced arable strips, and the Great Meadow, which adjoins Llanrhidian village on its north side, was communally occupied.

Similar field patterns existed around Landimore and Llanmadoc villages and a map of the local estates of Thomas Mansel Talbot, made by John Williams in 1780, shows that the Penrice lands and those of several other owners were intricately intermingled in strips that were often unfenced, and were grouped under such names as Hoarstone, East Field, Great Park, Furzehill and Great Longfield. Between Llangennith village and its Burrows lies part of Westown manor of Llangennith (Priorstown was the "East Town" of Llangennith). This area is an undulating and largely arable slope, with Llangennith Marsh at its foot. By 1844 when the tithe commissioners surveyed this parish, the Marsh had been enclosed, but the meadows and withy-bed on its eastern side were described as "in landshares" and were partly unfenced. South of Broughton, in the north of the Manor, a field called Longstone was still in four landshares, and one east of Broughton, called Landshare by the tithemen, was in six.

Holdings of the farmers of Broughton and Llangennith settlements were scattered throughout the cultivable area. Llanmadoc Down backed the bigger cluster of farms at Llangennith and provided an extensive common pasture. The large hill and dune commons of the parish of Llangennith are described in the tithe award as Lord's Waste. In most awards this older form is not used by the tithemen to describe common land.

> Margaret Davies, 'Rhosili Open Field and Related South Wales Field Patterns,' in *The Agricultural History Review*, 1956.

18.   *The Map Makers*

Although Sheet 37 (Swansea) of the 1″ Ordnance Survey "Old Series" was not published until 1830, the original triangulations of South Wales, including Gower, was carried out between 1800 and 1809 under the direction of Lt. Col. William Mudge and Captain Thomas Colby:

While the survey was under way, some of the basic triangulation to establish the 'great triangles' of the area was carried out from key trigonometrical stations within the area of Sheet 37, such as Margam Down and Cefn Bryn. Rays were plotted not only to other points in South Wales, but to Lundy Island and to Dunkery Beacon, Somerset.

As the survey went on, interior triangulation extended the network from local points such as Swansea Castle and the Mumbles Lighthouse. These original survey stations were thus the forerunners of the solid, whitewashed, triangulation points which we can see today in Gower. They can be found not only on Cefn Bryn, but on the Beacon above Rhossili, Llanmadoc Hill, Clyne Common, as well as at the deserted Hills Farm above Overton where there are splendid views with an unusual perspective of West Gower.

But the basic triangulation was only the first step in the map makers' task. Next came a field survey, completed for our area during 1813-14, and carried out by Royal Military Surveyors and Draftsmen, probably helped by local surveyors.

Then, after 1820, Colby decided that a systematic revision was necessary before publication, and this was made by assistant surveyors. Careful attention was paid to detail, including place names, and local gentry were consulted in this process . . . Soon the copper plate engraving was complete, the printing was done from a Board of Ordnance press in the Tower of London, and Sheet 37 of the "Old Series" was published by Lt. Colonel Colby, Royal Engineers, in May 1830 . . .

Besides depicting . . . lost highways of long ago, Colby's Ordnance Map is especially interesting in showing some Gower farms and settlements that have vanished since Napoleonic times. For some of the place names recorded here, we will look in vain on the latest Ordnance maps.

Here on Colby's map is *Oldmoor*, a pile of rubble and nettles a few hundred yards east of Kingshall on the green way to Henllys. Also vanished is *Moor House*, on the way from Corner House, Scurlage, to *Cold Comfort*, another lost settlement on what was the eastern edge of Port Eynon Moor, enclosed at the end of the seventeenth century. A few miles away is *Limerick*, now a roofless byre on Oxwich Point. At Pennard, far out on West Cliff, is *Jamesgrove*, now a ruin, but once owned in other times by the Knights of St. John, and a sometime home of the Vicar of the parish. At the crest of Welsh Moor, there is *Maddocks Hill*, recorded in an eighteenth century Margam manuscript.

On Fairwood Moor, Colby records, there lay *Melin Hafod*, the summer mill, where the track to Wimblewood Isaf crosses the upper Ilston stream. Further west there is *Bush Park*, on the old Leg Lane which runs south-westwards from Cwm Lane, and *The Plough* at Burry Head. While Newton Farm, Scurlage, called 'Low Newton' by Colby, has only recently been abandoned, *High Newton*, a few hundred yards away on the track to the South Road, has disappeared. Here the searching wind blows over empty grass.

David Rees, 'Map Making in Gower,'
Gower XXI, 1970.

19. *The Great Frost*

Some few years ago, an old MS. commonplace book of one Mr. Leyshon Rogers, of Llangennith, came into my hands; it was commenced in 1784, and as it contains some very interesting information as to the scale of labourers' and artisans' wages one hundred years ago, the price of cattle and game at that time, together with a great variety of other matter, I have made a few extracts, and give them without any alteration, just as they appear in this curious old book, which begins with an account of a very severe frost in 1784.

"January the 17th, 1784, the great frost and snow began, and held till February the 21st, which is 5 weeks before it came to change, there was some snow till the 5th of March before it went clear off."

"the frost began the 7th day of December in the year 1784, came to rain the third day of February in the year 1785, Saturday the 18th day of December in the year 1784 was the most dangerous time that was ever remembered in any age by any person that is living, some horses lost their lives, the turnpike roads was all in a plate of ice."

He then speaks of a great drought following this hard frost.

"From the 18th day of February 1785 there was no rain of any value till the 1st day of June, that was three months and most three weeks, and after that it was very dry, till the beginning of September, and then there was so much rain that the late corn was all most lost, that the corn groud fast to the ground, and some was carried off the ground that could not be bound."

"January the 6th in the year 1786 there was so much water upon the

face of the ground as was ever seen by any age now living. Coome
Kiln[1] was every bit under water, that it ran along the road towards
Burry . . ."

The Rev. J. D. Davies, *A History of West
Gower,* Vol. III, 1885.

20. *Gower: A Land of Yesterdays*

Linger with me this olden land to spy:
  A land of sleepy hollows, hemmed with woods
  And hill-slopes dense with deep-roof'd solitudes;
Of wind-racked moors o'er which the curlews cry,
And the red waves of rolling gorse-fires fly;
  Of capes and scaurs, sea-hewn in stormiest moods,
  And roaring caves, that nurse the kestrel broods,
Where once old-world carnivora crawled to die.

A land whereon the breath of Arthur's praise
  Floats like a mist; around whose rock-bound coast
  Lie Philip's galleons rooted fast in sand,
Hovers in storm-time many a drowned ghost;
A shore for song, a land of yesterdays:
  Linger with me about this haunted land.

James Chapman Woods, *A Complete and Reliable
Guide to Swansea, and the Mumbles, Gower . . .,*
1883.

---

1. The ruins of Cwm Lane Kiln can still be seen on the overgrown track from
Muzzard to Burry.

VI

Ships and the Sea

1. Oxwyche Lieth Agenste Combe

Following a tour of the Welsh coast, probably in the early 1550s, Thomas Phaer of Cilgerran wrote a survey which was presented to Queen Elizabeth's government during 1562. Phaer paid close attention to the Gower coast:

Mombles . . . is a road for small ships at 2 fathom low water to serve in necessity at all winds saving easterly winds. It lieth against Hangman Hill in Devon, 3 mile from Combe. There is also a barred haven that serveth upon a spring [tide] to bring a ship of 60 [tons] into Swansey with a southerly wind or westerly.

The Town of Swanseye and country very plenteous. And at Swansey lieth Sir George Herbert Kt., Steward and deputy to the Earl of Worcester being chief Lord of all that coast and country and the port is under the lord's customer that giveth license and cockette.

Oxwyche bay four miles from Mombles is a good road of 4 fathom by shore and deep enough a sea board for all ships and all winds saving easterly. It lieth agenste Combe in Devon the country full of corne and the sea coast under the Earl of Worcester.

Portynon from thence two miles. No haven but a pier and common passage from Wales into Cornwall and Devon with cattle and other things. And this also under the Earl of Worcester and his officers . . .

Then the land turneth in northwards from Wormes hedd and maketh a baye called Tynbye bay nought in a sotherly winds and in that bay is two barred havens Burry and Carmarthen . . . There be dyvers olde Castles decayed . . .

Thomas Phaer, 'Anglia Wallia,' *Archaeologia Cambrensis,* 1911.

2. Coves and Headlands

The Gower cliffs therefore show five main features: the level plateau surface, the steep fall to the *Patella* beach, the *Patella* beach platform, the fall to the modern beach, and and finally the modern beach platform. Since the last is planed across inclined limestone beds and is often very perfect in form, it clearly demands a long period of erosion. There are good reasons for thinking, therefore, that it is not wholly modern, and that it was largely cut in Heatherslade times to be brought later once again to that level. The actual configuration of the Gower coasts is thus the result of several oscillations, and although structural control is clear the more detailed forms are evidently the outcome of many shifts of sea level relative to the land.

A walk along the coasts of Gower is, for the reasons already given, of great physiographical interest. It is also one of great beauty and variety. The magnificent range of Carboniferous Limestone cliffs between Worm's Head and Port-Eynon is probably the finest in the peninsula. They are high and cut into coves and headlands. Usually the sea is now cutting into the lower part of the cliffs only, and these extend a little seaward as a low platform (the *Patella* beach). The views from the headland overlooking Worm's Head are excellent, both eastwards along these cliffs, and northwards across Rhossili Bay with its very marked platform at about 100ft. This feature is of uncertain origin, and is banked against the high Old Red Sandstone mass of Rhossili Down. the marsh on the northern coast lies under the old cliffs, and its setting is impressive.

The great sweeps of Port-Eynon and Oxwich Bays with their sand dunes and woods, break the general trend of the south coast east of Port-Eynon and add much to its interest. Further east, the alternation of smaller bays and lines of good cliffs, with in nearly all places the lower platform still prominent, make the coast perhaps less imposing, but nevertheless most attractive.

J. A. Steers, *The Coastline of England and Wales*, 1969 ed.

3.   *Abertawe, Fair Mother of Ships*

When King John went over to Ireland in 1210 he requisitioned four ships from the burgesses of "Suineshei".

In 1305 William de Braose allowed then timber from his forests to repair and build "four great ships at a time" and as many small ships as might "carry twenty hogsheads of wine or less". Edward the Second and Edward the Third, to assist them in paving and walling the town, granted them "customs" on, *interalia*, pickled herrings, Aberdeen cod-fish and oil, wines, web and canvas cloth of Galway and Ireland, flax, cloth, of silk with gold of samite, diapre and bawdkin, merceries, tallows, tin, brass, copper, copperas and alum—imports which were balanced partially, even in those days, by the "sea-coles" which they exported in fair quantity. So the port of Swansea was not inconsiderable seven and a half centuries ago, and it is likely that it may have been such even two centuries earlier, when Sweyne "Forkbeard" is said to have given it his name.

The late David Lleufer Thomas's rather free translation of the words of Dafydd Benfras which head this article, as "Abertawe, fair mother of ships," may thus be appropriate. They were written in relation to the events which followed the Battle of Kemereu in 1257, and clearly Dafydd was projecting the image of a gem-like estuary of some importance. It was not important, however, in official records. Only the "Royal Ports" like Carmarthen, Caernarvon and Haverfordwest were important then, but these held the limelight by an influence of politics which far exceeded that of commerce. In the fourteenth century, Bristol was made the chief port of the Severn Sea. All other ports of the Channel—on both sides, from Bridgwater to Milford—were subordinated to it, and made "creeks," but it is doubtful if Bristol itself, at that time, enjoyed more transmarine commerce than Swansea.

The Act of Union of 1536 constituted only three head ports for the whole of Wales, namely Cardiff, Milford and Chester, and every port from Worm's Head to Chepstow became a creek of Cardiff, which was itslef one of the least important creeks of the whole extent of coast specified. Thus we read of "the Creeke of Swanze in the Port of Cardiff" in the Port Books of the sixteenth century. Henceforth, nevertheless, we shall talk of the "port" of Swansea.

King John gave Swansea to William de Braose in 1203, as part of "totam terram de Guher," and this word "terram" connected not merely the land of Gower but all its foreshore too, from "Pulcanan" to "Logherne," which is to say, from Pwll Cynon in Crymlyn Bog to the junction of the Loughor and Amman rivers, inclusive of the beds of the Tawe and Loughor rivers.

Therefore, the grantee could claim the anchorage, moorage, keelage and tolls of all ships, and all flotsam and jetsam, but in fact the moorage, keelage and the tolls of ships had for centuries been taken by the Portreeve of Swansea for the use of the common coffer, and the lord of Gower did not manage the port, nor build its quays, and landing places, nor dredge "the paddocks in the river and the rise of Swansea Bar." He did not repair the port, nor erect barrel posts to define the channels, nor fix capstans, bollards and mooring rings, nor "regulate" the ballast thrown out from vessels entering without cargo. He did appoint the Water Bailiff and the Layer Keeper who, under the Portreeve, managed the port.

It was necessary, he said, that these officers should be in his right of appointment, since the Corporation received the benefit of the collections and should incur the responsibilities going with them. They had these benefits because some of his own privileges and franchises as lord-marcher had been demised to them in return for a rent which had been paid to him and his predecessors over centuries, if not from time immemorial. Records, from the sixteenth century, show that £18 1s. 6d. per annum was paid by the town to the lord of the borough for markets and fairs, assize of ale, weighing, moorage and keelage and other things. The "fee-farm rent," as it was called, was paid until 1935, when it was extinguished by a capital payment of thirty three years' purchase.

> W. C. Rogers, 'Aber Tawy Teg Esgorfa: The Port of Swansea—A Retrospect,' in *Glamorgan Historian,* Vol. V, 1968.

4. *The Vice-Admiral of Gower*

The Lord [of Gower] is Vice-Admiral to the Seignory, and as such intituled to all the Profits and Advantages belonging to the office of Admiral, to the holding of an Admiralty Court for the trying of all offences on the sea within the Precincts of the Seingory; but that has never been done within my memory. He is intituled to all Wrecks, Flotsam, Jetsam and Logan. In Virtue of his said office of Vice-Admiral the Lord appoints an Officer called a Water Bailiff who receives a fee of . . . from every vessel . . .

> Gabriel Powell, *Survey of Gower,* 1764.

5. *The Gower Customs*

We say that David Bennett[1] holdeth the Customs of the keyes of Oxwich and Port Eynon, and that he hath the grant thereof under the late Lord's hand for a long term yet enduring, and there hath been

---

1. Of Pitt in the parish of Penrice.

some limestones digged and transported thence, and also some other carriadges, and there is of custom due unto the Lord received for every horse transported there 2d, for every beast 1d, every sheep a farthing, for every hog a half a penny etc.; and the marks and colours of all horses, cattle, and sheep have been accustomedly kept in writing by such as received the said customs for the Lord, with the names of those who transported them, the name of the boat and the master thereof . . . and there is for every ship, bark, or boat that hath a cock-boat unto it, which shall come on ground 4d due unto the Lord for keelage (vizt.) for every keel 2d.

Survey of the Manor of Oxwich, 1632, in Baker
and Francis, *Surveys of Gower,* 1870.

6.   *Channel Crossing*

Until the coming of the railways there was extensive trading between Swansea, Oystermouth, Oxwich, Port Eynon and the West Country. The short crossing, however, was not always an easy one:

Swansea, June 6, 1728

Sail'd for Cornwall, was drove back ye 9th. Sail'd again the 10th. Got within sight of St. Ives, and then by a violent wind drove up almost as high as Swansea. Now landed at Clovelly in Devon, and proceeded by land. Went to St Columb's 45 miles on ye way to the ore district. Sail'd again from St. Ives about 28th June, and got to Swansea July 2nd. Aug. 24, same year, again to Cornwall. Horseback: *via* Bristol . . .

Robert Morris, History of the Copper Concern,
Morris MSS, University College of Swansea.

7.   *French Frigates Off Gower*

In February 1797, a French squadron, from the force which took part in the famous landing near Fishguard, Pembrokeshire, was seen "hovering about off the Worm's Head":

It was from Swansea that the first report of the presence of the French squadron in the Bristol Channel had been sent. The consternation of the merchants and principal citizens of that seaport on learning that four enemy ships were in their nieghbourhood, and their realisation of how ill-prepared they were to meet an attack, is reflected in a letter which the Portreeve was induced to send to the Marquess of Bute for transmission to the Home Secretary. On the same day that the Collector of Customs at Swansea had sent his report of the enemy to the Duke of Portland, the Portreeve wrote as follows:

Swansea, 22nd Feb. 1797

My Lord,

An application having been made to me as Chief Magistrate of this town, by several justices of the peace merchants and other gentlemen of property residing here; stating the necessity of taking some measure for the defence of the trade & sea coasts, three French frigates and a corvette having been seen a few days since hovering about off the Worm's Head—and in case a small vessel with 40 or 50 men should come to the Mumbles (where there are frequently from sixty to one hundred sail of coasting vessels lying at anchor unprotected) they may very easily take and destroy the greatest part of them and do other serious mischief,—In consequence of which I consulted Captain Gibbes, the Regulating Officer at this Port, on the subject, who from the situation of the place is of opinion that some mode of preventing it is absolutely necessary, and that were a dozen or fifteen long twelve or eighteen pounders, sent down by Government with the necessary ammunition they may be placed to such advantage upon different parts of the coast as to secure it effectively from any attempt of the kind, that may be made by the enemy.

I have therefore taken the liberty of troubling your Lordship upon this subject, and have to request that your Lordship will be pleased to obtain an order for sending down the guns &c. necessary for the purpose, there being none between Milford and Bristol: I also beg leave to mention to your Lordship that the Royal Swansea Volunteers—consisting of 180 men are stationed at Swansea, two thirds of whom have been ordered by the War Office to exercise great guns for the defence of the coast, if any can be obtained.

I have the honour to be &c.

Gabl. Jeffreys

Portreeve of Swansea.

The Marquess of Bute forwarded this letter to the Duke of Portland with the comment that it was very important, and he hoped that he would be empowered to return a favourable answer. The Duke of Portland sent the request to the Master General of the Ordnance, but apparently the inhabitants of Swansea never got their guns until the great Napoleonic Invasion scare of 1803, and then they had to pay for them by a public subscription. The battery consisted of two-six-pounders, and the guns may be seen at the present time mounted on the terrace in front of the Mansion House.

E. H. Stuart Jones, *The Last Invasion of Britain,* 1950.

8. *Blinkers on the Moon*

Smuggling first began in the 13th century when a law was passed which forbade the export of English wool to the Netherlands. The early smugglers were called *Owlers,* and they specialised in smuggling wool out of the country. This illicit traffic continued for nearly five hundred years, in spite of a succession of laws which was passed in attempt to suppress it. By the mid-seventeenth century Britons had acquired a taste for spirits, tea, and tobacco. Smugglers therefore turned their attention to these commodities which affected a much larger section of the community, and opened up new avenues of potential profit.

The eighteenth century saw smuggling gain ground rapidly and reach the peak of its activities about 1750. The steps taken by the authorities to cope with these *free traders* were ineffective, and the diversion caused by the Napoleonic wars further prevented the enforcement of existing laws. In 1822, however, the navy co-operated with the Customs, and an effective blockade of the Channel was maintained. By 1830, the Coastguard Office was in operation, and Coastguards—as we know them today—were appointed. This latter ruling finally sealed the fate of the smuggler, who had virtually been put out of business since the blockade.

Smuggling had been given an impetus in the 18th century for three very cogent reasons. In the first place, the Enclosures Act had made labourers of the smallholders and commoners, and had also increased unemployment. Secondly, half the population contenanced smuggling because, in a century of rising prices, it enabled them to live more cheaply. A third, and impelling reason, was that the profits were large: the *trade* also attracted men who were liable to be seized by pressgangs. Smugglers had only to *run* one cargo out of every three to make a profit; actually they averaged four out of five.

Smuggling in West Gower started in a small way early in the 18th century, particularly at Porteynon, where the oyster trade was in full swing, and landings were easily made with the co-operation of the oystermen. In those early days the Revenue cutter visited the Gower coast only rarely, but in the latter half of the century events at Porteynon attracted attention, and strong measures were taken to suppress the practice there. Smugglers were driven to seek more isolated places to land their *stuff*. Men like William Arthur, at Pennard, and Thomas Knight, at Lundy, were at the head of highly-organised gangs which operated both on land and sea some time after the traffic was diverted from Porteynon. Traditional stories tell that about this time, there were eight excisemen stationed at the village, with a boat at their disposal. This boat was mounted on a wheeled carriage and could be launched at short notice. A watch-house was erected on Porteynon Point where a continuous watch was maintained. The ruins of this old house, known locally as Davy Chissel's house, are still to be seen; Davy Chissel died in 1814, and is buried at Porteynon.

About the middle of the 18th century, French smugglers were frequent visitors to the bay. Their contempt for the *Rev'nue* was such that they dropped anchor in broad daylight, and waited for darkness to dispose of their cargo. The contraband, on being landed, was sometimes buried in the sand dunes, but more often was transferred to pack-horses and distributed around the countryside under cover of darkness. Dwellers on the byways, on being awakened by the clatter of hooves, did not have to be told that Johnny Frenchman was at *Partennan* [Porteynon].

A story is told concerning one, Moses Gibb of Uvverton [Overton], who on a winter's day, was dredging with the Porteynon oyster fleet in the Channel. Moses had witnessed the arrival of a French lugger which had anchored in the bay, when he spied the Revenue cutter beating up from the west'ard close inshore. He quickly sized up the situation, *hove* up his dredge and headed for the bay with all the speed he could muster. He contrived to warn Barneo Farneaux, the French captain, who hastily slipped his cable and stood out for the south-east as the cutter rounded Porteynon point, but not before dropping a keg overboard for Moses. Mr. Gibb promptly recovered the bobbing keg and stood by to await developments. The Revenue cutter accepted the challenge, but the Frenchman gradually drew away and eventually was lost in the distance. Moses died in 1765, but this incident has served to keep green his memory.

In spite of the presence of so many King's men at the village, a few cargoes of contraband were handled successfully, even after the turn of the century. One of the last *runs* ever to be made at Porteynon took place about the time of Trafalgar. The *stuff* was alleged to have been hidden in the church, thus escaping the attention of the argus-eyed Preventive men. Thereafter, local worthies had to venture further afield for their eau-de-vie.

Rhossili men, who did more than their fair share of smuggling, must have been more discreet than their compatriots at Porteynon, for their activities were not effectively curbed till long after the *trade* had virtually ceased at the latter village. They were a bold and fearless fraternity; and it is stated on good authority that the women also took part in the landings and even attacked the Customs officers. If Mally Rogers (Mrs. Stote) was representative of them, then they were opportunities of a high order, and their resourcefulness was beyond question. Local tradition relates that towards the end of the 18th century, two Customs officers, accompanied by a servant, rode up to Mally's cottage at Middleton and asked to stable their horses—a request which she readily acceded to.

At the time, a cargo of brandy was lying in a secret cellar nearby, and Mally suspected that the Revenue men had knowledge of it. She persuaded them to enter her cottage and to partake of something a little warming on such a cold morning. They accepted, and she regaled them with brandy, which she diluted not with water, but with the best *Hollands,* out of the kettle on the hob. They remarked, as they rose to go, that she kept some good stuff, whereupon she prevailed upon them to have one for the road, which they did. The kettle of *Hollands* was again in evidence; soon the officers got drowsy and eventually fell asleep. Mally immediately sent word around the village to remove the *stuff,* and at the same time saw to it that the serving man had his share of the potent mixture. By the time the Customs men had recovered their composure, the cellar was empty and the kegs were distributed far and wide.

At a later date, however, a kinsman of Mally's, one William Stote, spent three months in Carmarthen Jail for being concerned on the release of impounded horses from a farmyard in Pitton, the animals having been seized in a smuggling raid on Rhossili sands.

The *Cambrian* of 1805 recalls the seizure on Rhossili sands of a hundred casks of spirits and wine. Customs officer George Beynon, assisted by Lieutenant Sawyers and the Sea Fencibles, attacked the smuggling gang, who fled, leaving the sand littered with kegs. On June 3rd, 1805, the same paper reports that Mr. Beynon seized one hundred and fifteen casks on Rhossili sands.

Mr. A. R. Dawson, of Cardiff, however, tells another side of the story in the *Western Mail* of January 31st, 1934, when he recalls an affray on the same sands on March 11th, 1805. Customs officers William Webb and Thomas Seward from Llanmadoc were severely manhandled by a smuggling gang. Webb, suffering from wounds, was locked up for the night in Stote's cottage in Middleton, but Seward was allowed to limp home. Mr. Dawson also reports that some time after 1807, Thomas Prance, the armless Customs officer from Whitford, surprised a gang at Rhossili hiding *stuff* in a haystack. He seized seventy-five kegs of spirit and over twelve hundred pounds of tobacco.

These incidents, in the spring of Trafalgar year, emphasise the extent of the free trade at Rhossili. The successful runs naturally escaped mention, but there can be no doubt of their prevalence. Under the cloak of night the ploughman, the quarryman and the village craftsman cast aside their robes of respectability and hurried resolutely shorewards to lose their identity in the darkness. These Hydes of the dark moon were the jovial Jekylls who assisted George Beynon and Thomas Prance in shepherding their midnight captures into the fold of the Customs Authority.

All this provides a contrast with the Rhossili of today, where one has not been able to procure liquor since the *Ship* at Middleton closed its doors many years ago. Stote is now a forgotten family name, both at Rhossili and at Porteynon—Isaac Stote was formerly landlord of the *Ship* in the latter village—but the story of Mally will ever figure prominently in the smuggling annals of West Gower.

H. M. Tucker, *Gower Gleanings,* 1951.

9.   Loss of the 'City of Bristol'

. . . We have the melancholy task of recording the entire loss on our shores on Wednesday evening last of the fine steam vessel, the 'City of Bristol,' Stacey, Commander, trading between Waterford and Bristol. The following particulars of this melancholy event may be relied on, having been communicated to us by a respectable person who visited the wreck yesterday.

The vessel, he states, foundered at six o'clock in the afternoon on the sands at Llangennith, near the Holms, in consequence it is thought, of the Commander mistaking the Worm's Head for those dangerous sands, the Helwicks, from the appearance of the breakers; which by endeavouring to steer clear he got on the Llangennith sands, about two miles from the Worm's Head where she almost immediately foundered. There were twenty nine persons aboard, including seven passengers . . . and of whom, with the exception of two seamen, all were drowned . . . Seventy two pigs and four head of cattle swam ashore, and are present at the farm of Cwm Ivy, belonging to Mr. Holland, the agent for Lloyd's. The steamer is gone to pieces, and the fragments are scattered along the shore . . .

. . . In connexion with this lamentable occurrence, it is due to the inhabitants of the lower district of Gower to state that their conduct, both as respects the property and the two survivors has been most praiseworthy. For several days property to a considerable amount, and some of which easily might have been taken away, lay on the beach and yet not an article of the slightest value was removed . . .

The Cambrian, Swansea, 20 and 28
November 1840.

10.   *August Storms, 1850*

One of the worst storms ever known in Gower occurred about 1850. Picture a harvest scene in August. About 30 people of all ages were reaping the New Meadow, a field of wheat on Mrs. Beynon's Great Pitton Farm. The men reaped with hooks, the women bound the sheaves and the children gleaned the heads of wheat. The older men were putting up the stooks.

There was plenty of fresh mutton and home-brewed beer for all, also a great hunk of harvest pudding for everyone to take home at night. The morning was fine and still with the sea smooth as glass.

At dinner-time it was seen that a very big circle had formed around the sun. Then the sun was covered and the wind freshened from the south. By the time the reapers had finished, the wind was blowing down the stocks of wheat.

That day, the schooner *Margaret,* commanded and owned by Captain Thomas of Rhossili, had anchored in Rhossili Bay. His fiancee was Miss Beynon of Pitton.

When the reapers got in from the field in the evening, they heard that Mr. Beynon, with his brother and sister, had gone aboard the vessel with Capt. Thomas, who had gone to Pitton to see them. In those days there was a lot of smuggling done in Rhossili Bay: silks and other goods were brought in, as well as wines and spirits. After they had boarded the *Margaret,* the wind freshened and they could not put a boat ashore.

As the wind was dropping sou'west, the captain was afraid he would be caught on a lee shore, so he sent all his guests below and put out to sea. Then it started to blow a full gale.

The men of the village went down to see what had become of the vessel, but they could not walk over the top of the cliff, having to get down and crawl—but they could see nothing of any ship.

Meanwhile, the vessel got out into Carmarthen Bay, but failed to reach Tenby Roads as the wind had now dropped west. She was driven on the Hooper Sands off Burry Holms, and at high water she got over the sands and finishes up ashore in Broughton Bay, with both masts broken and a lot of other damage.

The Beynon family were shut down below and were very frightened. All got ashore, thankful to escape with their lives.

The vessel was eventually taken off, lashed to two empty barges and repaired. She went to sea again, but was never seen in Rhossili Bay.

After the storm, incidentally, it was found that all the wheat reaped in New Meadow had been blown away. The sheaves had been blown on to the next farm and most of it was saved. The corn cut in swathes had been blown two or three fields away, while the corn which had not been cut could not be cut with any implements and had to be hand-picked and put into sacks.

It was the greatest storm ever known in the month of August, and resulted in near starvation for many poor families in Gower.

John Beynon, *An Eye-Witness Account of
Shipwrecks on the Gower Coast,* 1964.

11.   *Disaster at Broughton*

Probably the most dreadful disaster that ever happened on this coast took place in Broughton Bay, on the night of January the 22nd,

1868, when no less than sixteen vessels varying from 80 and 90 to 400 tons burden, were totally lost, and most of the crews perished. The disaster was caused by an extraordinary heavy ground sea, and the wind dying away. The ill-fated vessels, numbering about eighteen or nineteen sail, were outward bound from Llanelly. When they left that port they were unaware of this ground sea, which was not perceived until they reached Whiteford Lighthouse; here, however, one or two of them very prudently anchored; but as there was a little wind, the rest, having been let go by the steam tug, supposed they would be able to clear the Burry Holms, and with the help of the ebb tide, make a good offing, in which case they would have been all right; one or two only of the number were fortunate enough to do this, but before the remainder could clear the high land up to this point, the flood tide set in against them, and the wind died completely away; the result was they were drifted helplessly back, some dashing against the rocks, and some against each other, while a few sank in the middle of the river, having their bottoms knocked out by thumping on the sand; for such was the extraordinary character of the heavy swell that at one moment a vessel would be floating on the crest of a wave, and the next weeping down its hollow, would be aground on the sand.

At this time a Pilot ship, called the Hulk, was stationed in Broughton Bay, and taking to their boats a few of the crews of these unfortunate vessels managed to get on board of her, and remained there in safety until the morning. The dismal disaster happened between nine and ten o'clock at night, none of the people in the village being at all aware of the terrible catastrophe that was taking place so close at hand. In the morning—as may easily be supposed—there was much excitement in the neighbourhood, and those who went to the sands beheld a sight that will not soon be forgotten. From Whiteford Sker to the Burry Holms, the shore was covered with seamen's clothes, broken spars, shattered hulls of stranded vessels, ropes, sails, tarpaulins, carpenters' tools, and vast quantities of coal, with which latter article the vessels were laden. The bodies of the poor sailors, as they came on shore, were interred in the churchyards of the parishes where they were picked up.

A rather remarkable and somewhat mysterious occurence took place in connection with this wreck, which I cannot help mentioning. The choir of the Parish happened on the evening in question, to be holding their weekly practice in the church, when suddenly an indescribable scream of terror was heard in the churchyard, as of one in the last extremity of mortal fear. I immediately ran out to see what was the matter, and saw a young lad, whom I knew very well, standing in the middle of the walk, not far from the church, with his face not only blanched, but actually distorted with fright. "What is the matter, my lad?" I said. "Oh," he replied, "I saw a man without his hat come and look in through the window." I brought the poor terrified lad into the church, where he remained some little time before he came to himself.

It was currently believed that what he saw was the apparition of one of the poor seamen who was drowned, as it was just about the time when the wreck took place.

The Rev. J. D. Davies, *A History of West Gower*, Vol. II, 1879.

12. *Mary Stenhouse, 1879*

There had been only one practice drill when the company in 1879 attended its first wreck on Rhossili sands. Mr. W. H. Betts had then been sent as Coastguard to Rhossili. He was stationed at Hoarstone.

On a very dark night when the *Mary Stenhouse,* on tow from Liverpool to Swansea, ran ashore near the Old Rectory. Whether the towing tug slipped her cable or parted it when she found herself in the breakers was never discovered, but the vessel ran aground in very heavy seas.

With Coastguard Betts in charge, the Rhossili Life-Saving Apparatus Company were soon on the scene. The first rocket missed and after the smoke had cleared, the rocket tube was missing over the cliff, and members of the company were sent to look for it. It was recovered from the surf and brought back on shore. The second shot found its target, landing on board.

Quickly, the gear was rigged up and a man brought ashore asked if any boats had been found. It was learned that when the ship struck, some of the crew launched a boat and ten men with a woman—the captain's wife—went aboard. But the boat swamped and broke up, all the occupants being drowned. The other ten members of the crew, with the carpenter's wife, had stayed aboard, all being saved.

On the following day. Mr. G. Gibbs of Overton rode a horse to Llanelly and got a tug to go out to the vessel. She went in close and one of the crew jumped aboard the *Mary Stenhouse* with a line. A tow rope was made fast, and eventually the ship was taken off.

Her crew having left her, they were on shore, watching as she rounded Worm's Head and was made a prize of by the Llanelly tug. Standing off in the bay was the tug which had towed the ship from Liverpool, with her crew also watching.

Safely taken to Swansea by the Llanelly tug, all that was left were the remains of the small boat and some bodies. The Llanelly folk claimed a substantial sum for salvage.

John Beynon, *An Eye-Witness Account of Shipwrecks on the Gower Coast,* 1964.

13. *Helvetia, 1887*

On November 1st, 1887, the Pilot Cutter was unable to leave the shelter of Swansea Bay to respond to the signals for a pilot being flown by two vessels standing off Mumbles Head. The south-easterly gale increased as the morning passed, and the vessels, both laden with timber, were blown down channel. One reached the shelter of Lundy.

The other, the *Helvetia,* is the subject of this tale. She struck on the Helwick sands but, being timber-laden, and a fine old oak ship, was lifted across the sands. Under one bare mast, she was blown around Worm's Head into the bay, in a smother of broken water, and was able to anchor in the shelter of the Inner Head.

Coastguard Darch led the Rhossili Life-Saving Apparatus Company to her, firing a rocket aboard, but although the captain came ashore, he refused to leave her altogether, being afraid someone might board and make a prize of her.

Then, however, the wind veered west and the vessel began to drag her anchor. The order came, "Abandon ship!" and next morning, the *Helvetia* was ashore on Rhossili sands, where her remains still lie.

Her 500 tons cargo of wood was discharged on to the beach. Every available man, horse and cart was employed for weeks—and there was timber everywhere! Eventually, there was an auction sale and South Wales timber merchants bought the cargo for a mere song, ordering ships to take the timber away in the summer . . .

It was said that the *Helvetia* brought the most money to the neighbourhood of all the local wrecks.

John Beynon, *An Eye-Witness Account of Shipwrecks on the Gower Coast,* 1964.

14. *Winter Harvest*

The oyster beds in the Bristol Channel have been famous since Roman times. In 1674, one writer described them as the best in Britain. At that time, the fishery at Oystermouth was known to be flourishing, but it was probably early in the 18th century before dredging operations on a large scale commenced at Porteynon. One decided drawback at the latter place was, and still is, the lack of a protected lay-up for ships. The old causeway, built in the late 17th century in order to facilitate the loading of paint mineral, perhaps helped to break the force of southerly gales, and may have influenced the Porteynon men in their decision to expand their oyster fishery.

By the mid-eighteenth century the industry was well established, and for the next hundred years—and longer—offered lucrative employment for many south Gower men. In the early 19th century, oystermen received one penny for two dozen oysters, but later prices rose till, in the early seventies, the shell-fish fetched nearly a penny each. But the industry was by this time on the wane; oysters became scarcer, possibly from disease, and by 1870, the fishing fleet was considerably reduced in strength. Finally, in 1879, the last haul of oysters was landed at the Quay.

In the thirties and forties of last century, the heyday of the industry at Porteynon, the village reached the zenith of its prosperity and fully justified its name of "Port." One can visualise at this period, the bustle and activity which attended the embarkation of as many as forty skiffs for the fishing grounds, each boat manned by a crew of four, not to mention the attendant longshoremen, the smiths and other craftsmen necessary for the successful and sustained operation of the fleet.

More than half a dozen smacks were in commission as auxiliaries for transporting the oysters to Bristol and even to Liverpool. These smacks later traded to Swansea only, where the oysters were transferred to the Steam Packets, which had commenced regular services to the more distant ports. Prior to dispatch, the shellfish were stored in *Perches pools,* still to be seen sectioned off by lines of pitched stones on the foreshore near Salthouse. Since at the height of the season, each skiff would land seven to eight thousand oysters after a day's fishing, it will be appreciated that provision had to be made for storage on a generous scale.

The oyster season lasted from September till the end of March. In the summer months, the dredgermen were employed in the quarries on the cliff-top, while the skiffs were beached and made shipshape for the next season's fishing. The fishing area usually exploited by the *Partennan* fleet was known as *Bantum,* and lay outside the Helwick Sands in a westerly direction from the bay. It was reached by sailing due south from the Quay until the "Corner of the Coombe," in Overton Mere could be seen simultaneously with the "Barley Mow" at Nicholaston. The course was then changed to west, but as the prevailing winds were from that direction, the skiffs usually beat down as far as the Worm, or the *shoord bwee* (sited on the Helwicks off Pilton), turned about, dropped their dredges, and came up-Channel before the wind. The avoidance of certain well-known obstructions on the sea-bed, which caused the dredges to overturn, also involved careful navigation. Successful dredging runs were again ensured by observing landmarks: the dredgermen's rule in the case of one particular run was remembered by the rhyme:

> "Three Cliffs bay and Crowtor clear,
> through the *shoord* and never fear."

Unfortunately, some of these old landmarks have long disappeared.

The early skiffs were open boats, but were replaced about 1850 by larger decked vessels. These considerably lessened the hardship in winter and offered better protection to the crew in rough weather. The oystermen carried no compass, so it was a matter of skill and experience to *fetch* the bay if caught at sea in thick fog or darkness. It is said that on such occasions the church bells were rung as a guide to the benighted stragglers, while dwellers in the Quay cottages kept a lamp burning in their windows. It is related that the crew of one vessel, after beating about in thick darkness for sometime, saw a light, which they judged was in the window of one of the cottages at the Quay, so they anchored till daylight. At first break of day they found themselves alongside Caldey Island, on the Pembrokeshire coast.

Well aware of the vagaries of winter weather, the oystermen assembled at dawn each morning to discuss the weather signs and portents. They decided by majority vote on the advisability of embarking: this conference was known as *making almanacks.* In spite of all precautions disasters did sometimes occur. In 1851, the *Spring Flower* foundered in heavy weather off Slade's foot drowning the four occupants. It so happened that they were four skippers whose crews, that particular morning, had failed to turn up, so they agreed to go together in one skiff: they were Henry Chalk of Porteynon, John Jenkins of Slade, William Jones of Horton, and James Rees of Kitehole.

In 1823, a similar disaster occurred in the Channel. Two of the crew clung to the oars and were rescued, but John Morgan of Moorcorner and William Guy of *Italy* lost their lives. A previous incident, at the beginning of the century, involved the loss of two lives, George Taylor and a man named Haywood. Their skiff was overtaken by a storm and was forced to beach on Oxwich sands. In 1870, William Horwood lost his life at *Bantum,* his leg having been caught in a coil of rope when a dredge was being dropped: he was pulled under and drowned. Considering the risks accepted during seventy-five years of fishing in all weathers (the period for which there are records), the small total of nine lives lost at sea is a tribute to the seamanship of the oystermen. The smacks, in spite of their ventures further afield, seem to have escaped any serious incidents, though David Stephens of Overton, a seaman on one of the Porteynon boats, was drowned at Bristol in 1844. When dredging ceased at Porteynon many oyster-men and their families moved to the Mumbles, where the oyster fishery was carried on well into the 20th century.

By virtue of their sea-going experience, Porteynon men formed the nucleus of the "Home Guard" of Napoleonic times, when the village was selected as the headquarters of the Sea Fencibles. This unit was formed in 1798, but was disbanded in 1802, only to be recalled later when the threat of invasion became imminent. The men, armed with cutlasses and pikes, drilled on the Bowling Green, a level stretch of turf on the burrows.

The passing of the old *Industrial,* the only remaining skiff, severed the last link with the oyster fleet. It had been ten long years since she had yawed to the sudden pull of the dredge ropes, and during the period of her idleness, her presence in the Quay was a constant reminder of *Bantum,* and of the succulent shellfish. She was sold to Cardiff on March 29th, 1899.

Very few people today would assoicate oysters with Porteynon. The only evidence which recall the old oyster days are the shells which lie among the stones in the Quay and are strewn around the arc of the Bay. The barely visible signs of orderliness within the perimeter of the *Perches Pools* will escape all but the sharpest eyes. The old ship-wright's workshop on the Quay is now a dwelling house. The forges which fashioned the framework of the dredges have long ago dis-appeared. The memory of a calling which attracted men from as far away as Rhossili and Oxwich, has now passed into the limbo of forgotten things.

H. M. Tucker, *Gower Gleanings*, 1951.

15. *The Mumbles Lighthouse*

. . . It shall and may be lawful to and for the said Trustees, with the consent of the Duke of Beaufort, his heirs of assigns, and of the owners of the property whereon such Light House shall be built, but not otherwise, and making him or them full and adequate compensation for the same by rent or otherwise, to erect a Pier at *The Mumbles,* and sufficient building for the keeping of coal or any other light at or near *The Mumbles* aforesaid, and to cause such light to be kept constantly burning in the night from one hour after sunset to one hour before sunrising throughout the year, for the benefit and security of the ships and vessels passing the said place called *The Mumbles Head* . . .

—*Swansea Harbour Act, 1791.*

16. *Mixon Shoal*

We have no early records of any system of lighting the dangerous headland of the Mumbles. The safe anchorage of the roadstead was well known to mariners from ancient days, and the navigation of the approaches to it was always attended with much difficulty. The lesser fishing crafts could choose their time for coming in and leaving, but the sea-going vessels running hither in heavy weather would have run many risks of catastrophe ere they came into quiet waters.

There were the dangerous Mixon Sands, the accumulation of sand moved by the current from Swansea Bay to the sunken rocky ridge south west of the Mumbles islets, which are now sentinelled by a buoy and bell. These sands, covered as they usually are, always offered a menace to navigation in the calmest of days:

But when the tempest crash and the storm fiends roar
And the breakers dash on the rocky shore,
And the Mixon is drowned in the thundering gale,

then the peril of approach along the Gower coast to the Mumbles or to Swansea was most imminent; and if the Mixon was safely passed, there remained the Cherry-stone rock, on the east-south-east margin of the outer Mumbles head, an ugly reef just hidden by an ordinary tide, to be reckoned with.

But it is mainly for the Mixon shoal that the lighthouse is maintained. These sands are about a mile long and half a mile wide, and only at exceptionally low tides is the bank at all visible. About six years ago this condition arose, and the incident was marked by a couple of Mumbles boatmen going thither to play pitch-and-toss on the sand.

W. H. Jones, *History of the Port of Swansea*, 1922.

17.   *Sir Christophers Knoll*

Sir Christophers Knoll, with a depth of 9 feet (2m7), rock, near its southern extremity, extends about 8 cables southward from the coast on the north-eastern side of [Oxwich] bay. Mumbles Head lighthouse, bearing 073°, and open southward of Tutt head leads southward of the knoll; and the cairn on Cefn Bryn bearing more than 320° and open westward of Little tor, situated about 1¼ miles north-eastward of Oxwich point, leads westward of it.

Admiralty West Coast of England Pilot, 1960.

18.   *Worm's Head*

Wormshead Island next Caldey in the Severn Sea, distant from Caldey about 20 miles, and in length about half a mile, and in breadth about a bowshot.

William of Worcester, *Itinerary,* 1478, from James Nasmyth's ed., 1778.

19.   *Helwick Sands*

Helwick sands, with depths of less than 6 fathoms (11m0), extend about 7 miles westward, from a position about 3 cables south of Port-

Eynon point. They form the southern side of Helwick channel, which
lies between them and the coast westward of Port-Eynon point.

There is a least depth of 6 feet (1m8), over the western part, which is
named West Helwick, and 12 feet (3m7) over the eastern part named
East Helwick; whilst there is a least depth of 17 feet (5m2) in Helwick
swatch, which crosses the sands about midway between West and
East Helwick sands.

Helwick sands are steep-to on their southern side; on the northern
side they are not so steep-to; whilst at the western end, the shoaling is
gradual.

There is a least depth of 18 feet (5m5) in the fairway of Helwick
pass, the narrow channel which separates the eastern end of the sands
from Port-Eynon point; this channel is advantageous for coasting
craft as, towards low water, it offers comparatively smooth water
during both northerly and southerly winds . . .

Directions.—A vessel should not approach Helwick sands from
southward into depths of less than 13 fathoms (23m8), not only on
account of the steepness of the sands in that direction, but also because, within that depth, there is a heavy cross sea during the west-
going tidal stream in strong westerly winds. Pwlldu head bearing
071° and well open southward of Oxwich point, leads southward of
Helwick sands. Mumbles head bearing o75° and open southward of
Oxwich point (Lat. 51° 33' N., Long. 4° 09' W.), also leads southward
of but closer to the sands.

Rhossili rectory, bearing 049° and just open south-eastward of
Worms tableland, leads over the western end of the sands in depths of
25 feet (7m6). The rectory seen westward of the tablelands leads well
westward of the sands.

Burry Holms, bearing 359° and seen through the middle of Worms
sound, leads through Helwick swatch in a least depth of 21 feet (6m4),
but close westward of a 17-foot (5m2) patch.

At night, a vessel should not bring Helwick light-vessel to bear less
than 275° until Mumbles Head light bears less than 072°.

Admirality West Coast of England Pilot, 1960.

20. A Hundred Sail

In the early eighteenth century Daniel Defoe saw Swansea, long
before the Age of Industry, as a thriving seaport with 'a very good
trade for coals':

. . . Swanzey, a very considerable town for trade and has a very good harbour. Here is also a very good trade for coals, and culm, which they export to all ports of Somerset, Devon, and Cornwall and even to Ireland; so that sometimes may be seen a hundred sail of ships at a time loading coals here; which greatly enriches the country, and particularly this town of Swanzey, which is really a very thriving place . . .

Daniel Defoe, *A Tour through the whole island of Britain*, 1724-26.

VII

Churches, Chapels & Castles

1. *The Priory at Llangenydd*

Cenydd, the sixth Celtic saint who gave his name to the village of Llangennydd or Llangennith, made a most lively appeal to the imaginations of old Gowermen judging by the gusto with which they commemorated his wake or *mabsant* well into the nineteenth century.

It fell on July the fifth and was traditionally the most hectic day in the calendar of old Gower. The stories woven round his name, too, are among the most charming of Gower legends. Fruit of an incestuous union, he was punished for his parents' sin by being born lame with the calf of one leg attached to the thigh. He was thrust out of Arthur's court, then being held at Casllwchwr or Loughor, and cast, Moses-like, in a basket into the river Lliw. Borne out to sea by the river Llwchwr, he was miraculously preserved by divinely-directed seagulls and fed from a wonderful breast-shaped bell. He remained under divine protection and was instructed by an angel until he grew to manhood, when he became the associate of Saint David and other notabilities of the Celtic Church.

Although we must reject, not without reluctance perhaps, these flights of hagiographical fancy, we can be quite certain that there was in Llangenydd in pre-Norman days, an ancient *clas,* or semimonastic church, of some significance, presumably bearing its founder's name. In company with many others of the more celebrated and long-standing fanes in Wales, its wealth and its defenceless position near the sea-coast made it an unusally easy and attractive object of violation by Scandinavian sea-raiders from Ireland. In 986, these most-feared marauders of the Dark Ages, appearing unheralded in their swift and graceful dragon ships, sacked the church of Cenydd and left it desolate. And desolate it still remained a century later when Caradog of Llancarfan settled there for a short while.

The church was probably rebuilt and reconsecrated round about the end of the eleventh century or the beginning of the twelfth. Almost certainly, the Normans had a hand in its reconstruction. One of the earliest acts of Henry de Newburgh, earl of Warwick, (in all likelihood the first Norman lord of Gower), was to issue, early in the twelfth century, a charter to the abbey of St. Taurin at Evreux in Normandy. It granted to the French monastery "for the souls of his lord, King William, and Queen Matilda" and of de Newburgh himself, "the church of St. Kenetus (i.e. Cenydd) and land for two ploughs in the vicinity of that church, and the tithe of the vill of Llanguene (namely Llangenydd—and interestingly enough that is the way it is still pronounced by natives of the village) and a suitable spot for a mill, and enough of his wood for all their necessities, and the tithe of all his rents and his hunting and fishing, and of all his demesne, and the churches of Taurin (probably Knelston) and Pennart, with the tithes and the church of the Isle (the little chapel on Burry Holm), free of all claim." The French monastery sent over some of its monks to take possession and to establish a daughter priory.

Henry de Newburgh was only one of the many Norman lords in South Wales who were thus transferring the possessions of ancient Welsh churches to monasteries in England or on the Continent. They were inspired partly by feelings of filial piety for mother church, but also by the more mundane consideration that the alien priory, no less than the castle and the borough, was an instrument of conquest. It was uncommonly satisfying to ensure security in both worlds by generosity at other people's expense.

The priory established at Llangenydd remained a small and un-pretentious one. Its monks were too few to have had much in the way of conventual buildings, though they would probably have had a small cloister, a refectory, a dormitory, and various outbuildings. Nearly all traces of these have now disappeared. Only the priory church, which served also as the parish church, remains intact. With its unusual saddleback tower, it is the largest of Gower churches; and there may still be seen that curious stone slab which local lore insists is Cenydd's tombstone.

What little is known of its history in the Middle Ages suggests that it enjoyed little of that leisured tranquility we usually associate with mediaeval cloisters. For nearly two centuries, its handful of monks must have gone in almost daily dread of the neighbouring "Welshry," who were always prone to revolt against their foreign overlords, and to attack Norman knight and trader and monk alike. When danger from the Welsh need no longer alarm them very greatly, the un-fortunate inmates of the priory were beset by fresh vexations arising from the loss of Normandy by the English crown, and the endemic wars between France and England. In time of war, the possessions of those alien priories which acknowledged French monasteries as their mother houses were not unnaturally seized by the king. Such confiscation hit them hard. The register of the bishop of St. David's of 1399 has a dismal tale to tell of the alien priories of Pembroke and of Llangenydd being "above measure destroyed, dilapidated and wasted, as well in houses as in things and possessions, that the divine worship and regular observances therein are at an end, and hospitalities and alms and other works of charity besides, of old established and accustomed to be done there, are withdrawn, and also the pious vows of the founders are in manifold ways defrauded and frustrated, to the no small offence and displeasure of Almighty God as we believe."

Within a few years, in 1414, all the alien priories were suppressed and their property finally transferred to royal hands. By this time, there may have been no more than two monks at Llangenydd to mourn the loss of Gower's only monastary. The priory remained in royal possession for nearly forty years until in 1442 it was granted to the new foundation of all Souls' College, Oxford.

It would seem from petition sent to King Henry VI by the Warden and Fellows of All Souls that they were meeting with considerable difficulty in enforcing their title to their newly-acquired Gower properties. They complained that "Richard Baddelsey, priest, and Hugh John, knight rejoicing them of the great and inconvenient riots of late fallen" (i.e. the Wars of the Roses), accompanied by the "most misruled and mishievous people" of the neighbourhood, caring nothing for the "sentence of God, nor of our mother holy church, neither of the king's laws," had seized the priory, the priest taking its tithes, and the knight its temporal revenues. However, when these troubled days of civil war were over, All Souls' College seems to have had no difficulty in making good its claims.

Thus began that long connection between the Oxford college and the parishes of Llangennydd and Pennard, whereby the college because the patron of both livings and nominated all the vicars down to the middle of the nineteenth century.

Glanmor Williams, *Gower III,* 1950.

2. *Llangyfelach*

Llangyfelach on its hill, overlooks a wide view of the surrounding uplands. In spite of being only a small country village clustered about its massive and isolated tower, Llangyfelach is a home of lost causes. It began when Dewi Sant founded there one of the most important Christian settlements in Wales, a glory which is now represented only by a few stone relics. On its mapsant, the First of March, a great fair sprang up, at first in the churchyard, then spilling out into the road and then into the fields opposite, a fair to which over fifty thousand people came on St. David's Day—Ffair Llangyfelach, now defunct but rosy in the memory of plenty of men still living. Even more recently it might have had a great steel plant, but nothing is left of that project but a flattened desert stretching north towards Felindre. All lost causes, and recorded even in song by the immortal "Farwel i Llangyfelach Lon." Still, in our day, it has two glories, its Celtic Cross and Evan Walters.

They say in Mynyddbach that Llangyfelach church tower was the first Nonconformist in Wales, but from Colonel W. Ll. Morgan's *Antiquarian Survey of East Gower* we learn that it was the church which could not conform with the tower, for it collapsed during the Napoleonic Wars and was rebuilt on the site of an old tithe barn further down the hill, leaving the famous tower of the Llan in its solitary grandeur. Detached church towers are by no means uncommon in Wales, and they can be seen at Bronllys in Breconshire, Manorbier in Pembrokeshire and Henllan in Denbighshire. This tower is over thirty yards to the south of the church and still contains the belfry. Three periods of restoration can be recognised distinctly, and over a door on the north side of the tower is a badly weathered inscribed slab-stone with a Celtic Cross. But the gem of Llangyfelach is its inscribed cross-base, a delightfully carved boulder of local stone which belongs to the tenth century, or even earlier. It stands at the foot of the tower, and elaborate spiral designs in an excellent state of preservation enhance all its four sides. It is one of the finest examples in Wales, and unique in Gower.

The church is modern and plain, but inside there are several features of interest. First of these is an inscribed stone slab inserted into the north wall of the nave, having upon it a Celtic Cross and the letters CRUX XPI, "the cross of Christ,"—this is a relic from the monastic origin of the early Christian settlement and dates probably from the same century as the cross-base. Memorial brasses are uncommon in Gower, so a fine specimen here should not be missed, especially as it has historic associations. It is a small brass dated 1631 with a Latin inscription by Marmaduke Mathews to his parents. He was the Vicar of Swansea who left the Church with John Myles, Rector of Ilston, as a protest against the compulsory reading of the Book of Sports in churches. On the north side there is the small sepulchral chapel of the Penllergaer family. It is now a children's chapel, dominated by a large painting by Evan Walters, over the altar. It is called "Holy Communion at Pentonville Prison," and was given to the church by the artist as a memorial to his mother. It is considered among the most important of the artist's works, and it is so suitably illuminated in its setting that the characterisation of faces, which is such an important feature of Evan Walters' work, can be properly and comfortably studied.

The foundation of this church is one of the few certainly pre-Norman churches we have in Gower, and as one passes through the lych-gate and takes a last look at the ancient tower, the field opposite where the fair was held, and the great desert of mud that might have been a steel-works, but is now the haunt of buzzards and foxes, one tarries not with these thoughts, but with the emotional experience of the rugged and lovely Cross of Cyfelach, and the painting in the chapel which is a son's tribute to his dead mother.

Gwent Jones, *Gower I,* 1948.

3. *The 23 Churches of Gower*

. . . Within the circuit of the said Lordship is contained twenty three churches, viz't, Llangiwg, Llangyfelach, Llandeilo Talybont, Loughor, Swansea, St. John's, Oystermouth, Pennard, Bishopston, Ilston, Penmaen, Penrice, Oxwich, Nicholaston, Porteynon, Rhossili, Llangennith, Llanmadoc, Cheriton, Llanddewi, Knelston, Reynoldston and Llanrhidian.

Survey of Gower Anglicana, 1583, in Baker
and Francis, *Surveys of Gower,* 1870.

4. *St. Mary's, Swansea*

In Swensey one church called St. Mary's church. Within ye same is a monument of Sir Matho Cradog . . .

Rice Merrick, c. 1584.

5.   *St. John's, Swansea*

To judge from all traditions this was a beautiful church with good monuments.

When it was destroyed is uncertain, as the church pulled down in 1820 was a very inferior building of no great date. The monuments have perished, and a brass to some extinct family, which is mentioned as extant in 1845, has disappeared. In the Register of the Banns of Marriage there is a note made by one Watkin Jones to the effect that a stone was found at the time the old church in High Street was rebuilt, bearing date 1124. This has also disappeared, it it ever existed.

The church was again restored and a small chancel added a few years ago. In the north wall of the 1820 church, which was left intact, there is a large flat stone at a considerable height; no inscription or carving is at present discernible upon it; it is supposed to have come out of the original church, and if so it is the only relic known to exist.

The most interesting event relating to this church is its connection with Marmaduke Matthews, the celebrated Nonconformist divine, who, after his return from the West Indies, was appointed by his friend, Col. Jones, to St. John's Church, Swansea, 1658, from which he was afterwards ejected . . .

Col. W. Ll. Morgan, *Antiquarian Survey
of East Gower,* 1899.

6.   *Ilston (St. Illtyd)*

August 1851.

An interesting specimen of a church in Gower, lately put into a state of order and repair, and beautifully situated on a sloping bank finely shaded by trees.

It comprises a chancel with south chapel, nave, and a tower on the south side of the nave. The latter is peculiar, being low and rude, and unusually large and massive, partaking quite of a castellated character. It has no openings, but mere slits and no stringcourse, a plain battlement, which in the centre of the south side rises into a low gable, and a roof of saddle form. The east and west faces have corbel tables under the battlement.

The tower is vaulted, and opens to the nave by a low, rude, obtuse arch. The chancel arch is pointed, and springs immediately from the wall without moulding. The West end of the nave has a middle-pointed window of two lights. On the north is a lancet trefoiled, and one transitional from first to middle-pointed; also of two lights with foiled circle above and no hood. There seems to have been no windows originally on the north. The east window has three lancet lights beneath a pointed arch, the hood having crowned heads for corbels. On the north of the chancel is a lancet restored, if not quite new.

The ground being very uneven causes an unusual ascent eastwards, and there are two sets of steps in the chancel. The chancel arch is not in the centre, whence arises a crooked appearance. The font has an octagonal bowl on a similar base. In the north wall of the chancel is an arched recess. The chapel on the south of the chancel is perhaps debased, with little architectural character. The roofs are newly slated, and there is a good cross on the east gable and the south chapel. The whole interior is very neat, with new open benches, and the general appearance of this church contrasts sgreeably with the neglected state of most churches in Gower.

The churchyard is beautiful and secluded.

Sir Stephen R. Glynne, 'Notes on the Older Churches in the Four Welsh Dioceses, 'Archaeologia Cambrensis, 1897.

The church is referred to as 'Llan Ildut in the letter of Pope Calixtus II to Urban, Bishop of Llandaff in 1119, where it is confirmed as part of the possessions of the lattter. It was also known as "Llanilldut Gwyr" and "Llanilltyd-Verwallt."

Gower as ecclesiatical property had been debateable land since the 7th century. At that date there was a dispute as to which was the territory of Bishop Oudacius and that of the abbot of St. Illtyd. Part of that disputed territory was no doubt the site of the present church of Ilston. From the 10th to the 12th centuries the dispute continued between Llandaff and St. David's. The latter diocese eventually secured the whole of Gower with the exception of Bishopston, which was part of Llandaff until 10 years ago.

In 1221 the church of St Illtyd was given by William de Breos to the knights of St. John, who retained the patronage until the order was dissolved. The present church dates from this period. The tower appears to have been built over a small chantry chapel, and this may have been originally the cell of the monk who started this little colony of the monastery of Llantwit Major . . .

The Rev. Latimer Davies, Pennard and West
Gower, 1928.

7.   Trinity Well Chapel

This chapel must not be confused with St. Kenyd's Chapel at Trinity Well. The old chapel of St. Kenyd was situated a short distance away. Trinity Well Chapel was built in the 17th century, and the ruins are claimed to be that of the oldest Baptist chapel in Wales.

The well here was probably regarded as a holy well in very early times . . .

In the Act of Parliament for the better propagation of the Gospel in Wales, 1649, we find among the commissioners the names of several from this locality—William Herbert, Bussy Mansel, Roland Dawkins, John Bowen, and John Daniel. Any five of these could take action.

William Edwards, rector of Ilston, was one of the first deprived of his living. He was succeeded by John Houghton, who was removed in favour of John Myles, 1649-1660, styled "Cromwellian Minister," a graduate of Brasenose College, Oxford. Local tradition states that Houghton, on being deprived of the incumbency of Ilston, built a chapel at Trinity Well from the stones of the ruined oratory of St. Kenyd.

At the Restoration of Charles II, Houghton was reappointed rector of Ilston, and his name appears as such in the church registers. During the Interregnum the registers were signed by Roland Dawkins and John Bowen, commissioners, the banns of marriage were read by them in the market place, Swansea, on Saturdays.

It is said that William Houghton allowed John Myles to occupy the chapel the former had built at Trinity Well. While parochial minister, Myles appears to have also held services for the Baptists at the meeting house, Ilston, where he baptized many members, in all 46 people, among them were numbered, Jane Lloyd, Paviland; Margaret Davies, Ilston; Matthew Davies, Killay; Elizabeth Harris, Llanmadoc; Elizabeth Hills, Rhossili; W. Thomas, Llangennith; W. Morgan, Bishopston; H. Griffiths, Bishopston; Mary Griffiths, Bishopston; Margaret Bowen, Ilston; Jane Austin, Ilston.

The minister and his congregation migrated to America in 1660, where they founded the town of Swansea in Massachusetts.

The Rev. Latimer Davies, Pennard and West
Gower, 1928.

8. Nicholaston Church

An extremely small church, with only a diminutive low nave and chancel, and a bell-gable over the west end. The situation quite solitary, on a height overlooking Oxwich Bay. There is a large south porch. The west window, a single lancet now closed; the eastern, a double lancet. On the north another lancet stopped, and on the south a poor square-headed Perpendicular window. The chancel arch rude and pointed, upon imposts; the font a square bowl on a cylindrical shaft.

Sir Stephen R. Glynne, 'Notes on the Older
Churches in the Four Welsh Dioceses,'<br>'Archaeologia Cambrensis, 1897.

9. Penrice Church Unroofed

The Rev. David Evans, Rector of Nicholaston, to Lord Mansel of Margam.

Llanrhidian, November 28, 1720.

My Most honoured Lord,

Having heard that your Lordship designs for London ere long, I hope your Lordship will pardon my freedom herein, having little else to com'unicate to your Lordship than an assurance, as in duty bound, of my hearty Prayers for your Lordship's good journey and safe return home, and as soon as business will permit. I am overjoyed to hear yt there will be (by your Lordship's meanes) a period put to ye differences between Mr. Mansel & Mr. Hancorne; it was a great heart-breaking to me to have 2 of my Parishoners, and ye chief of them, & also so near relations, at such an enmity, but I doubt not but your Lordship will speedily reconcile them.

Last Sunday, in ye evening, I did (with much adoe, for ye weather), get to Penrice, tho I could not get into church by reason of ye head of ye church was stript by ye violence of the storm, where I saw Mr. Hancorne, who told me, when I exprest my grief for ye variances, yt all was refer'd to your Lordship. Mr. Hancorne then desired me to acquaint your Lordship yt our chancel at Llanrhidian was put into good order, w'ch I can assure is true, and beyond my expectation, considering ye time of the year. And it was well it was finished before last Sunday, else both sides wd. have been down, and if ye north side had not been pointed, it wd. have infallibly have been stript. Llanrhidian, as your Lordship knows, stands low, yet 2 large elms upon your Lordship's estate just by ye village, were blown up by ye roots, of w'ch yr. Lordship has had an acc't ere this.

Heavens favoured us with brave weather while ye chancel was in doing, yet we had no frost nor rain, so yt I hope it is as well done as if it had been in the middle of su'mer, and ye work as I take it is well done. I am sure I attended them from first to last, & I do design to prevent playing of Tenis upon it, w'ch is almost ye only thing yt can do it any damage. I again heartily assure your Lordship of my sincere prayers for yor. Lordship's safe return, which concludes from, my Lord

Your Lordship's most dutiful and
most obedient humble servant,
°   DA. EVANS.

The Rev. J. D. Davies, *A History of West Gower,
Vol. IV, 1894.*

10.   *Gower Churches, 1721*

Livings above 50£ per Ann.

Bishopston R.
Cheriton R.
Ilston R.
Loughor R.
Llanmadoc R.
Llangyfelach V.
Port Eynon R.
Rhossili R.

Living not exceeding 50£ per Ann.

St. John's *Chap.*	05	00	00
Llanrhidian V.	10	00	00
Llangennith V.	15	00	00
Llanguick C.	10	00	00
Llanddewi V.	08	00	00
Llansamlet C.	12	00	00[1]
Nicholaston R.	29	00	00
Oxwich R.	40	00	00
Oystermouth C.	10	00	00
Penmaen R.	35	00	00
Pennard V.	08	00	00
Penrice C.	05	00	00
Reynoldston R.	35	00	00
Swansea V.	36	00	00
Talybont V.	41	00	00

Erasmus Saunders, *A view of the State
of Religion in the Diocese of St
David's,* 1721.

11. *The Church at Knelston*

Isaac Hamon, the steward of the manor of Bishopston, who in July 1697 sent a detailed description of Gower to Edward Lhuyd, claimed that he was "not very well acquainted" in West Gower. It is true that he is at his most certain when describing places in the eastern part of the peninsula, but even when on less familiar ground he can give information which is now of value. He describes "Knoylston of Knowlston" as "a very small parish . . . there was in the time of King Charles I a pretty church, but it hath been ever since open & un-covered & nothing done there but burialles".

Today the church at Knelston is an ivy-choked ruin which the frosts of each succeeding winter are alowly reducing to a meaningless heap of rubble; if you went to look at it you would be likely to have

1. Llansamlet church was in the Manor of Kilvey. Erasmus Saunders recorded that Knelston, the remaining church of the Lordship of Gower, was one of those in the Diocese which was "totally neglected" and which served for "the solitary habitations of owles and jackdaws."

some difficulty in imagining its original appearance. What follows is an attempt to gather together the scattered references to the building and, by presenting that information together with a group of previously unpublished illustrations, show something of its history and of what existed there before time and decay took a hand.

In about 1875 the site of Knelston church was visited by Rev. J. D. Davies, who was then compiling his *History of West Gower*. He made a series of sketches, which have unfortunately disappeared, and extensive notes about the church, which are now preserved with some of his other unpublished papers at the Swansea Museum. By combining these notes with information from surviving photographs and drawings, and with measurements of the ruins, it is possible to build up a fairly complete picture of the church as it once was.

It must have been a small, rather low building, consisting of a simple nave and chancel. The chancel occupied just under half the length of the building. Entry was through a doorway on the south side, the semi-circular tympanum of which was a solid block of breccia. On the outside of this tympanum was a scratched dial-plate, the existence of which confirms the impression given by the plan of the church on the map of Knelston manor made in 1784 that there was no porch attached to the building. The same plan makes it clear that the church had no tower, and it may be safely assumed that part of the west wall which rises above the level of the side walls in the old photograph of the church is the remains of a bell-gable.

In 1875 Mary Hoskins of Knelston, who died three years later at the age of 78, told the Rector of Reynodlston that she remembered a bell hanging in the old church. It finally fell down and remained in the Hoskins's barn until boys knocked it to pieces. Davies noted that the quoins of the nave were dressed with breccia and that the small window on the eastern side of the doorway was 2ft. high, but only 4ins. wide. Some holes which he noted in the interior of the east wall, and which were similar to those in the external wall shown in Mrs. Wood's drawing, were probably no more than holes used to secure the scaffolding when building the church. No record exists of the shape of the east window of the church, which appears as a rather formless opening in both drawing and photographs, but perhaps some reminiscence of it may be found in the windows of Providence Baptist Chapel at Knelston, which are not particularly characteristic of chapel-building.

The name of the village is variously spelt in manorial-surveys made between the 14th and 18th centuries as *Knoylston, Knowelston,*

Nolston, and *Nelson.* Of these, *Nelson* is the earliest, appearing in 1302, and it is the one still favoured by local pronunciation. Among the Penrice and Margam manuscripts at Aberystwyth is a 16th century pedigree of Pierre de Bien Scavoire "who came to Gower (in 1279) to serve William de Bruse, who gave him in marriage the only daughter and heiress of Thomas ap Griffith Gower and had by her the lordship of Llan y tayre mayre, and had issue . . . Adam de Bien Scavoire, called . . . Adam Knowell, who named the lordship of Llan y tayre after his name, Knowelston".

This facile explanation of the name comes from too late a source to satisfy everyone, but is as likely as that in the *Gower Guide* which, while suggesting that *Knelston* derives from *Knoyle's Farm,* takes no account of the fact that *Knoyle* has never been a Gower name. This pedigree also gives the earliest evidence which I know for the name of the church. Rees Merrick's notes, written over a century before Lhuyd's *Parochial Queries,* become illegible at the point where it is given, and all other early sources refer to it by its Norman dedication to St. Taurin. A few late sources which state that the dedication was to St. Maurice are certainly mistaken. The existence in the village of a St. Mary's Well and references to a lost chapel of St. Anne tie the church firmly down to the group dedicated to the Virgin Mary. If the reference to *Llan y Tayre Mayre* is accepted, two other Marys must be included in the dedication. These may have been Mary Magdalene and Mary of Bethany, or it may be that we have here a reference to the once popular legend that the Virgin had two sisters, also named Mary the wives of Cleopas and Salome. The Virgin Mary, Mary Cleopas and Mary Salome are engraved on the early 17th century chalice of Beddgelert church, but no instance is known in Britain of a church dedicated to the Three Marys, so that in one way Knelston is perhaps unique.

In the 12th century the advowson and tithes of Knelston were presented to the Abbey of St. Taurin at Evreux in Normandy by Roger Bellomont, Earl of Warwick: after this the church appears to have been known as the church of St. Taurin at Knelston. Knelston now became an offshoot of an alien monastery, and subject to confiscation by the Crown in the event of war with France. Early in the Hundred Years War, according to Fenton, the king "granted to Bishop Gower to appropriate the tythes of Knelston for the building of a wall round the close of the Cathedral of St. David's, and keeping it in repair".

Whether Bishop Gower did have "power" to appropriate the tithes is a matter of some doubt, for in 1367 the tithes were granted to Adam Horton, Gower's successor, by the Abbott of Evreux, a grant which was confirmed by Richard II in 1393. From this time onwards, the church seems to have remained in the hands of the Bishops of St. David's, whose interest in it was seemingly confined to the collection of tithes. It is said that for a time the services of the church were performed by the Vicar of Llanddewi, whose only payment for this duty was a new hat once a year. If this was the limit of the finances available to the church it is hardly surprising that it was allowed to fall into ruin early in the 17th century. When a survey was made of the manor of Knelston in 1688, the jurors stated confidently that there was "no church or chapel within this manor", which ought to be the end of the story, but is not.

The same Mary Hoskins who remembered the bell hanging in the church also recalled that she had heard her grandfather say that he had attended the funeral of a person who was buried in Knelston old church. This was probably the last occasion on which the churchyard was so used, but it means that even in the 18th century the old church was still being used for one of the purpose for which it was built. What is now a shapeless ruin had probably given five hundred years of service before it was abandoned to nettles, ivy and the scratching of hens.

Michael Gibbs, *Gower XXI,* 1970.

12.   *Llanddewi in Gower*

2nd August, 1871

A small neglected church, much out of repair; consists of nave, chancel, south porch, and west tower. The tower is low, of very rude construction, and little architectural character; without buttresses, but having the north and south sides gabled at the top.

There is a battlement and corbel tabel on the east side; the openings are mere slits, save the north belfry window which is Pointed. The chancel arch is very rude, and of obtuse form; but one half has mouldings, the other not. On the north side of it is an obtusely pointed recess. There is a trace of a similar arched recess on the south of the chancel arch. On the north of the nave is a Norman window, much splayed but closed. On the south is a single-light window with ogee head. In the chancel on the north is a trefoil-headed lancet; at the north-east, a two light window without foliation.

Other windows are modern. The porch is large with stone seats, the doorway pointed.

Sir Stephen R. Glynne, 'Notes on the Older
Churches in the Four Welsh Dioceses,'
Archaeologia Cambrensis, 1897.

13. *The Free Chapel of Henllys*

Another non-parochial benefice described in the chantry certificates was the free chapel of Henllys in Llanddewi parish.

The commissioners who reported on the chapel in 1546 were unable to say by whom or for what purpose it had been founded. They stated that it had been a free chapel time out of mind and that its income was derived from certain mountain lands worth 7s. a year and the tithe corn of the township of Henllys, worth 33s. 4d. a year. Sir George Herbert, the steward of Gower under the earl of Worcester and one of the largest landowners in the lordship, recieved the rent and the tithe corn. The commissioners noted that, apart from 3s. 4d. for the king's tenth, the 37s. which constituted the income of the benefice was for the priest's (or rector's) stipend "when there is one."

However, the 1548 certificate, which otherwise gives few details of the chapel, records that Sir George Herbert was its incumbent. There is nothing in this certificate to indicate how this situation had arisen, but the earlier certificate notes that the advowson of the chapel was in controversy between the Barrett family and the bishop of St. David's, and from proceedings concerning the chapel instituted some years previously it appears that Herbert had been given the chapel by Henry Barrett. Apparently the bishop claimed the chapel by virtue of an earlier grant by the Barrett family, but whatever the merits of his title may have been, it was evidently Herbert who occupied the chapel at the time when the chantry certificates were made.

W. R. B. Robinson, 'The Church in Gower Before
the Reformation,' *Morgannwg*, Vol. XII, 1968.

14. *Cheriton*

We are going to see Cheriton Church, which stands at the bottom of the hill in the bosom of the valley—a sweet brook glides merrily along, sighing or laughing like a merry girl as it races on to the sea. This little brook flows close to the churchyard, and we must cross a little stone bridge that spans the stream to gain the church . . .

Cheriton Church is very pretty—one of the finest in Gower. The tower stands between the nave and chancel without aisles or transepts. This may be called a transitional example, as it has a small saddle-back roof within the parapet, and not interfering with it.

We notice the two arches under the tower; they are really beautiful—the best early English well-chamfered, and rising from graceful corbel shafts of four different patterns, including some magnificent specimens of foliage. We also cannot help admiring the inner doorway with its banded shafts, fluted capitals, and well-cut mouldings. There is a very ancient Norman font on the east side of the porch outside the church. The interior of the church has been renovated, and is now very comfortable. The minister is the Rev. J. D. Davies, Rector of Llanmadoc.

There is a very large attendance here in the evening service. The worthy minister has cultivated music, or at least taken great pains to improve the singing, and to get a good choir, and I believe he has been pretty successful, the singing being now of a very respectable order. They have a harmonium with stops, which is very well played.

C. D. Morgan, *Wanderings in Gower,* 1886 ed.

15. *Llanmadoc Church*

The plan of this Church (the smallest in Gower) is of the plainest description, consisting of a nave, chancel, and saddleback tower at the western end. The probable date of the present structure is the 18th century. Much of the south side of the nave, with a portion of the upper part of the tower, and the greater part of the east wall of the chancel, being in a very decayed and loosened condition, had to be taken down and rebuilt when the Church was restored in the years 1865 and '66. A new window was then inserted in the east end of the chancel, and another in the south side of the nave.

There are no windows on the north side, but in scraping off the whitewash and plaster, two round headed, blocked up apertures were met with. A new porch was also built at the same time, replacing a former one (modern) but constructed in such bad taste that the architect was compelled to remove it. The ancient Holy Water stoup was found by me in a garden in the village, but whether it had been fixed in the porch, or within the Church, there were no means of knowing. The restoration was carried out from plans prepared by Mr. John Pritchard, of Llandaff, and the Church was re-opened for service on the 26th of April, 1866.

These saddle-back roofs, and the decidedly military character of the towers, are the peculiar feature of the Gower Churches. At Llanmadoc the gables are connected by a overhanging parapet, supported by a number of rude small red sandstone corbels. In the present instance the roof takes the direction of the Church; but at Llanddewi and Rhossili it is transverse to it, and runs north and south.

The opening on the north side of the wall, dividing the nave from the chancel, is the entrance to the Rood Loft, sometimes called the "Jube," a sort of gallery, which, in former days, stretched across the Church, immediately above the chancel arch and supported by what is called the "Holy Rood," generally of large dimensions, and fequently accompanied by figures of Our Lady and St. John on either side. The representation of the Rood, placed over the screen dividing the nave from the chancel conveyed to our ancestors the full type of the Christian Church, the nave representing the Church militant, and the chancel the Church triumphant, denoting that all who would go from the one to the other must pass under the Rood, that is, carry the Cross and suffer affliction. It was from this place the Epistle and Gospel were usually read in pre-reformation times, access being obtained by a staircase.

There is, however, one feature which it is necessary to explain here: it will be seen that the bottom part of this aperture in the wall is considerably below the top of the chancel arch. It was not so much so originally . . . But when the Church was being restored, it was found that the soil had accumulated to such an extent in the Churchyard, that it was at least four feet higher than the level inside the Church. The floor had therefore to be raised, the consequence of which was to diminish the height of the entrance into the chancel so much, that it became necessary to raise the crown of the arch; but the entrance to the Rood Loft not being interfered with, this now appears much lower down than it ought to be . . .

The Rev. J. D. Davies, A History of West Gower,
Vol. II, 1879.

16.   *Llanelen Yew Tree*

This old church stands in a small wood about a quarter-of-a-mile distant west by south from the dwelling house of Llanelen farm.

Little is left of the building save a confused heap of stones, overgrown with brambles and brushwood, the walls above ground having almost entirely disappeared. In the wouth-west corner, and within the boundary wall of the churchyard, which can be traced on the west, south and east, stands a venerable yew tree, measuring in girth about fourteen feet at three feet from the ground. It is a noble tree, and I hope it will long remain untouched by the woodman's axe. The Rev. N. R. Rees, and his brother, the Rev. C. G. Rees, accompanied me on a visit to the place in May, 1886. Of course it is impossible to say what may be buried beneath the rubbish, the removal of which would certainly disclose the plan of the church and other things might possible be discovered.

The church was dedicated to St. Helena, whence its Welsh name Llan-elen (i.e., the church of St. Helena). The place took its name from the church, and from the remains of old buildings found round about it is evident that a small hamlet or village existed here in former days.

The presence of yew trees in churchyards has given rise to a vast deal of discussion: pretty nearly all the opinion advanced on the subject may be found in "Brand's Popular Antiquities," Vol. 2, p. 164. But as Fosbrook remarks, in his "Encyclopaedia of Antiquities"—"This tree has come down to us as a funeral plant, from times long prior to the introduction of Christianity; death was symbolized by it both in respect of its poisonous qualities, and its gloomy aspect. The common tradition that it was planted in churchyards to supply the parishioners with bows is not supported by history; and as a matter of fact, yew staves for bows were imported from abroad, as being of superior quality to English yew." Humboldt, in his "Aspects of Nature," speaking of the age of trees, says, "Of all trees, the yew is that which attains the greatest age; that in the churchyard of Gresford, N. Wales, which measures 52 feet in girth below the branches, is computed to be fourteen hundred years old."

Taking this as a standard, that in Llanelen churchyard may be four hundred years old, which takes us back to the beginning of the sixteenth century; but the church is much older than that, for mention is made of Llanelen, under this name in 1319, in one of the Penrice MSS.   The Rev. J. D. Davies,
The Gower Church Magazine, June 1903.

17. Llangiwg Church

Dedicated to St. Ciwg. The chancel and nave are built together, without any division or distinction between them; a tower at the west end communicates with the church by a small modern doorway, which, however, is made through an old archway, 6ft. 6in. wide, by 4ft. 2in. to springing, and 5ft. to crown of arch; this is almost the only remnant of old work to be seen inside the church.

The main doorway is on the south side of the nave, about two-thirds of the distance down the church.

The four pointed windows on the south side, as well as the east window, are modern, as is also a south door to the chancel, which probably replaced an older doorway on the same site. In the east wall, close to the north corner, is a small square-headed window very much modernized, which from its position looks as if it had been a leper window.

The level of the floor of the church from inside the doorway has been raised nine inches. The chancel is raised to a level with the tops of the pews, 3ft. 4in. above the ground, but the upper two steps are, I believe, modern; the lower platform, 1ft. 9in. above the present body of the church, being the original level, is at a most convenient height for the leper window, which is four feet above it, though only a little over 2ft above the ground outside—on which the recipient would kneel.

The roof is modern; there are no signs of sedilla or piscina.

The doorway and porch are old to the height of about seven feet only, the arches of both porch and doorway have been rebuilt. The stoup and seats on either side of the porch are original. The stoup is a very good specimen of Norman work, 12½ in. in diameter, circular in shape, inserted in the wall which partly overhangs it, with a spherical bottom 4in. in depth.

The font is a very curious one; a circular tub 8ft. 1in. in circumference, 2ft. 6½in. in diameter, and 2ft. 3in. high, thickness varying from 2¾in. to 3in., 13in. deep inside, bevelled down at the bottom to 1ft. 6in. across. Below this tub is a rude rim 4¼in. deep, projecting 1½in., bevelled top bottom; and another base 4 in. deep, similar to the top, but this lower portion is most certainly set not quite true with the upper part.

The north part of the west wall, i.e., beyond the tower, shows externally a pointed doorway now blocked up, inserted in a square recess. Over it is a window, 2ft. in height to the spring and 5in. to the crown of the arch, with a 1in. bevel all round and a further 5in. chamfer. The shape of this window is remarkable, as the north side has a wide splay. There are holes for iron bars still visible, and it would almost seem as if at some time there had been a turret to the tower of which this was a window.

There is a window similar in shape, now blocked up and partly defaced, to be seen externally on the north side of the nave, but in this instance the head of the window is formed of one stone only (though now cracked); in the other the head is formed of two stones.

Tower. The tower, which is 9ft. 9in. square internal measurement, has been much patched and altered. The east wall is, however, old, as there are visible signs on it of the line of the roof, marked by the remains of stone tiles. The windows are only straight slits and the embattlements are new. The west wall has a decided bend outwards, but it seems to be due to bad building more than anything else; probably most of this side has been patched and rebuilt.

The interior of the tower is very plain and appears completely modernized. Three feet above the doorway between the tower and the nave is a small window, now blocked up, with widely splayed opening on the inside, and a square-headed top formed of one large stone.

Churchyard: Sculptured Stone. A circular stone, about three inches thick, evidently the head of a wheel cross, with a Latin cross inscibed on it. One-half of the cross is quite complete, the other two arms being more or less mutilated. A plain margin, about four inches, was left all round. There can be no doubt that within the last sixty years the cross was removed from the churchyard, but from what site is doubtful. Some say it was part of a sundial, the base of which is still *in situ.* It was taken to and fixed in the garden of the late Dr. Price, of Glantwrch, whose son-in-law, Mr. Ernest Benthall, sent it back to the church about nine years ago.

Col. W. Ll. Morgan, *Antiquarian Survey of East Gower,* 1899.

18. *The Castle of Swansea*

The town of Swansea was part of the honour, or barony, or lordship of Gower, but comparatively an inferior part, whilst the castle was superior, capital, metropolitan . . . The important status of the castle of Swansea was always recognised by its being, in official documents, ranked as of equal significance with the lordship itself—"the castle of Swansea and the lordship of Gower"—and when after the death of a lord, possession of livery of the lordship was given to his successor, it was usually the entering into occupation or seisin of the castle of Swansea that signified the legal transfer.

Besides the departments of administration already mentioned, there was within the castle precincts the shire-hall, wherein all manner of pleas of the people of Swansea, as the shire fee, were heard at regular intervals before the lord's sheriff or steward. In everyone of the thirty manors into which the lordship was divided, there was also a court kept monthly for the hearing of similar pleas before the steward of the manors or members, so that the administration of the laws of the lordship was decentralised, appeals lying to the lord's court at Swansea in the manner already stated. The records of the lordship and of all its manors were brought into the exchequer at Swansea Castle, to be preserved there . . .

W. H. Jones, History of Swansea and of the
Lordship of Gower, 1920.

19. Oystermoth Castle

The existence of two neighbouring castles in the possession of the chief lord at Swansea and at Oystermouth raises the question of the relationship of Oystermouth with Swansea as the caput of the lordship.

The answer seems to be bound up with the Norman occupation of Gower when, about the year 1106, its conquest was assigned by the Crown to Henry de Newburgh, Earl of Warwick, who established his castle in the district of Seinhenydd or Swansea. Among the fiefs granted by Henry to his supporters was that of Oystermouth which was made over to William de Londres (who had already participated in the conquest of Glamorgan, to receive there the sub-lordship of Ogmore), for William later gave the church of Oystermouth to the newly-created Priory of Ewenny which, as lord of Ogmore, he had recently founded. William seems also to have been involved in the conquest of the neighbouring lordship of Kidwelly, assigned by the king to Roger, Bishop of Salisbury but there is no clear indication that he himself was ever lord of Kidwelly, though later his son, Maurice took over the lordship on the withdrawal of Roger.

William de Londres clearly held Oystermouth for a time as a fief from de Newburgh and the first castle raised there—doubtless of timber—would have been of his construction. The castle, however, was attacked and burnt in 1116 by Gruffydd ap Rhys of Deheubarth, many of the garrison being killed, so that William, so it was said, "through fear of Gruffydd, left his castle and all his cattle and all his wealth," probably never to return, his estate escheating to the chief lord in whose hands it remained, to pass in succession through the families of de Newburgh, Braose and Mowbray. Henceforth, therefore, the history of Oystermouth was closely associated with that of Swansea.

Three periods of castle-building on the site seem to be indicated, viz., the original Norman castle, the rebuilding in the thirteenth century under de Braose (possible following on the destruction of the castle by the Welsh in 1215), and the reconstruction of the interior buildings in the fourteenth century, especially in the time of Alina, heiress of the last William de Braose and wife of John de Mowbray, who seems to have made Oystermouth her favourite residence.

A plan of the castle was prepared for the visit of the Association to Gower in 1886 and will be found in *Archaeologia Cambrensis* 1887. It shows the relatively small gateway with flanking towers and portcullis room above and, in the open courtyard, in the interior, the keep, the State apartments, the Hall, kitchens and chapel, the last-named with fine windows of the Decorated period probably of the time of Alina.

The origin of the name *Oystermouth, Ostremewe,* and its Welsh counterpart, *Ystum Llwynarth,* has been the subject of much discussion. *Llwynarth* is probably the *Loyngarth* mentioned by Nennius as the site of the church on the Gower coast founded by Illtyd to mark the place of the landing of the body of a saint brought by sea. The form *Ostremewe,* oyster mouth, may well have arisen from the trade in oysters which was carried on with Bristol and other markets since the sixteenth century, and traditionally since Roman times. Oyster beds were still being laid on the sands under the cliffs here in the mid-eighteenth century. The late Dr. Seyler put forward the interesting suggestion that the name *llwynarth* in its mediaeval form *luinarth,* could in mediaeval script be more correctly written as *lumarch,* signifying the Welsh *llymarch,* an oyster, in which case the form Oystermouth is but a translation of *Ystum Llymarch.*

William Rees, 'Oystermouth Castle,' Cambrian
Archaeological Association *Programme,*
1960.

20.   *Pennard Castle, 1650*

. . . The Castle of Pennard, desolate and ruinous, and so long time unrepaired that scarcely there remaineth one whole wall. It standeth upon a rock near ajoining to the sea, now encompassed with much sand. And for Demesnes thereof we find in an ancient paper which is in the nature of a Survey that the Demesnes thereof is between the old Church besanded to the said Castle and from thence to Pennard's Bridge, and from thence to the Three Cleeves.

Survey of Gower, 1650, in Baker and
Francis, *Surveys of Gower,* 1870.

21.   *Penrice*

The most extensive military ruin in Gower is *Penrice Castle,* occupying a moderate elevation facing Oxwich Bay. It is the property of C. R. M. Talbot, Esq., M.P., whose modern mansion, a plain structure . . . of the same name, stands close by . . .

Pen-Rhys, the Ancient Welsh name, was possibly the designation of the rock or eminence upon which the castle is planted, and adopted by the *Penrhys* family who lived here before the Mansels of Margam, through marriage with the heiress, entered into possession. We read in the pedigrees that "Sir Hugh Mansel, Kt., son of Richard Mansel by Lucy, daughter of Philip Scurlage, Lord of Scurlage Castle (the ruins of which are still traceable near Llanddewi in Gower), *temp.* Richard II, married Isabel, daughter of Sir John Penrees, Lord of Oxwich and other large possessions in Glamorganshire," and that "this Sir Hugh was the great-grandfather of Anthony Mansel, Esq., who was slain in the war between the houses of York and Lancaster."

The property continued in the Mansels until 1750, when by default of heirs male, it passed to the second son of Mary youngest daughter of Sir Thomas, by her husband, J. Ivory Talbot, Esq., of Lacock Abbey, Wiltshire . . .

Standing on any favourable point near Oxwich village, the view of Penrice Castle and its richly wooded park, occupying the mid-scene between you and healthy heights of Cefn Bryn, is extremely fine. The luxuriant and extensive woodland, broken sufficiently to afford the eye here and there the variety of verdant meads, and the gravelled walks and terraces of the modern mansion, receives a picturesque and perfect finish in the grey and broken ramparts of the great castle, which mount up defiant of time and elements in the midst.

It must be confessed, however, that the venerable pile is much neglected, no care is taken to preserve it from dilapidation, and if it were not for the friendly ivy—ever partial to the old and neglected—its disappearance would hasten apace.

Thomas Nicholas, *The History and Antiquities of Glamorgan,* 1874.

22.   *Oxwich Castle*

Here we have a manifest case of transition between the old type of fortress, only accidentally domestic, and fortified mansion . . . only accidently military. The result at Oxwich is certainly not satisfactory; the appearance being that of a large Perpendicular mansion carried along at the complete elevation of a castle tower.

There are a multitude of small square-headed windows, of two lights, and chiefly in the more exposed front—of broad single-light windows with depressed heads, a most untoward form but which is probably owing to a retention of castellated ideas. In the upper range is a row of Perpendicular windows, showing that the hall and other principal apartments must have been placed in this elevated and airy position.

A great part of this castle is converted into a farmhouse, which contains some very good bits of domestic work, of which it is not always easy to say whether they are parts of original building, or have been added at a subsequent, though not very distant, period.

E. A. Freeman, 'On the Architectural Antiquities of Gower,' *Archaeologia Cambrensis,* 1850.

23.   *Bishop Gower's Castle*

We follow the road, and before us we see Llanddewi Church, and a farm-house adjoining it, called Llanddewi Castle.

This castle was erected by Bishop Gower [of St. David's] about the year 1320, and intended for one of the episcopal residences; but Bishop Horton, in 1374, ordered this castle built by his predecessor in his native place, Gowerland, where he had but one ploughland of ground, and the place destitute of water, to be taken down and the materials sold. There is nothing to interest the antiquarian about the church.

The Castle is now a very fine farm-house, very clean, and the mullioned windows covered with white-wash. All is very quiet and peace reigns paramount; fertile fileds surround us on every side—blooming meadows and waving masses of golden grain, when the breath of autumn spreads rich robes over the earth, delight the eye.

C. D. Morgan, *Wanderings in Gower*, 1886 ed.

24. Landimore

The Manor was held as one knight's fee, and came into the possession of Llywelyn ap Iorwerth, who was connected with Gower by the marriage of two of his daughters with two members of the de Breos family, 1215-19.

With the Manor passed a not inconsiderable castle, the possession of which strengthened the position of the Turbervilles, already very considerable people in Glamorgan; and in the same degree excited the jealousy of William de Breos, then Lord of Gower, who seems to have forced a sale to Sir Robert de Penrice, and in other ways to have broken up the property, until the manor fell into the hands of the chief Lord [of Gower] in the person of Thomas de Mowbray, Duke of Norfolk, from whom it came, probably by grant, to Sir Hugh Johnys . . . There was a castle known as Bovehill here, which was the residence of Sir Hugh Johnys . . .

G. T. Clark, 'The Signory of Gower,'
Archaeologia Cambrensis, 1893-4.

25. Weobley Castle

Weobley Castle is, to my mind, a more interesting structure than any in the peninsula. Two sides only are at all perfect, and these have a character of their own, not that of pure and perfect military defence, like Kidwelly, but simply that of a picturesque range of irregular walls and towers, which, as they do not equally affect the pure military type with Oystermouth, do not equally offend by their dereliction from its most perfect form.

The multitude of breaks, angles, and projections, square, round, and octagonal, and the number of elegant little windows, two expecially, one a quatrefoil, the other, I think, a sexfoil, produce a very peasing effect. On the other hand, the only remaining entrance is

very poor, but as a great part of the castle has been destroyed, it may
not have been the principal one.

'On the Architectural Antiquities of Gower,'
E. A. Freeman, *Archaeologia Cambrensis,*
1850.

26. *Llandeilo Talybont*

The main interest of the site, sometimes known as Castell Du,
arises from its association with the Norman conquest of Gower
making, as it does, an early crossing-place of the River Llwchwr by
the more direct inland—possible Roman—road, linking Gower with
Carmarthen.

The ancient road follows here the raised edge of the flood-plain of
the tidal river, the later turnpike road having been diverted to cross
the river further up-stream at Pontardulais. The importance of the
site is further indicated by the existence on this route of the ancient
church of Teilo foundation, claimed by Llandaff as being within its
diocese immediately after the Norman conquest, also of the motte,
known as Ystum Enlle, on the opposite bank within the adjoining
lordship of Carnwyllion, the two mottes being connected by the ford
which here crosses the tidal river near the church. The road continues in direct line through Hendy to the top of the rise, there to be
joined by the present road through Pontardulais, leaving the Llandeilo site today isolated. There remain no traces of a bridge across the
river such as is indicated by the name Talybont, which name occurs at
least as early as the year 1119.

Both mounds, moated, with steep sides and of early Norman date,
about 30 feet high and with platform top, are alike in that they occupy
similar sites on opposite sides of the river on the edge of the flood-
plain. The Llandeilo motte is more oval in shape in conformity with
the ground, while that of Ystum Enlle, with its entrance on the south
side, shows signs of a bailey attached. Both mounds are today cleared
of any stone structure, though the Llandeilo motte is described in the
fourteenth century as having a tower.

Little is known of Ystum Enlle and it was probably abandoned
early in face of the strong Welsh revival especially after the death of
Henry I in 1135. Llandeilo Talybont, however, remained in the
occupation of the family of de Villers from the twelfth to the end of
the fourteenth century in the persons of Henry, Hugh and John de

Villers, the successive members holding from the lords of Gower, by the service of two knights' fees, the castles and lordships of Talybont and Loughor (Aber Llychwr), being thus charged with the defence of the two routes leading into Gower from West Wales.

Both castles suffered a serious blow in 1215 at the hands of the Welsh under the leadership of Rhys Ieuanc, who, after capturing Loughor besieged the castle of Hugh at Talybont which he took by force, burning the castle and slaying the entire garrison. According to the *Brut,* the castle was, at the time, in the charge of Hugh de Meules, though whether the entry is here in error for Hugh de Villers, or whether it was temporarily in the charge of de Meules (de Molis), a possible member of a West Wales family of that name, which in the 40's of that century supplied the king's lordship of Carmarthen with its seneschal, is not clear. Herein may be the explanation of the name *Castell Hu* (rather than *Castell Du*) given by the chronicler to the site.

The chapel of St. Michael within the lordship of Llandeilo Talybont was early granted by Hugh de Villers, one of the first of his line in the twelfth century to the Abbey of Neath to serve as a grange of the Abbey. Under the name of *Cwrt Carnau* and *Tir yr Abad,* it remained in possession of the Abbey until the Dissolution, after which it passed under the name *Tir y Brenin,* and it has continued as a separate property until our own day.

The church of Llandeilo stands near the ford of the river on a site slightly raised above the level of the high tides. In its isolation it is almost abandoned, but three services a year are still being held there.

> William Rees, 'Llandeilo Talybont,' Cambrian
> Archaeological Association *Programme,*
> 1960.

27.   *Penlle'r Castell*

. . . Ller Castle now in utter ruine . . .

> Rice Merrick, c. 1584

This is situated about 300 yards to the right of the Llandeilo road, near the 11th mile stone, and almost overlooking the brow of the hill.

Absolutely nothing is known about this Castle, when or by whom erected, or what it was called.

It is mentioned on Kitchin's and other maps as a castle, as if, a couple of centuries ago, there were more remains than we see at present, but Rees, in his *Beauties of Wales,* page 537, written in 1810, describes its condition very much as it is now. He called it—"An oval with the longer sides about 100 yards, the shorter 50," but in this case he is certainly not very correct.

On reference to the plan in the wood-cut it will be seen that the Castle lies N.W. and S. E.

The S. E. end, where was situated the moated mound, or keep, is round and much narrower than the N.W. end, where was the base-court, which was square with rounded angles; the whole enclosed within a ditch 12 feet deep. The *terre plein* of the base-court is very little above the surface of the ground, though that of the keep is considerably higher.

It is uncertain if a ditch formerly existed between the base-court and the keep; probably it did not, as they are still connected on a level on the western side: the present ditch is only the result of quarrying, although this was done before 1819 (as it is mentioned by Rees), most likely when the turnpike road was made.

There are no remains of masonry now visible, although I have no doubt that if the *debris* were cleared away along the line of the rampart the foundations would be found still intact. Outside the counterscarp, especially on the southern and western sides, are the remains of mounds which look like the ruins of a walled covered way.

Although the work has been so much destroyed there can be no doubt that it is the remains of a stone castle with a round tower as a keep, and a walled base-court, but never of any very great importance and holding only a small garrison.

It should be noticed that from the keep of Penlle'r Castell the watch tower of Carreg Cennen castle just appears above the intervening ridge of hill . . .

Col. W. Ll. Morgan, *Antiquarian Survey of East Gower,* 1899.

28.   *Loughor*

Loughor Castle, like the village of which it forms a part and was once the chief constituent, is a desolate-looking object. The position of this place on the ferry of the Loughor river (Llwchwr) naturally give it importance from the earliest times; the Romans added to this importance by establishing here one of their stations on the *Via Julia,* giving it the name *Leucarum,* in imitation of works left by the

Romans; and this the Norman lord who first took this district—probably the same Henry de Beaumont already mentioned in connection with the other castles in Gower—fixed upon a site for a Norman castle.

The river Llwchwr washes its base; the mound on which it stands indicates a place of strength and considerable extent; but for many ages the ponderous ivy-covered fragments which remains has only been a habitation for the sparrow and the owl . . .

Thomas Nicholas, *The History and Antiquities of Glamorgan*, 1874.

29. *St. David's Hospital, Swansea*

This hospital or priory was founded in 1332 by Bishop Gower of St. David's for the support of 6 chaplains and laymen deprived of bodily health and for the celebration of Divine Service every day. It was situated in St. Mary Street, and part of the ruins may still be seen. The principal benefactor was Alinora de Breos, mother of John Mowbray. She gave to the hospital the small manor of Brynawel in Ilston. Among the other grants were:

A curtilage with a garden and 10 acres of arable land which Robert de Weston held in Pennard. A messuage, 58 acres of arable and 8 acres of rough land at Kilvrough, from our aforesaid patrimony in the fee of Pennard. 2 messuages, 60 acres of arable land, 8 acres of mountain land, and 12 acres of rough land, and the profits of a water-mill in Sketty (Ynis Ketti) in the parish of Swansea.

The advowson of Swansea, at this time held by the priory of Llangennith, was now given to St. David's Hospital.

All this land given to the hospital would appear to be old land of the "Monastery of Llangennith." The Swansea portion of it, together with the advowson, by agreement with the prior of Llangennith, being now restored to the town.

The abbot of St. Peter's, Gloucester, granted to the Hospital the glebe and advowson of Oystermouth, subject to an annuity of 10 marks a year to Ewenny Priory. The master of the hospital pledging the hospital lands at Kilvrough as security.

In 1380, Thomas de Campo Bello, earl of Warwick, grants to Richard Colet of Sutton, master of the hospital of Blessed in Sweynese, the chaplain-general of the same, a confirmation of former gifts, given by his progenitors, and further adds 20 Librates of churches, lands, and rents within the precinct of his land of Gower.

All the endowments of this priory were seized and confiscated by King Edward VI, and became the property of the Crown, which, for sometime, leased them for a term of years and eventually sold them, The Kilvrough lands were bought by Sir George Herbert, Kt., who sold them in 1543 to William ap Hopkin Dawkin, of Gellyhir, in Ilston, in part exchange for lands at Pantygwydr.

The Rev. Latimer Davies, *Pennard and West Gower,* 1928.

VIII

Houses and Families

1. Stouthall and the Lucas Family

The Lucases of West Gower are now remembered mainly for their romantic legends. Ask the older inhabitants of Reynoldston about the Mansion of Stouthall and you may still be told of the underground passage from Brynfield to Stouthall through which a man might ride on horse back; of that still more fabulous secret passage from Stouthall to the old family stronghold at the Salt House, Port Eynon; of the bloodstained floorboards in the North-West bedroom; of smugglers' tales and pirates.

But whatever you may think of the legends, Stouthall is plain enough, perhaps too plain one may feel, at first sight of the old house through the tracery of the beech trees along the main road to Port Eynon. From this aspect the house with its gaunt outline and tall empty windows appears out of sympathy with its surroundings. Viewed from Reynoldston the effect is very different. The light grey facade beneath the low pitched slate roof, against a dark background of trees, has a comfortably dignified air and makes a pleasing focal point in the landscape. One is too far away for the eye to be distracted by the war time offices clapped on either side of the main entrance, yet near enough to distinguish the splashes of red from the rhododendrons, and to hear the distant cawing of the rooks. Here indeed is that "elegant residence" on which John Lucas set his heart in the closing years of the 18th century and upon which he lavished "all those softer beauties which taste could dictate."

John Lucas was born in 1756 according to the transcript of the Register of Reynodlston Parish Church. He was the youngest of the six children of John Lucas the elder whose family had lived at Stouthall for many generations, having moved there from Brynfield on the North side of Reynoldston village probably at the beginning of the fifteenth century. Young John's mother Hannah was a Miss Nicholas, heiress to the Nicholas estates at Garth "opposite the village of Clydach in the vale of Towe". In her reputea portrait we see a handsome fine featured girl with brown eyes and the flicker of a smile. One must say "reputed" portrait since her dress with its low square cut neck trimmed with lace and adorned with red roses, the ringlets down her neck and the feathers in her hair, may perhaps accord better with the fashions of the end of the 18th century than the middle.

John the elder must have suffered much family sorrow. Two daughters and a son died in infancy. Hannah herself died in 1766, at the age of 48. The next year saw the death of their only surviving daughter at 17 and a year later Henry the eldest son and heir died in Southern France, while on a tour with his father, leaving young John the only surviving child. John the elder thenceforward busied himself with public affairs, becoming High Sheriff of the County in 1778. As a Justice of the Peace he became involved with Sir Gabriel Powell in the controversy over the paving of Swansea's streets and we find him making presentments before the old Manorial Court Leet in the interminable legal wrangles over road repairs, which were populary thought to be of little benefit to anyone but Sir Gabriel as Steward of the Court.

At this time young John and his father lived in the Old Mansion House of Stouthall. No pictures of this house are known but there is a tiny drawing of it in John Williams' map of Reynoldston Parish made in 1784. This map is one of a series covering Gower Parishes and was made to show the estates of Thomas M. Talbot of Penrice Castle. The map is drawn to a scale of about 20 inches to one mile and shows the roads, buildings and field boundaries. In the margin is a schedule giving the field areas and cultivations and the names of the tenants of the farms belonging to the Penrice estate. The ownership of the land which did not belong to Penrice is also shown.

The map is very accurately surveyed as can be verified by comparing it with the 25 inch ordnance survey done about 90 years later. A number of the fields are the same on both maps and where reference points can be identified the measurements correspond closely. Penrice Estate farms and cottages are shown pictorially; other dwellings are shown by a conventional black rectangle, with the exception of Stouthall and Fairy hill (then called Peartree), both Lucas properties, which are also shown pictorially. The drawing of the South front of Fairyhill is accurately plotted and oriented and has features in common with the house as shown in a 19th century photograph after various alterations had been carried out. It is therefore reasonable to assume that the drawing of Stouthall is also accurate.

This shows and L shaped two storey building between the site of the present house and the main road, from which it is set back about 25 yards.

This is in fact the traditional site of the old building according to the Rev. J. D. Davies whose father was Rector of Reynoldston. The drawing shows that one wing of the house faced South, parallel with the road. The other wing projected from its Eastern end and contained the main entrance facing East. Chimneys are shown at the ends of each wing and there is a central chimney opposite the entrance. The impressions is of a substantial but unpretentious farmhouse. It would be interesting to know whether any features can be verified by excavation on the site.

John Williams' map shows that in 1784 the Penrice Estate owned 248 acres of enclosed land in Reynoldston Parish. The land owned by the Lucas family may estimated at between 250 and 300 acres and the remaining land, perhaps 175 acres, was divided between nine other owners, Edward Sneed, William Bennett, Mrs. Mancorne, Samuel Hughes, George Lord Vernon, John Popkins, Mrs. Price, George Thomas and Margaret Thomas. We do not know to what extent the Lucas land was let to tenants, but in the case of Penrice Estate the largest farm in the Parish was Hill End farm of 45 acres. There were four other farms of over 25 acres, Mansel Fold, Reynoldston Farm, Evans Land and Reynodlston Glebe. The remaining Penrice properties in the Parish were small holdings of less than 10 acres each.

But although John Lucas the elder was a substantial land owner he did not enjoy around Stouthall anything resembling the park land bequeathed to posterity by his son. The land between Reynoldston village and Stouthall was a jumble of small enclosed fields in varying ownership, part meadow, part arable, interspersed with undivided strip cultivations introduced into Gower by the Normans. At the back of old Stouthall and within a few hundred yards of the house were a 5 acre field owned by the Penrice Estate and let to Mrs. Evans, 4 acres belonging to Samuel Hughes, a 2 acre field of Lord George Vernon, detached acre of Reynoldston Farm, and four elongated undivided strips known as The Half Acres, each about 11 yards wide and separately owned. On the southern edge of the village were some larger undivided fields known as the Landshares, owned alternately by the Stouthall and Penrice Estates . . .

In 1777, John Lucas the younger of Stouthall married Catherine Powell, a girl of 16, and the young couple went to live at Peartree which they re-named Fairyhill. Catherine was the daughter of

William Powell, the illegitimate son of Walter Powell, a prominent Carmarthenshire landowner at one time High Sheriff of the County and a relative of Sir Gabriel Powell of Swansea . . . A portrait in oils of John Lucas painted a few years after his marriage shows an elegant young man, slight of build, with delicate features, grey eyes and the corners of his mouth a little pursed in determination or perhaps obstinacy.

John's father died in 1787 and no doubt John and Catherine and their young family would then have moved back to Stouthall from Fairyhill. It seems likely that John embarked on the building of the present mansion during the 1790's and that the work was completed in about 1800. The traditional date of 1754 is almost certainly wrong. The new house is not shown on John Williams' map of 1784. The Swansea Guide published in 1802 and in the preparation of which John Lucas is said to have taken part, refers to the house as having been built by Jernegan, a well-known Swansea architect. Jernegan was born in 1750 and his known work in Swansea was done mainly between 1790 and 1800. The Swansea Borough Architect, the late Mr. Ernest Morgan, who converted Stouthall into a maternity hospital in 1942 found masons' marks of 1800 on the stonework. The latest mark found was a plumber's mark of 1803 in the roof.

The house is built in the Palladian style so popular in the 18th century and shows the strong influence of the Adams brothers, both in the design of the building and the interior decoration. The main entrance and portico form the central feature in the North facade. The hall rises through two floors and is surrounded by a gallery on three sides giving access to the principal bedrooms. This gallery is decorated with columns and approached by a fine stairway. The cornice mouldings of the hall have an unusual design of bulls' skulls. This design also appears on the coat-of-arms of the Powell family. The large West drawing-room and the dining room decorated with columns, moulded cornices and low relief ceiling mouldings, are separated by the library, a most unusual and beautiful room of elliptical shape and very fine decorative treatment.

Opposite the Adam style fireplace in this room is the well-known secret door in the library shelves giving access to the drawing-room and providing, no doubt, a most convenient bolt-hole for any member of the family trapped in the drawing room by the arrival of unexpected guests in the front hall. The Southern end of the library projects to form a bow window in the Southern facade of the house. The house and its furnishings as they were some 100 years later, are

described by Mr. C. E. Vulliamy in an earlier volume of *Gower*.
Outside, John Lucas managed to acquire the various fields and
strips of land lying between the house and the village. He planted
trees and laid out a park of some 40 acres. He built stables and other
outbuildings, including and elaborate grotto in the romantic style,
excavated and ice-house and probably established the walled garden.
John also indulged in what Mr. Davies, the then Rector of Reynoldston, used to describe as Mr. Lucas' whims. He erected a "prehistoric" stone circle in a field on the left of the road as you enter
Reynoldston village from the South, and buried a favourite horse
under a burial mound in a field on the opposite of the road near
Stouthall farm surmounting it by a sculptured pillar stone which he
had probably found elsewhere in Gower. The 10th or 11th century
carving on this stone is described byn the late Dr. Iorwerth Hughes
Jones in *Gower X*.

John and Catherine had five children, three girls and two boys. The
elder son, Colonel John Nicholas Lucas inherited the Stouthall
Estate on his father's death in 1831. Colonel Lucas served for over 40
years in the Royal Glamorgan Militia. He seems to have been a rather
careful, conventional, and unambitious man. His few surviving
letters show a preoccupation with hunting and a fear of Chartists
about whom he comes to the comforting conclusion that "they can't
reach us here". Though twice married he had only one child, a
daughter Mary. One of the early census returns, that of 1841, shows
him living at Stouthall with his second wife, his daughter Mary, his
unmarried sister Matilda, also his wife's unmarried sister and five
resident servants, two male and three female. One suspects that the
Returning Officer did not dare to approach the Colonel for the ages
of himself and his family. He is entered as "50" and his wife a tactful
"40". They were really 61 and 56. In 1843 Mary married Colonel E. R.
Wood of the 12th Lancers who "hung up his hat" as the saying goes at
Stouthall. Colonel Lucas moved to Brynfield where he died in 1861.
A photograph shows him in his old age in a wheel-chair drawn by a
donkey, and accompanied by a groom and members of the family, the
ladies in crinolines and the gentlemen in tall top hats.

Colonel Lucas' younger brother, Henry, was a man of very
different stamp. Genial, debonair and extravagant by nature, he was
popular with his friends, and the despair of his family. On his coming
of age in 1818 his father transferred to him the Fairyhill and Cheriton
Estates, perhaps unwisely without any legal strings attached. The
following year he married Caroline Tottenham daughter of a former

Member for Wexford in the old Irish Parliament at Dublin and began to devote himself to horse racing. Fairyhill had been leased in 1814 to Lady Barham. On her death in 1823 Henry took up residence there and his strings of horses exercising along the crest of Cefn Bryn became a familiar sight to the villagers of Reynoldston. At about this time Henry built himself the house known as Uplands Villa on the outskirts of Swansea, and for a few and no doubt expensive years he lived with his growing family at the imposing old mansion of Taliaris near Llandeilo. It was not long before the Fairyhill and Cheriton Estates, and even his wife's jewellery were sold to meet the losses on the horses.

A characteristic account of Henry at Swansea Races by an unknown diarist has appeared in an earlier volume of *Gower* and is worth repeating. "As a small boy I have a vivid recollection of Mr. Henry Lucas on one occasion winning a large and valuable cup, with a horse called 'Bay Hampton' or 'Totten ham,' I forget which. He had had ill luck and been constantly losing, and there was now great joy amongst his friends and the onlookers at his success, a joy not confined to them, but vastly appreciated by himself who, kind amiable man as he was, came round to all the carriages with a servant carrying bottles of champagne, from which he from time to time filled his cup, with a request that each lady should drink his horse's health. One lady I know, said, "I drink your health, Mr. Lucas,' when he at once checked her saying 'No, my horse's health, if you please.' "

John Lucas in his old age must have seen with sadness that the Stouthall Estate would pass into other hands at his granddaughter Mary's marriage, and that Henry's family (he was married twice and had nine children) would be reduced to comparative poverty through their father's extravagance.

Something of John's firm and kindly character appears in a letter he wrote from Stouthall in 1830, a few months before his death, to his grandson, Henry Loftus, Henry's eldest son, at the age of 9. "My dear Loftus," he wrote, "Be assured it afforded me infinite pleasure to have the satisfaction of hearing of your obtaining a prize particularly so soon after your going to school; and I have no doubt of your proceeding in the same way, with diligent attention to your learning; for education and good principles make a *gentleman;* which I hope you will prove in every respect. I shall be very proud to be informed of your next success and at all times of the progress in learning; and when you have a holiday, I shall be very happy to see you here with your Papa. With best love, my dear Boy, you ever affectionate grand-papa. John Lucas. Give my best love and many kisses to all your dear little sisters and to John and tell him I hope he will follow your good example when he goes to school. My affectionate love to your Papa and Mamma, and a waistcoat is sent that was left here."

After John's death in 1831 at the age of 74, his widow Catherine went to live in Gloucester Place, Swansea, where she died in 1841. The Stouthall Estate which they had so largely created survived almost intact until 1920 and even today the old house looking very much as John built it, still stands in rich and unspoilt farm land, flanked by splendid trees, and awaiting an uncertain future.

R. L. T. Lucas, *Gower XXIII,* 1972.

2. *The Bowens of Court House*

The surname "Bowen" is derived from the Welsh "ab Owen," or "ap Owen"—by Grimm's law the two consonants are interchangeable. "Ap," or "ab," "son of." Welsh surnames of an early date were represented by a string of Christian names divided by "ap"; thus, you got a man called "David ap John ap Rees ap Thomas." But when a member of a family amassed money and became important he would take simply, as surname, the Christian name of his father, discarding, as a unnecessary distinction, the names of those who had gone before. Any man whose father was Christened Owen *could,* of course, call himself "ap Owen." Alongside, therefore, of the main Glamorganshire family of ap Owen there came to be a number of people who, though using the name, did not, strictly, belong to the main stock. Again, the whole of the brothers of one family did not always choose to take the same surname.

The Bowens of Court House, Ilston, Glamorganshire, became "ap Owen" about 1441. The Bowens of Llangyvelach, in the same county, did not take "ap Owen" till 1550. (The Court House and the Llangyvelach Bowens trace back to a common ancestor, Owen Gethyn.) In both branches, "ap Owen" was changed to "Bowen" early in the reign of Queen Elizabeth. In the will, proved 1582, of Henry Bowen of Court House, the testator refers to his two brothers and to his eldest son as "ap Owen," but to his two younger sons as "Bowen." The transition from the old form to the new was thus, clearly, not made all at once: it remained a matter for individual choice.

The coat of arms borne by the various Bowens seems to have varied slightly from branch to branch; it always, however, featured a stag. The Bowen's Court (originally the Court House) Bowens' coat of arms, as now entered with the Ulster King of Arms, is: *"Azure, a stag lodged argent, attired or, vulned in the back of an arrow gules, feathered of the second,* and for motto "Cautus a futero."

Pedigrees tracing back the Bowens of Court House to Bleddin ap Maenerch, last British sovereign of Brecknock are recorded in *Limbus Patrum Morganiae et Glamorganiae,* by G. T. Clark, and in *The Golden Grove Book,* by Hugh Thomas, Deputy Herald, 1703. These pedigrees, however, differ considerably and do not appear to be complete. Covering a space of three hundred and seventy-nine years—from the death of Bleddin in 1098 to the death of Morgan ap Owen in 1467—they represent only nine generations.

This all—the number of Bowens, the slightly differing stags, in consistencies or lacunae in pedigrees—goes to create confusion in the present-day mind, to which at the best all origins are obscure. Glamorganshire, and the Gower Peninsula in particular, came to be congested with an increasing number of Bowens—some *bona fide,* others people who made use of the promising name. Living-room shrank as families multiplied, and the resulting pressure expelled, from time to time, various Bowens in search of expansion elsewhere. Two different Bowens went to New England, one went to Ireland, to Queens County (where his family later built Balle Adam), one settled in Devonshire, one again went to Ireland, to County Cork—and he was my ancestor. Stationary Bowens were those of Llangyvelach, Kittlehill, Pennard, Ilston, Llanmadoc and Bishopston—all in Gower.

The founder of the family of Court House Bowens was the Morgan ap Owen of Swansea who in 1441 purchased Court House and Mawr House, and lands pertaining thereto in Ilston, with the lands of Wogan Hill in Pennard, from Geoffrey de la Mare. Morgan ap Owen died in 1467 and is buried at Swansea, St. Mary's Church. He left three sons, of whom the eldest, Richard, for some time Receiver of Gower and Carnwyllion, inherited Court House.

Richard became the father of Harry ap Owen, who married Elizabeth Hopkin and had by her one son, Thomas. Thomas inherited Court House and married Jennet, daughter of David ap Evan of Yehan. Henry, the eldest of their three sons, in time got Court House. This Henry now shed the ap Owen chrysalis and called himself Henry Bowen. He married Ellen Franklyn of Park le Brewys, had three sons, made the will I have mentioned, and died 1582.

This Henry Bowen of Court House seems to have favoured the third of his sons, Harry. Court House had to go to Thomas, the eldest son, but Harry, a child at the time of his father's death, was left substantial property in the Llanellan [Llanelen] lands. He got, also, his father's "best brasen pan, and best crock, with a couple of round pans, and my pewter platten, my standing bell and appurtenances, being upon my loft." A Paternal uncle John (still) ap Owen was to be tutor and guardian to the little boy.

We are Harry's descendants, therefore from this point on the history of what were to be the Bowen's Court Bowens branches off from that of the Bowens of Court House. The Court House line continued (through the descendants of Harry Bowen's eldest brother Thomas) but soon no longer meant much to us.

The fortunate Harry settled down in his house on his lands at Llanellan, and married Margaret, daughter of Harry Holland, rector of Cheriton. When he died, in 1641, he left two sons, Henry and Thomas, and one daughter who married a Henry Morgan. The elder son, Henry, inherited Llanellan. He was that Henry Bowen who was to leave Gower, to (as a lieutenant-colonel in the Cromwellian Army) to Ireland and get the County Cork lands. He was the first of our Bowens to die in Ireland, he was the founder of the Bowen's Court family, so from now on I shall call him Henry I.

Elizabeth Bowen, *Bowen's Court*, 1964 ed.

3. *Thomas Penrice of Kilvrough*

Our story begins in 1820, when Major Thomas Penrice of Great Yarmouth purchased the manor and demesne of Kilvrough in the parish of Penard.

Kilvrough Manor, still surrounded by its high walls and well-tended parkland, stands about a mile south-west of Fairwood Common, where the South Gower Road drops into the shallow cwm leading down to Parkmill. The house here was first built by Rowland Dawkin, scion of the old Gower family, in 1585, but the place may once have been the site of the original manor of Langrove. Moreover, the Dawkins themselves were descended from the even older family of Langton, contemporaries of the De Breoses, Lords of Gower, in the thirteenth and fourteenth centuries.

The present Kilvrough Manor was built by William Dawkin in the mid-eighteenth century. William was Sheriff of Glamorgan in 1773, but his daughter Mary, the last of the Kilvrough Dawkins, sold the house to Major Penrice in 1820. Yet the sale in no way broke the circling line of association that linked Kilvrough with some of the oldest families in Gower. Thomas Nicholas, in his *History of Antiquities of Glamorgan,* tells us that Major Penrice's family traced its descent from a branch of the Penrice family of Gower, lords of Oxwich and Penrice, and whose inheritance passed to the Mansels by marriage probably late in the fourteenth century.

The new owner of Kilvrough was a distinguished soldier and had fought in the Peninsular Wars under Wellington as a captain in the XVIth Lancers. So it was only fitting that in 1829 he became Major-Commandant of the "Swansea and Fairwood Corps of Yeomanry Cavalry". This was a volunteer corps which had been created towards the end of the Napoleonic Wars by the amalgamation of separate units in Swansea and at Fairwood. It consisted for the most part of gentry and farmers from Swansea and Gower, and its total establishment was about 160 men. There were similar corps in Central and Eastern Glamorgan.

However, within a short time of Major Penrice taking over his new command, quite unforseeable events perhaps even inconceivable by the standards of a distinguished regular soldier, were to involve him in a controversy which reached all the way to Whitehall, far away from Kilvrough. The story, not without its drama, is told in a slim volume of letters published by Major Penrice, probably during 1832, and printed by the press of *The Cambrian* newspapaer in Swansea. This volume, *The Swansea and Fairwood Cavalry 1831,* may be found in the Swansea Reference Library, and it is on these letters that this account is based.

These events began on Friday, 3rd June, 1831, when Thomas R. Guest, the ironmaster of Dowlais, and a magistrate, arrived in Swansea on the evening mail coach with orders for Major Penrice from the Lord-Lieutenant of Glamorgan, the Marquess of Bute. The Yeomanry were to be mustered and to march to Merthyr. Here riots and industrial unrest, long to be remembered in legend and literature, had broken out. The authorities were worried, and in the background was the great controversy in the nation over the Reform Bill. According to G. M. Trevelyan, in *History of England,* the fifteen months between March 1831 and May 1832—when the Bill was eventually passed—was a period of "political agitation unparalleled in the history of Great Britain". There was even a threat of revolution in the air.

From the Swansea, Guest rode on to Kilvrough, arriving about 10.30 p.m. Major Penrice had gone to bed. But speed was of the essence. Penrice was given his orders from Lord Bute, and runners were sent out all over Gower and the environs of Swansea to alert the corps. By midnight Major Penrice was in Swansea with his officers, and when about 25 men were assembled, he ordered them, at the request of Guest, the "civil authority", to go as an advance detachment to "The Lamb and Flag" at Aberpergwm in the Neath Valley. This tavern was of course on the direct route from Swansea to Merthyr via Hirwaun.

Penrice soon followed. At the "Lamb and Flag" the horses were fed, and led by the Major, the forward detachment of over 30 officers and men set off for Merthyr on Saturday morning. They were accompanied by Guest, who was urging a quick advance to Merthyr. However, at the top of the escarpment above Flyn Neath, before reaching Hirwaun, the men were told "that a vast number of armed rioters were waiting for the Swansea Cavalry a short distance from Merthyr."

Now came the critical moment, and with it Major Penrice's dilema, for according to the Major's later report for Lord Bute, Guest "at this time left us". Penrice went on to record in his report that with Guest's departure he was not in a position of "having any civil authority with me to direct me on the offensive". At the first sign of serious trouble it seems clear that "the civil authority" had decamped, leaving Penrice to cope as best he could.

The Cavalry detachment pushed on to within two miles of Merthyr, where they were again warned of armed men, reportedly based on the spoil tips that now lined the road. Deciding to investigate, Penrice and one of his officers Captain Collins, left the detachment but were soon surrounded by "a body of the mob", hitherto out of sight. The would-be insurgents were armed with muskets, pistols, scythes, pikes and other weapons not found in the armouries of the best cavalry regiments. They cried out that they were starving and offered no overt violence. But in the *melee* Major Penrice's sword, which he had carried through the Peninsula, was stolen from its scabbard. Captain Collins was similarly disarmed.

A few hundred yards away, the main detachment of the Cavalry was also surrounded by thousands of rioters, and easily disarmed. There was no violence again, but now the banks above the road were suddenly lined with muskets. Penrice had been ambushed. Quickly forcing his way back to his men, the Major secured the ammunition,

and managed to lead the detachment back the way they had come,
The retreat ended at the "Lamb and Flag", where the rest of the
Yeomanry had come up from Swansea. It was still only Saturday
afternoon.

That night, Penrice and his corps rested in Neath. New arms were
sent from Swansea, and on Sunday, 5th June the Cavalry set off for
Merthyr via Bridgend, Llantrisant and so northwards along the Taff
valley. This time there were no hitches, and by the 6th Penrice was
safely based in Dowlais, "one of the disaffected parts". The following
day, "order having been restored" in the area, the Yeomanry were
directed back to Swansea, and they rode down the Neath valley on
the 8th. But on the 9th, the Cavalry were still on duty in Swansea because of "disturbances" in the neighbourhood.

However, later that day, order reigned in Swansea too, and the (unreformed) Corporation voted each man of the Corps a shilling to
drink the King's health. The Yeomanry remained on duty until 10th
June, and then Major Penrice returned to Kilvrough, a week after his
departure for Merthyr. But the Swansea and Fairwood Cavalry were
never to see service again.

Indeed, by the time that Penrice returned to Kilvrough the disarming of his detachment was already the subject of attention in
Whitehall. On the 10th June Bute wrote to Penrice stating that he had
received a letter from Lord Melbourne, Home Secretary in Lord
Grey's Whig Administration, asking for a full report on the disarming of the Yeomanry. Bute wrote, almost ominously, that he
thought Melbourne had seen "an exaggerated account" of the story in
the press.

Penrice now immediately wrote the report of the incident that we
have quoted from, and forwarded it to Bute. But by 3rd July he was
again writing to the Lord-Lieutenant saying that his officers were
"anxiously awaiting" Bute's sentiments on the episode. Bute then
notified Penrice on 5th July that Melbourne wanted to have an
official military enquiry into the disarming of the Yeomanry; this
investigation was held by a Court sitting at Merthyr, and then in Pyle,
later in July 1831. The long summer weeks dragged by at Kilvrough.

The blow fell in a letter from Bute to Penrice at Kilvrough on 22nd
August 1831:

"I have received his Majesty's commands to dissolve the Corps
of Yeomanry in Glamorganshire. You will have the goodness to
make known the same to the Corps under your command, which
is hereby dissolved accordingly; and you are directed to hold the

arms and accoutrements which have been furnished by the Government at the disposal of the Board of Ordnance".

A separate note informed Penrice that it was proposed to reorganise the Yeomanry in the County into merely three troops. But at Penrice wrote back in early September, "it will be thought by this corps, as well as the others in the County, that the cause of their dissolution is on account of that unfortunate affair [at Merthyr]". Penrice had also gone to London, he informed Bute, and waited on Melbourne's brother, who promised that he would speak to the Secretary of State. But this came to nothing.

Realising the extent of Penrice's concern, Bute told him that the Court of Enquiry had forwarded two separate reports. The first concerned the Merthyr incident, and this Melbourne had merely acknowledged. The second report had proposed a reorganised Glamorgan Yeomanry, and this was the report on which the Government had acted. There was no imputation upon the courage of either Major Penrice or of his Corps.

Penrice asked for, and received on 17th September a copy of the report on "that unfortunate affair". The Yeomanry were recommended for their alacrity in turning out, but were criticised because reconnaissance during Penrice's initial march to Merthyr had been inadequate, so allowing the men to fall "into the ambuscade so successfully laid for them". Penrice had also been in error in allowing himself to be separated from his main detachment, together with Captain Collins. But the Court did not consider "that the slightest imputation of want of courage can be laid to the charge of either officers or men on this unfortunate occasion; but that on the contrary they evinced every disposition to do their duty to the utmost of their ability".

Penrice's judgement had been questioned, but of course his honour was unsullied. Nevertheless, the autumn of 1831 must have been a bad time for the owner of Kilvrough. Indeed, Penrice felt strongly enough about the matter to attempt to reopen the case. He wrote to Bute regretting that the Official Enquiry "did not take notice of the neglect of the Magistrate who accompanied the detachment, and who was constantly urging the necessity of the march of any small number of men, and then left it, and without whom I could not act . . ."

But the matter was concluded, as Penrice must have realised, for on 22nd October, 1831 he wrote to the War Office in London stating that the Swansea and Fairwood Cavalry were dissolved: "The arms are packed up, ready to be sent to the Ordnance Office . . ."

The final letter in this collection, later made public by Penrice, bears the date of 5th December, 1831. It was the receipt of the Bank of England for the funds of the Corps. But Penrice ended his collection of letters on the events of 1831 with a farewell message to his men, surveying what had passed, a farewell laden with a sense of injustice. Put in what was probably an impossible position, trapped by a mob and not an enemy, and then abolished by a distant authority, perhaps for reasons of political expediency, the Swansea and Fairwood Cavalry were now no more.

After this disturbing involvement with some of the birthpangs of modern Britain, life returned to a more even tempo at Kilvrough. Like William Dawkin before him, Thomas Penrice was made Sheriff of Glamorgan in 1836. Then, in 1838, he exchanged his estates in Northamptonshire for land owned by All Souls College, Oxford, in Gower, including the patronage of Pennard and Llangennith. Eight years later, in November 1846, Thomas Penrice died, and he is commemorated by a tablet in the chancel of Pennard Church. Other old Gower families commemorated in the same church include the Bowens and the Bennets of Kittlehill, and also the Dawkins.

Kilvrough Manor itself descended from Major Penrice to his nephew, also named Thomas Penrice, and so to the latter's daughter, Lady Lyons. Leet Courts of the manor continued to be held as late as the early 1920s, in the "Bishopston Valley Hotel". Then, in the 1930s, the home of the Dawkins and Major Penrice passed to the Swansea businessman, Arthur Thomas, the last private owner of Kilvrough. After the Second World War, in 1949, the house was sold to a foundation and is at present held by the Oxfordshire Education Committee.

So the past lingered on Kilvrough for well over a century after "that unfortunate affair" outside Merthyr in the late spring of 1831. Curiously enough, perhaps, only with the sale of the Clyne, Park-le-Breos and Penrice Castle estates in the early 1950s did the age of the squirearchy really come to an end in rural Gower.

David Rees, *Gower XXIII*, 1972.

4. *Gellihir*

The recent purchase of Gellihir Wood by the Glamorgan County Naturalists' Trust has drawn many people's attention to a name they may not have heard before. It is in the parish of Ilston (Llanilltyd Ferwallt) bordering on Llanrhidian Higher. Although having lived since 1911 within two miles it was not until 1954 that I realized there was an estate, and ruins of a mansion near the present farm house, which had a history going back to 1305 and probably before. In this year there was a great lawsuit when "William de Langton of Kilvrough and others complained that William de Breos by and with force of arms came to the house of Langton at Kilvrough and carried him to the manor of de Breos at Oystermouth."

In 1307 Sir William de Langton is described as Lord of Henllys, Langrove and Kellyhir. (Note the similar meaning of Langrove and Kelyhir). By 1328 Gellyhir, Killonan and Brynwas were the possessions of Robert Penres and Isabel his wife from the grant of John de Horton and Joan his wife. Later it became the house of Ifan ab Owen (alive in 1468) and brother of Morgan ab Owen (circa 1400-68) a devoted Papist. The heiress Sisyl daughter of Ifan married Hopkin Dawkin, fifth generation in descent from Dawkin Langton son of Sir William Langton and Eva daughter of Lord William de Breos, Lord of Swansea and Gower.

In 1396 Ilston Manor was stated to be part of the possessions of the Lord of Gower and was held by the De la Mare family, but by 1441 the estates were forfeited for rebellion against Henry VI and sold to Morgan ab Owen of Court House. He died in 1467, and his will was proved at Llandeilo Ferwallt (Bishopston) before Sir John Franklin. In 1543 the Kilvrough lands were bought by Sir George Herbert who then sold them the same year to William ap Hopkin Dawkin of Gellyhir in Ilston, in part exchange for lands at Pant-y-gwydr. Rowland Dawkin, his son, built a new Kilvrough in 1585. Col. Rowland Dawkin fought for Parliament at the Battle of St. Fagans in 1649 and was made Governor of Carmarthen and one of the Comissioners for Wales during the Commonwealth.

In 1557 William Hopkin Dawkin of Gellihir was involved in the attack on Oxwich Castle when Anne Mansel was killed. His granddaughter Elen by her marriage to John Price second son of John Price of Cwrt y Carne (on the left bank of Afon Llwchwr) brought the Gellihir estate to the long line of Price. His grandfather Rhys ab Ifan of Ynys y Maerdy, Briton Ferry, and Cwrt y Carne had married Elizabeth daughter of David Mansel, and one of his sons, John Price (ap Rhys) of Cwrt y Carne was Crown Commissioner for the lands of the dissolved Abbey of Neath (1575). In 1634 William Price, Esquire, of Gellihir was Sheriff of Glamorgan.

This cell of Cromwellian supporters, Dawkin, Price and Bowen (ancestors of Elizabeth Bowen, the Irish novelist, of Bowen's Court in County Cork, named after Court House) were behind the Baptist foundation and John Myles at Ilston.

1662:-"Evan Lewis a prisoner about to be released is a most dangerous person and took part against the late King." He fled to Elizabeth Price in Glamorgan who entertained him as servant to her son John Price, one of the Judges who condemned Col. Gerrard and Dr. Hewitt to death. A daughter Jane became the wife of Col. Phillip Jones later of Ffonmon Castle. Catherine her sister became the wife of Col. Henry Bowen of Llanelen.

In 1651 John Price was on the Bench of the High Court of Justice and in 1655 arranged the Cromwellian Charter of Swansea. In 1658 he was a member of the Commission to protect the person of Cromwell. An Indenture dated 12 May, 1679, is for a lease from Leyson Price of a messuage and lands at Cwm Mawr to build an Independent Chapel there. This was the beginning of Crwys Chapel and the Price family were members.

John Watkins of Pen-yr-Wrlodd, in County Brecon, came to Gower after a duel when he killed his antagonist. He married Anne daughter of Evan Lewis and his wife, daughter of John Price. He died in 1708 and there is a memorial tablet in Ilston Church. He had been Steward of his Grace the Duke of Beaufort and also to two Earls of Leicester.

Sir Gabriel Powell married a Gellihir daughter, Mary Price. He was Recorder of Swansea and Steward to the Duke of Beaufort.

There is an outside memorial tablet fixed to the east wall of the vestry at Ilston to Joseph Pryce of Gellihir. Mary's father, who died in 1785, aged 60 years. It says he was "religious without hypocrisy, humble without meanness, charitable without ostentation, humane, benevolent, hospitable, an affectionate husband, indulgent father, sincere friend, impartial magistrate, his life exemplary, his death happy. Quod Mori Potuit".

Gellihir is marked on Malkin's map as a gentleman's house, but on the 13 January, 1788, it was destroyed by fire and Sir Gabriel Powell (knighted 1800) and his wife, Mary Pryce (d. 1793) moved to Fairwood Lodge and to the new Heathfield in 1793.

Through Laetitia Pryce, born 1812 and married to Nathaniel Cameron of Erracht, the estate passed to the first Reform Mayor of Swansea of 1836-37. They had ten daughters and lived at Danygraig House (now pulled down). He was the son of Sir Alan Cameron who raised the 79th Cameron Highlanders in 1793 and 1798 and Ann

Phillips of Slebech Hall, Pembrokeshire, daughter of a wealthy sugar planter in the West Indies. The Penrice estate wished to acquire the lands of Gellihir and were very angry at the sale when they passed to the Vivians. Relics of their possession are the Cornish granite gate posts in north Gower.

Sid Porter, an old man in 1954, remembered Lord Swansea as landlord and described the ruined mansion to me as a "Toff's Place", John M. Leeder & Son auctioned the estate in lots in 1919.

In this long history names well known to us recur apart from Gellihir; Bryngwas, Cwrt-y-Carne, Killan, Park-le-Breos, Mor Parc, Langrove, Kilvrough, Court House and Llanelen. The families lived, inter-married and died through turbulent times and many were heavily involved in the troubles.

It is a long story and I have been able to refer in brief only to a few of the people but in particular I like to imagine Sisyl, daughter of Ifan ab Owen, coming on horse back with her bridal cavalcade maybe along the old road through Gellihir Wood on her way to Ilston Church to be married to Hopkin in the mid-fifteenth century. This is the overgrown road, to the entrance of which the Naturalists have recently placed a very solid and handsome wooden gate.

Iorwerth Hughes Jones, *Gower XIX*, 1968.

GELLIHIR

Descent of Dawkin to Price and to Cameron

Sir Wm. Langton = Eva, daughter of Lord William de Breos, Lord of Sweynsey and Gower. Lord of Langrove. Henllys and Gellihir, temp. Edward II.
|
Dawkin Langton
|
Robert David Langton
|
Walter Dawkin
|
Evan Dawkin
|
Thomas Dawkin
|
Hopkin Dawkin = Sisyl, heiress of Ifan ab Owen of Kellyhir.
|
David Dawkin = daughter of Thomas William Jenkin of Glyn Nedd.
|
Hopkin Dawkin = Elen, daughter of Gethyn ap Howel Melin of Gower. ob. 1554.
Wm. Hopkin Dawkin = Margaret, daughter of Henry Barrett of Pendine. ob. 1564.
Jenkin Dawkin of Gellihir ob. 1581 = Elizabeth, daughter of Wm. Jenkin of Baglan by Eliz., daughter of Sir George Mathew.
|
Elen = John Price, 2nd son of John Price of Cwrt y Carne, viv, 1594, will proved 1623.
|
William Price = Elizabeth, daughter of Humphrey Lloyd of Llwyn Adam. viv. 1610, of gellihir.
|
John Price = Cecilia, daughter of Rhys Arney of Nash, Sheriff 1647. M.P. for
Gellihir   Cardiff 1654/5 and 1656/9.
|
William Price
|
Joseph Pryce of Killan, will 5 Feb., 1766, makes bequests to poor of Killan hamlet in parish of Llanrhidian.
|
Maththew Pryce of Cwrt y Carne.
|
Joseph Pryce, d. 1785.
|
Mary, d. 1793 = Gabriel Powel of Swansea. Mayzod Eliz. = Rev. J. Powel Cuny.
|
Laetitia Pryce 1812-49 = Nathaniel Cameron, first Mayor of Swansea, of Danygraig House, 1836-37.
|
Nathaniel Pryce Cameron of Murton House, Bishopston, d. 1899.

(From *Gellihir* by Iorwerth Hughes Jones)

5. *Plas House*

Under the Tudors, the Swansea branch of the Herbert family acquired great political power. Sir George Herbert (d. 1570), Steward of the Lordship of Gower, was the first Sheriff of the new county of Glamorgan in 1541, and the shire's first Member of Parliament in 1542. His younger brother, William, was made Earl of Pembroke (second creation) in 1551. Another member of the family, Sir John Herbert (d. 1617), later achieved fame as a courtier and diplomatist. The family home was Plas House:

The Manor House of Swansea formerly stood in the block formed by Castle Bailey Street, Caer Street and Goat Street, and extended some distance beyond Temple Street, but a fringe of small houses divided it from both Castle Street and Caer Street. A good model, made before it was destroyed, is now in the Royal Institution, and there is a picture at Singleton which shews it was a building of Elizabethan character with a very unusual octagaonal shaped tower.

There is no record of its first construction; probably the greater part was erected or rebuilt by Sir Mathew Cradock, as may be inferred from the terms of his will. His arms, with those of the Herberts and of the Earl of Worcester, appeared over the main gateway, destroyed when Temple Street was made. The rest of the house was pulled down in 1840, the materials removed, and for the most part re-erected at Singleton Farm.

Thomas, who died young in 1736, was the last of the Herberts who lived at the Plas House; at his death the male line became extinct. It is doubtful if the house was ever occupied again; at the time it was pulled down part was used for the ignoble purpose of barn and stable. During the alteration to Messrs Ben Evans' premises (1897) part of the S. W. wall and the projecting gable as shown in the model, with a large square-headed window, were once more exposed to view and taken down; these were probably the last fragments of the old house. It was then noticed that the small houses in Caer Street appeared to have been built over a filled-in ditch.

Col. George Grant Francis draws attention to the fact that though the Manor House was not supposed to have been erected earlier than Henry VIII, none of the coins found in 1840 in the building are later than Edward II, and infers that part of the building was older than it was considered to be.

Col. W. Ll. Morgan, *Antiquarian Survey of East Gower*, 1899.

6.   *Bennet of Kittlehill*

Here lye ye Bodies of John Bennet of Kittle-Hill, Esq., and of his son, John Bennet, by Mayzod his wife, daughter to the Rev. Richard Portrey, A. M. Rector of Rhosilly and Ystradgunlys, by Catherine, sole daughter of Morgan Aubrey of Yniskedwin, Esq., who erected this monumnet out of a due and affectionate regard to the memory of her husband, who died October 21, 1723, aged 63. And of her son who died November ye 21st, 1726, aged 34.

—In Pennard Church.

7.   *Cradock of Cheriton*

The Cradocks of Cheriton were a junior line, proceeding it, it is said, from *Robert* ap Evan, deriving from Einion ap Collwyn, while Sir Mathew Cradock of Swansea was descended from *Gwilim* ap Evan, an elder brother. These Cradocks settled at Cheriton about the time of Henry VII., by marriage of David Cradock with the heiress of Philip Delabere of that place, and maintained their surname in the male line for several generations.

They inter-married with Mansells, Flemings, Popkins, and Bassetts. Philip Cradock, the fifth possessor of Cheriton, sold that place "about 1657 to Thomas Philip of Swansey" (J. H.'s MS). His great-gr. son, Philip Cradock, is described as of Tir-Coch, and living in 1699, having *m*. Susan, dau. of Harry Mansel, Esq., by whom he had a son, Morgan, "a priest." The writer of the MS. just cited has this note respecting the arms of the Cradocks: "memdm. That the above-named Evan ap Cradock killed a monstrous, upon which occasion the arms were altered."

Thomas Nicholas, *History and Antiquities of Glamorgan*, 1874.

8.   *The Great House, Cheriton*

Formerly the Residence of the Cradocks of Cheriton

About sixty years ago there were to be seen not far from Cheriton Bridge extensive remains of what was once a very fine mansion. Little is now left save a portion of an ivy-covered wall with an archway in it. The late Mr. George Holland, of Cwm Ivy, who died in his 87th year, informed me that he remembered the house well—that it was large, and had a porch. On a stone over the outer doorway there were two letters, one of which was a C; he could not recollect the other. Mr. John Guy, of Cheriton, grocer, since deceased, was able to give a better account of these letters, and remembered the one that Mr. Holland had forgotten, which was an M, and supposed that M C meant "Made at Cheriton." They were probably the initials of Morgan Cradock, gent., who resided here in 1603, temp. James I.

When the house was taken down by the late Henry Lucas, Esq., about thirty years ago, a square stone, having a stag in high relief carved upon it, was removed from the doorway of the porch and conveyed to Stouthall, where it still remains, though in a somewhat mutilated condition, as shown in the engraving, which was made from a drawing given me by Mrs. Wood.

Mr. Holland described the house as being much out of repair in his time; but some of the rooms were in good order, and had oak wainscotting and gilt cornices. The latter had been whitewashed over. It was well supplied with water conveyed through lead pipes. The windows were all fitted with freestone jambs and mullions. A few years ago I found a piece of stone (resembling that of which a quarry is said to exist near Cil Ivor, in the parish of Llanrhidian), with some carving on it, placed for the hearthstone of a cottage in the village. It had evidently formed part of a chimney piece in the Great House.

In an old Parish Terrier, dated 1720, mention is made of Cheriton House Mill. This must have been a small water grist mill attached to the Great House; but the old people have no recollection of it, and the site of it is unknown.

The Rev. John Williams, M.A., Rector of Cheriton and Prebendary of Brecon, is said to have lived in the Great House. He died in 1787. His wife, Anne Lucas, daughter of Richard Lucas, Esq., of Peartree [Fairyhill] in the parish of Reynoldston, survived him, and was buried in her husband's grave in the chancel of Cheriton Church. They had three daughters, Elizabeth, Barbara, and Anne. The latter married the celebrated Dr. Spry, Rector of St. Mary-le-bone, London. The others remained single, and after living some years in the Great House, went to reside in Swansea, where they died, and were buried by the side of their parents.

The above-mentioned John Williams succeeded his father, the

Rev. John Williams, who was also incumbent of the parish, and lived at Glebe House . . .

The Rev. J. D. Davies, *A History of West Gower,*
Vol. II, 1879.

9.   *Price of Penlle'rgaer and Nydfywch*

Of the sept of Bleddyn ap Maenarch, Lord of Brecknock when the Normans under Newmarch attacked that country, AD 1091 or thereabouts, was David Evan *Fwya* (the "greater", or perhaps "senior"), whose father was Gwilyn *Ddu.* A junior gr. grandson of his, William ap David, founded the family of Nydfywch[1]; and a senior gr. grandson, brother of the former, named Evan ap David, was of Penlle'rgaer.

To Evan ap David succeeded at Penlle'rgaer his son Griffith, his grandson Rees, and gr. grandson John *ap Rees,* with whom originated the name Price. He lived in the time of Elizabeth; married Elizabeth, daughter of Roger Seys, Esq., of Boverton, Attorney-General for South Wales, by Elizabeth Voss, heiress of Boverton. His son Griffith Price succeeded at Penlle'rgaer, and was followed by four generations of his descendants (Thomas Price was Sheriff of Glamorganshire 1739), under the last of whom, Griffith Price, Esq., Barrister-at-law, issue male failed.

He married Jane, daughter and heir of Henry Matthew of Nydfywch, (thus reuniting the two families, the latter having adopted the surname Matthew from Matthew ap John ap William of that place), and had a daughter Mary who died without issue. He married a second time, but had no issue. By his will he devised the Penlle'rgaer estate to his cousin John Llewelyn, Esq., of Ynysgerwyn near Neath (Sheriff of Glamorgan in 1790), in whose family it still continues.

Thomas Nicholas, *History and Antiquities of
Glamorgan,* 1874.

10.   *The Salte House*

. . . On death of his father (notorious John Lucas of The Salte House), Philip Lucas and his wife, Joan of Essex, went from The Great

---

1.   No stone of this ancient house above the Afon Llan in Llangyvelach parish remains, but the name survives in a nearby bank still called 'Graig Neddfwch.' Until the end of the nineteenth century, snowdrops from the gardens appeared each spring.

House, Hortown, taking themselves unto the patrimonial mansion, The Salte House, Port-Eynon, his mother going unto The Great House, Hortown, the Dooer house, and this custom prevailed in The Salte House branch of the Lucas family for many generations . . .

Lucas Family Annotation No 1, 1826.

IX

Legend, Folklore, Old Customs

1. *Taliesin in Gower*

Late I return, O violent, colossal, reverberant, eavesdropping
  sea.
My country is here. I am foal and violet. Hawthorn breaks
  from my hands.
I watch the inquisitive cormorant pry from the praying rock
  of Pwlldu,
Then skim to the gulls' white colony, to Oxwich's cockle-
  strewn sands.

I have seen the curlew's triangular print, I know every inch
  of his way.
I have gone through the door of the foundered ship, I have
  slept in the winch of the cave
With pine-leg and unicorn-spiral shell secreting the colours
  of day;
I have been taught the script of the stones, and I know the
  tongue of the wave.

I witness here in a vision the landscape to which I was born,
Three smouldering bushes of willow, like trees of fire, and
  the course
Of the river under the stones of death, carrying the ear of
  corn
Withdrawn from the mood-dead chaos of rocks overlooking
  its secret force.

I see, a marvel in Winter's marshes, the iris break from its
  sheath
And the dripping branch in the ache of sunrise frost and
  shadow redeem
With wonder of patient, living leaf, while Winter, season of
  death,
Rebukes the sun, and grinds out men's groans in the voice of
  its underground stream.

Yet now my task is to weigh the rocks on the level wings of
    a bird,
To relate these undulations of time to a kestrel's motionless
    poise.
I speak, and the soft-running hour-glass answers; the core of
    the rock is a third:
Landscape survives, and these holy creatures proclaim their
    regenerate joys.

I know this mighty theatre, my footsole knows it for mine.
I am nearer the rising pewit's call than the shiver of her own
    wing.
I ascend in the loud waves' thunder, I am under the last of
    the nine.
In a hundred dramatic shapes I perish, in the last I love and
    sing.

All that I see with my sea-changed eyes is a vision too great for
    the brain.
The luminous country of auk and eagle rocks and shivers to
    earth.
In the hunter's quarry this landscape died; my vision restores
    it again.
These stones are prayers; every boulder is hung on a breath's
    miraculous birth.

Gorse breaks on the steep cliff-side, clings earth, in patches
    blackened for sheep,
For grazing fired; now the fair weather comes to the ravens'
    pinnacled knoll.
Larks break heaven from the thyme-breathing turf; far under
    flying through sleep,
Their black fins cutting the rainbow surf, the porpoises
    follow the shoal.

They are gone where the river runs out, there where the
    breakers divide
The lacework of Three Cliffs Bay in a music of two seas;
A heron flaps where the sandbank holds a dyke to the twofold
    tide,
A wave-encircled isthmus of sound which the white bird-
    parliament flees.

Rhinoceros, bear and reindeer haunt the crawling glaciers of
    age
Behold in the eye of the rock, where a javelin'd arm held stiff
Withdrawn from the vision of flying colours, reveals, like
    script on a page,
The unpassing moment's arrested glory, a life locked fast in
    the cliff.

Now let the great rock turn. I am safe with an ear of corn,
A repository of light once plucked, from all men hidden away.
I have passed through a million changes. In a butterfly
    coracle borne,
My faith surmounting the Titan. I greet the prodigious bay.

I celebrate you, marvellous forms. But first I must cut the
    wood.
Exactly measure the strings, to make manifest what shall be.
All Earth being weighed by an ear of corn, all heaven by
    a drop of blood.
How shall I loosen this music to the listening, eavesdropping
    sea?

Vernon Watkins, *The Death Bell,* 1954.

2. *The Red Lady of Paviland*

The red ochre, which stains her skeleton, is said to be an imitation
of blood, imparting a specious immortality. Specious! I spent the best
part of a week with the Lady. An ivory armlet had suggested a
woman's skeleton; now it is said to be a young man's. And I slept with
her each night in a cave! A *Guide to Gower* does not make the
mistake: "Leaping from crag to crag, the Red Lady of the Cavern
goes bounding on with wild and discordant screams, her long red
mantle streaming weird-like in the ghastly light of the sickly moon."
But how unlike the Lady I met on Yellow Top!

Under the headland was Paviland Cave, where also were discovered the remains of an elephant. We never descended; her burial-
place had memories for her, having been her home. Our walks were
mainly on the cliffs. One morning, however, I took her to Arthur's
Stone on Cefn-y-Bryn, imagining a monument three or four
thousand years old might edge me a little closer to her Paleolithic

Age; but she was not interested; to anyone buried in a cave a Bronze Age cromlech may seem ultra-modern.

Another time we walked on Rossili Down, but she was unaffected by its charm; the climate tropical in her day, stunted heather was a poor substitute for the jungle into which she had ventured as a girl, and rabbits were small deer compared with the animals her father trapped. She told me that after living for days on nuts, shell-fish and snails they made a great feast of a trapped animal. That night such a feast we had ourselves in our cave; if I remember rightly, the rhinoceros was tough, but of the elephant little was left.

Our parting was sudden. We had come round Brandy Cove to a cliff overlooking Pwlldu Bay. It was full of blue pebbles. Perhaps the Red Lady had an antipathy to blue, for she vanished. I felt it was more than a personal loss; I was bereaved of the adorable name, the Red Lady of Paviland. "What's in a name?" asked Juliet; she could not have cared greatly for her Romeo.

Andrew Young, *The New Poly-Olbion:*
Topographical Excursions, 1967.

3. *The Gower Wassail Song*

This was a song for Twelfth Night, January 6th—the old Christmas Day. The company would take their "wassail," in a can, around the villages, and sing at every door they thought might open to them. As can be seen, the occupants of the house also took part in the song. The contents of the wassail were a guarded secret, but some of the contents are mentioned in the song—good ale and cake, nutmeg and ginger, elderberry, apple, butter (old Colly) etc.:

Sung by the wassailiers outside the house.

A wassail, a wassail, throughout this town,
Our cup it is white and our ale it is brown;
Our wassail is made of good ale and cake,
Some nutmeg and ginger, the best we could get.

Chorus

Fal del dal, lal del dal de dal, lal de dal de dal,
lal de dal de dee,

Fal del dairal, lal de dah de, sing touralaydoh.
Our wassail is made of an old'berry bough,
Although my good neighbour will sing unto thou,
Beside all others we have apples in store,
Pray let us come in for 'tis cold by the door.
   Fal de dal . . .

We know by the moon that we are not too soon,
And we know by the sky that we are not too high,
And we know by the stars that we are not too far,
And we know by the ground that we are within sound.
   Fal de dal . . .

We're a company resigned for to drink of your ale,
Out of that little kildekin that's next to the wale,
We want none of your pale beer nor none of your smale,
But a drop from the kildekin that's next to the wale.
   Fal del dal . . .

Now master and mistress, if you are within,
Pray send out your maid with her lilywhite skin,
For to open the door without more delay,
Our time it is precious and we cannot stay.
   Fal de dal . . . .

   Sung by the family inside the house:

You've brought here your wssail which is very well known,
But I can assure you we've as good of our own;
As for your jolly wassail we care not one pin,
But it's for your good company we'll let you come in.

   (The door opens; the chorus is sung by those within
   and without; the wassailers come in and put their
   wassail by the fire to warm). After drinking
   the wassailers sing on leaving . . .

Here's a health to old Colly and her crooked horn,
May God send her master a good crop of corn,
Of barley and wheat and all sorts of grain,
May God send her mistress a long life to reign.
   Fal de dal . . .

Now master and mistress, thanks to you we'll give,
And for our jolly wassail as long as we live,
And if we should live till another New Year,
Perhaps we may come and see who do live here.
Fal de dal . . .

J. Mansel Thomas, *Gower I,* 1948.

4. *The Haunted Well at Lagadranta*

About one hundred years ago, a little old woman called at a farm-house at Lagadranta, and asked for the loan of a sieve, which, as my informant gravely remarked, "was to sifty gold, you know." The mistress of the house told her that she had not got such a thing. "Yes, you have," said the other; "and it is now over the vat straining the hops." Suspecting from this that she was one of the "Very folks,"[1] the sieve was handed to her immediately. Some days after this she returned, bringing the sieve with her. "Here," says she, "is your sieve; and as you were so good as to lend it me, the biggest cask in your house shall never be without beer." She then left, and being watched, was seen to enter the well and disappear.

This was the story as I first heard it related, but another version very similar to the above, gives the reason why the supply of beer was stopped. The fairy (for such she was) had laid it down as a condition, that the mistress of the house should never mention what had been told her. Of course she could not keep the secret, and after that the cask was soon empty.

The household at Lagadranta, for some reason or other, seems to have been in great favour, with the "good people," for not only did that happen which is related about the beer, but a short time previous, a servant girl belonging to the house used to find a new shilling in her pail every morning before she went to milk. This continued for some time, till at last, thinking it might be a trick of her employers to test her honesty, she mentioned the circumstance to them; but as everybody denied all knowledge of it, it was put down to the "Very folks." The girl, however, never had any more shillings. It seems to have been a rule among the "good people" to discontinue their kind offices whenever the recipients of their favours spoke of them to any other person.

1. The Fairy Folks.

I once asked an old woman, who was over ninety years of age, and knew many things about the "Very folks" if she could give any reason how it was that they were never seen now. Her answer was very peculiar. "Well," she said, "I suppose they have gone under the earth." A very singular opinion prevails in Ireland respecting the fairies. There they are supposed to be the angels who stood neuter when Satan rebelled against Jehovah, and that their destiny, which is now unknown, will be fixed at the Day or Judgement.

While dwelling on this subject I must not forget to mention the fairy ground at the foot of Cwm Ivy Tor. This used to be a very favourite spot for the little people to meet in former days. As in other places so here, their usual employment was dancing, and they were frequently seen on moonlight nights enjoying themselves in this way, frisking about, and all dressed in scarlet and green. It was, however, very dangerous to interfere with them on these occasions. A story is told of a man who once upon a time was bold enough to step into the ring where they were dancing, and was immediately ran through the foot with a fork. He was lame for many days, and could get no ease, till at last he consulted a wise woman, who told him to go and humbly put his foot again in the ring where he had the hurt, he did so, and he soon got well.

The Rev. J. D. Davies, *A History of West Gower,*
Vol. II, 1879.

5. *The Horse's Head*

The custom of going about with the Horse's Head at Christmas time is not peculiar to Wales, and answers to what in Kent is called "Hodening," the Welsh call it Mari Llwyd . . .

The practice is still kept up in Gower. Here the horse's head is profusely decorated with gay coloured ribbons, and a white sheet being attached to it, a lad gets underneath, the head being supported in the manner described above; a halter fitted to the skull is held by one of the party, who then go round the village, calling at the houses, the person concealed by the sheet causes much amusement and some terror to the inmates, by making the head snap and bite in every direction. The quaint old carol called, "The twelve joys of Mary," is usually sung. It is not unlikely that this curious custom of going about at Christmas time with the horse's head, may have some allusion to the birth of Our Saviour in the stable at Bethlehem.

I should mention, that when the Christmas festivities are over, these gamesome youngsters with mock gravity, bury the horse's head in some very secret place, known only to themselves, and at the ensuing Christmas dig it up again, and thus the same skull is made to do duty for many years.

The Rev. J. D. Davies, *A History of West Gower,*
Vol. II, 1879.

6. The Legend of Pennard Castle

There once lived in this Castle a bold and warlike chieftain, ever ready to rush madly to battle; he was a hasty and imperious man that feared no power visible or unvisible—rash and fierce in all his doings, admitting or acknowledging no power but might; war was his delight, and oft would he lead his warriors far away from this their homes (for tradition says that where these sand-hills now stand once stood a host of dwelling-places—a large hamlet or town) and return loaded with spoil. In those days every man's hand was against his fellow, and the fame of the chieftain of Pennard resounded through the land.

It appears that some of the Princes of North Wales were at deadly strife with each other, and one of them solicited this chieftain to join his side, promising him a rich reward. Nothing loth, but rather delighted, away marched the warrior with his fierce and savage band, and soon was engaged in the deadly feud. They say that the struggle was furious and long, but that the wonderous prowess of this chief, and the daring bravery of his warriors, at length turned the scale of victory in favour of the chieftain for whom he fought. It was now his time to receive his reward, and as he had to make his request, he asked for the daughter of the prince, a young and beauteous girl. It could not be denied—twice in the hot fury of the battle had he saved her father's life, and also had sacrificed a host of his staunch and bravest warriors, whose blood, he said, was as dear as his own.

The old prince called the young and timid maiden to him, and told her of the Pennard chieftain's request. She looked around, (for the chieftain was at hand), her heart fluttering like a bird, for the name of this chieftain was so terrible that she almost feared to look; but there was no cause for trembling—the hot blood in his veins flowed quietly on its course—the mad fire of passion leaped not from his eye—but love beamed in his glances, and his dark eyes seemed soft as a woman's. As she gazed on him love took the place of fear, and with a timid reluctance she consented to become his wife.

They were united at once, and a herald posted off to the Castle to prepare for the lady's reception. Proud, indeed, was the chief as he bore his young and blushing bride to his romantic wild fortress, and as they neared home he grew more and more elated. The evening they reached the Castle the wild rejoicings began—furious was the revelry, and the very walls shook with the sound of music and song. It was a calm sweet moonlight night, and the midnight hour was fast approaching; the wine cup passed merrily in the Castle, and cheer and shout rung joyously and loud. The sentinel pacing round the Castle walls paused once or twice in his walk, for sounds such as he had never heard floated by on the breeze; it came not from the Castle, but from a little green spot where the moonlight was flickering with strange yet glorious rays.

Again he heard the sounds—it was as if it were a song, and then a chorus of tiny notes seemed to swell on the air. He thought it could not be anything of earth, so inimitable was the bewitching melody; he trembled, for a strange feeling came over him, and he ran and aroused the warder of the Castle, who listened and heard the same. The warder went to the banqueting room and told the chief, who was maddened with wine, but he came and listened and also heard, as did the others that accompanied him. "I'll see," he said, "what it is? Come, men, we'll spoil the song, I warrant—buckle on your armour, we fight with man or spirit."

Down ran the wild and drunken troop, and there, on a little grassy knoll, dancing in the silvery moonlight, was a host of fairy elves. Among them rushed the grim and bearded warriors, and foremost was the chieftain, with his sword gleaming like lightning flashing in the moonlight, but it was vain to cut and thrust at bodiless creation, palpable to vision but not to touch; he grew as savage as a tiger baulked of its prey, and plunged with fearful vengeance into their very midst. His soldiers also clashed their spears and stabbed, but in vain—they panted and foamed with rage, when a low voice was heard saying, "Proud chief! thou warrest against those that shall now destroy thee; thou hast wantonly spoiled and marred our innocent sport—thy lofty Castle shall be a ruin, and thy proud township shall be no more."

He rose his wand—at once a tiny spirit swept its course towards the sky, and sang a strange incantation which rattled on the breeze. Clouds of sand came with whirlwind speed, overwhelming all before it; thicker and faster it came—pile upon pile— and in a few minutes the strong Castle was a ruin, and buried in the sand were the huts and houses of those warriors of the Castle.

C. D. Morgan, *Wanderings In Gower,*
1886 ed.

7. *The Comortha*

Originally it had been a free benevolence to relieve the victims of misfortune and impoverishment, but later it had been applied quite overtly by the contumacious lords and barons of the Welsh Marches to obtain funds for the maintenance and benefit of their retainers and mercenaries. The Act of Union that sealed the fate of the Lords Marcher had tried to deal a death blow to the system of *comortha* by expressly prohibiting it. But a custom that had proved its value as an instrument for raising money was too resilient to be suppressed by an Act of Parliament . . .

In the Lordship of Gower, the position of the tenantry was pitiable in the extreme in the face of this predatory practice. There the *comortha* was inflicted on them some twelve or thirteen times a year, generally by gentry of reduced circumstances who could hardly afford to marry off their daughters or keep up appearances. Despite the prohibition of the custom by the Lord of Gower, the Earl of Worcester, cattle, corn and money continued to pass into the hands of the impoverished squires through fear of reprisals.

G. Dyfnallt Owen, *Elizabethan Wales: The Social Scene,* 1962.

8. *Penrice Market*

In 1644 Charles II granted by charter to Sir Edward Mansel, Bart., the right to hold four fairs annually at Penrice on 6th May, 6th July, 6th September and 29th November. Also two weekly markets, on Tuesday and Friday, "at the village of Penrice, aforesaid, to be held for ever":

Both market and fair have now disappeared; the latter has been transferred in recent times to Reynoldston, and the market to Swansea.

The most aged person now living, does not remember the market twice a week at Penrice; there are some traditions of it, and that is all. It seems strange to us to think of people taking their butter, poultry and eggs, etc., for sale to Penrice, paying for their pitching (*picagium*) just in the same way as they now do in Swansea market, but such was undoubtedly the case, as the foregoing document plainly shows.

But we must remember that the population of Swansea in 1664 was very small; in 1563 it only amounted to about 900 inhabitants; so that in point of fact, as a centre for feeding purposes, and the disposal of commodities of every kind, the market at Penrice was even more necessary for the inhabitants of West Gower than Swansea was, and infinitely more convenient, when we remember the state of the roads, and the absence of all wheeled vehicles. Time and circumstances have, however, so altered the condition of things, that at the present day, Swansea, with its 100,000 inhabitants, consumes the whole produce of the Peninsula, and a great deal more besides,

This interesting old document gives us some idea of the changes that time brings in its train. Up to the year 1840, or thereabouts, Gower, as an agricultural district, was in a state of complete stagnation. The Gower farmer reaped and sowed, and ploughed and mowed, as his forefathers had done ages before him. In those days the land was ploughed with a wooden plough, and the only bit of iron in its composition was the share. A metal plough is now in use, all made of iron, and the only bit of wood in it is the two wooden handles. Although I am not old enough to recollect the old wooden plough, locally called the "zull," I can perfectly well remember the time when it was the custom to pound the young furze for the horses and cattle on a large flat stone with a wooden beetle. To this succeeded the old fashioned chaff-cutter, and hard work it was to turn that chaff-cutter; it was almost as bad as the beetle. The next improvement was the horse thrashing machine, and when the Gower farmer got that, it was supposed that human ingenuity could go no further.

We have now got the steam thrashing-machine, the reaping, mowing, hay-making and raking machines; and the traction engine and steam saw traverse the roads; truly we may exclaim: "Old things have passed away, behold all things have become new."

The Rev. J. D. Davies, *A History of West Gower,*
Vol. IV, 1894.

9.   *A Gower Fairing Song*

The farmer's boots are oakey and kittlebegs as well,
He wears a Sunday collar and a waistcoat like a swell;
Just now the spleets are idle, and the chimney corner there
Has a settle that is empty, for they're gwan to the fair.

The little pony's neighing in a newly-painted cart,
And tapping with its well-shod hoofs all anxious for a start;
Now they have put their weight down and settled in their
    seats
And left behind the whitpot and the lava bread and spleets.

They feel that they are vitte as they pass the pilmy roads,
And see a cavey cottager a-heaping in the loads;
The little pony's trotting as it carries them away
To the summer fair at Coity, and its hoof-beats seem to say,

> The Franklins and the Aces
> With their ruddy shining faces,
> The Tuckers and the Eynons,
> The Bevans and the Beynons
> Are gwan to the fair,
> Are gwan to the fair.

There be bargains to be buying and the selling should
    be good,
You casn't live for pleasure when you earn your livelihood;
Still there's real clever fairing to be got when you get theere,
Pies of mutton chopped, with currants, and a mug of Gower
    beere.

The cock towards the steeple a-climbing will be seen,
And lots of fun at Coity and dancing on the green;
And there the lads and lasses a-courting all will be,
And quiet joys for bright boys of the age of ninety-three.

There be many a vitte lello full of mischief at the fair,
To kiss a pretty gello and caffle all her hair;
They'll buy a stick with ribbons and sit beside the moon,
And folk will smile and whisper, "There's a bidding
    wedding soon."

And the evening shadows falling, they will hurry back again,
And sit within the farmer's cart while vather takes the rein;
The little pony's trotting as it carries them away
From the summer fair at Coity and its hoof-beats seem to
    say

> The Franklins and the Aces
> With their ruddy shining faces,
> The Tuckers and the Eynons,
> The Bevans and the Beynons,
> Are gwan to the fair,
> Are gwan to the fair.

E. Howard Harris, *A Swansea Boy*, 1959.

Oakey	— greased	cavey	— humble
kittlebegs	— gaiters	lello	— a card
spleets	— knitting needles	caffle	— tangle
whitpot	— Gower flour dish	Coity	— Coity Green,
vitte	— clever, smart		Llangennith.
pilmy	— dusty		

10.   *The Gower Bidding Wedding*

To St. David's Parish Church, Llanddewi, in February 1906 came the last beading or bidding wedding in Gower. These had been celebrated for many centuries with much feasting and merriment. The brides, as both bride and bridegroom were called, usually postponed their wedding day after the Banns had been called, thereby adding to the excitement as to who would be invited or beaded.

The wedding-house, where it was planned to hold the celebrations was not always the bride's home, but was chosen for convenience or because it had a large kitchen where the estimated number of guests could be entertained, and brewing commenced without delay.

When the wedding day was fixed, a beader was appointed to bead or invite the wedding guests and this was a ceremony in itself. The beader visited each house in the village and neighbouring villages, and discharged his duties with much pomp and phraseology, designed to impress the rustic mind, and incidentally to advertise the "good meat and tendance" to be expected at the wedding feast.

The guests gave, or heaved a substantial sum of money or kind, which all helped to fill the couple's purse and enabled them to set up housekeeping. When the money was heaved, it was contributed by young unmarried folk on the understanding that when their turn came to be married, the money would be returned in like manner. Heaving was paid at the wedding dinner, the amount being noted and recorded by the beader.

On the eve of the wedding day, relatives and friends visited the house bringing gifts of currant loaves, always referred to as "present". These were cut into slices and sold at the wedding supper at about ½d a slice. The eager purchasers were young men who presented them surreptitiously to the maidens of their choice. Later in the evening the girls displayed their collection of slices of present, and the possessor of the largest number was declared the belle of the ball.

The morning of the wedding day saw the brides leaving the wedding house, accompanied by their guests in procession to the church led by a fiddler. After the ceremony, they re-formed and marched to the local inn, where the brides officially thanked the innkeeper for his generosity in allowing them to "steal his trade". After leaving the inn, the procession was greeted by gunshots, and was several times halted by people holding a rope stretched across the road. This "chaining of the brides" was accompanied by a demand for a money toll, which was gladly paid. The rope was then lowered, and the merry company proceeded on their way to the wedding house, where dinner awaited them.

Tin-meat, mutton pies baked in the brick oven was the traditional dish at these wedding feasts, and at the ball which followed nearly everyone from the village attended, even if they had not been invited to the actual wedding ceremony. Partakers of supper bought their tin-meat at the table, one tin, costing five shillings, being sufficient for four persons. After supper the guests went to the barn, where the fiddler tuned up in preparation for the ball, which continued into the small hours.

The dancers rang the changes on the horn-pipe and the four-handed reel, and, for once in a while, the old threshing floor, accustomed to the slow and heavy rhythm of swinging flails, resounded to the quick beat of dancing feet. The evening sometimes ended with a fight, which may have been the climax of a long-missed grievance.

Vernon Richards, 1973.

11.   The Last Bidding Wedding

Parish of Llanddewi (with Knelston)

Vicar and Rector: Rev. John Hughes, B.A.

Marriage. Feb. 8, George Francis Nicholas, of Hardings' Down, Llangennith, to Margaret Anne Tucker, of Old Henllys, Llanddewi.

This marriage was looked forward to with great interest for some weeks prior to its celebration from the fact of it being a "Bidding Wedding," which is an old custom revived, but which has become almost obsolete, no marriage of the kind having for many years past taken place, so far as the writer is aware, in this part of the peninsula. In addition to the relatives and friends who attended the ceremony, and afterwards joined in the festivities, a great number came for miles around to see the bridal procession. Unfortunately, though they made every effort to enter the Church, they did not succeed in doing so, as it was more than full when they arrived. Another reason for the great interest in this marriage was the popularity of the bride. She was a special favourite, both in and out of the parish . . . The ceremony was partly choral, and Miss Wheeler kindly came and presided at the Harmonium.

The Gower Church Magazine, March 1906.

12.   The Last Days of Court Leet

I recall being present at one of the last of the Kilvrough Court Leets held at the Bishopston Valley Hotel. Then the deputy steward was the late Mr. C. J. C. Wilson, and the late Mr. Tom Jenkins appeared as agent.

When all presentments had been dealt with, the company retired to the converted barn across the yard of the hotel there to be regaled with a monumental meal, the deputy steward and the agent carving at two huge joints of meat, one at each end of the table, honest country fare for countrymen whose hard working days called for substantial food.

One of the early courts brought out a word which was later much used in discussions upon the faults of the old copyhold system. It was presented by the jurors that Thomas Penrice, Esq., late one of the freehold tenants of the manor, had died since the last court of the manor, seized of Knap, and divers other freehold tenements within the manor and that a fine of five shillings "in lieu of the Heriot," was therefore due to the Lord in respect thereof.

This was definitely a light fine when custom, which governed the law in such a matter, could have been very much more severe.

In another court the jurors were not so ready with an option.

When William Lewis, of Murton, died, "inasmuch as he died within the manor, a heriot of the best beast is due to the Lord in respect thereof."

The "heriot" was for long a sore point in the system. Technically, copyhold was tenure of the land by court roll, at the will of the Lord according to the custom of the manor. Thus a holder's title was evidenced by the court rolls of the manor, and the rights of the manor were in conformity with the immemorial customs of the manor.

The addition, "at the will of the Lord" served actually as a memorial of the derivation of this species of title from the estates granted in olden time to bondsmen, which were, naturally in those days, resumable at the pleasure of the Lord.

As the centuries passed, customs of the different manors varied. In some the lands were held for life only, but generally there was a customary right to renewal or to appoint a successor.

Descent, in some manors, was according to particular rules, but in most the ordinary rules of succession applied. Whatever was the custom in the particular manor, however, it could not be altered.

Under the system various money payments were due from the copyholder to the lord of the manor. They might, according to the custom of the manor, be rents, fines, payments on such occasions as alienation or succession, or heriots.

In the case of an heir succeeding, there was no surrender, but admittance to the roll of the manor upon payment of the customary fine. The heriot was a form of fine due to the lord upon the death of a person holding land of the manor. It could be the best beast, a jewel or a chattel that belonged to the dead person, or a money fine in lieu. This could be enforced by law. The origin of the heriot probably dates back to the days of the return of the horse and arms lent by the feudal lord to his tenant.

Claims for admittance to the roll of the manor had to be supported to the hilt. Thus we see in the case of Margaret Edwards who presented herself before Mr. John Gaskoin on March 7, 1857, she had to produce a copy of her father's will, and the will, in detail, had to

204 A GOWER ANTHOLOGY

be entered on the roll as evidence unassailable.

The will, couched in the language of the day, had a long preamble, but the scribe dutifully recorded it all. "In the name of God Amen," said David Jones, "I, David Jones, of Bishopston, in the parish of Bishopston, in the county of Glamorgan and diocese of St. David's, being of sound mind, memory, and understanding (praised be God for the same) and calling to mind the certainty of death and the great uncertainty of the time whereof, do make and ordain this to be my last will and testament in the manner and form following, that is to say in the first place I commend my soul in the hands of Almighty God, who gave it, and my body I commit to the earth to be decently buried at the discretion of my executrix hereafter named. And to such worldly estate as it has pleased Almighty God to entrust me with, I give and dispose therof as follows:"

Then came David Jones's wishes in regard to his "copyhold messuages, tenements or lands which are situate in Bishopston Hamlet and Murton Hamlet."

The record of the will is followed by that of the admission of both Margaret Edwards and her husband, Thomas Edwards, to the toll of tenants.

Throughout pages which can only be described as beautifully written are numerous such cases. Some of the wills recorded cover many pages with a maze of legal phraseology that the layman would find exceedingly difficult to follow.

Some, far less complicated, and the wishes of simple folk, are the products of unfettered minds, except perhaps for very human prejudices.

But now, of course, the last vestige of this old system in the manor of Bishopston has disappeared. The passing of the Law of Property Act in the early Twenties provided that every parcel of copyhold land should become enfranchised and freehold, subject, pending payment of compensation, to manorial incidents having money value such as fines and heriots, but free of other customary suits and services.

But even these fines and heriots had to cease either when, within five years after the Act came into operation there was agreement between the landlord and tenant upon the question of compensation, or when either served notice on the other to have compensation fixed by the Ministry of Agriculture, or, failing both, upon the expiry of ten years. Provision was made for the payment of compensation over a period of years.

Last record in the rolls of the Court Leet was on May 12, 1920, before the late Mr. C. J. C. Wilson, deputy steward for the then Lord of the Manor, Commander Algernon Edmund Penrice Lyons, while a later entry records a transaction resulting from the passing of the Act referred to a copyholder securing enfranchisement of his lands by payment of a small sum which suggested that the compensation payments made were by no means excessive.

George E. Long, *South Wales Evening Post,* March, 1957.

X

Epilogue

Ilston

The swallows are flying South.
They leave the familiar eaves.
It is the yellow month,
The time of broken leaves.

Nuts and blackberries fall.
Sloe and crab-apple tree
Still haunt a sunken wall
Whose windows none can see.

A leper's window there
Hides, and the stream runs slow
Under a town of air
Where tawny chestnuts blow.

Once a chapel was here.
Here before dawn they came.
Lit, in a withering year,
This altar's earlier flame.

Slow, the centuries crawled.
Time's caterpillar came,
Climbing the leaves grey-walled,
To eat away the name.

Leaves and the rose are strewn.
Not one fragment of glass
Breaks through the white cocoon
Of mist and rains that pass.

In the shadow of Ilston's yew
Spirits, purged of guilt,
Hear the dark rains renew
The house they have not built.

Vernon Watkins, *Gower V*, 1952.

Contributors

E. E. Allen
Lord Avebury (Sir John Lubbock)

John Beynon
Elizabeth Bowen
A. G. Bradley

William Camden
G. T. Clark

J. D. Davies
Latimer Davies
Margaret Davies
Walter Davies
Daniel Defoe
Thomas Dinely

David Evans
F. V. Emery

George Grant Francis
E. A. Freeman

Michael Gibbs
Giraldus Cambrensis
Stephen R. Glynne
Gordon T. Goodman
G. M. Griffiths
William Griffiths
Cyril Gwynn

Michael Hamburger
Isaac Hamon
E. Howard Harris
John Hughes

David Jones
Gwent Jones
Iorwerth Hughes Jones

E. H. Stuart Jones
Thomas Jones
W. H. Jones

Francis Kilvert

John Leland
Lewis Glyn Cothi
Samuel Lewis
J. E. Lloyd
George E. Long
R. L. T. Lucas

Benjamin Heath Malkin
Rice Merrick
C. D. Morgan
W. Llewellyn Morgan
Robert Morris

G. Dyfnallt Owen

Thomas Phaer
Olive Phillips
Gabriel Powell
T. B. Pugh

David Rees
William Rees
Vernon Richards
Tom Ridd
W. R. B. Robinson
W. C. Rogers
J. G. Rutter

Erasmus Saunders
Clarence A. Seyler
Henry Skrine
J. Beverley Smith
J. A. Steers

Dylan Thomas
Edward Thomas
J. Mansel Thomas
Horatio Tucker

Vernon Watkins
J. A. Webb
John Wesley
Henry Wigstead
William of Worcester
Glanmor Williams
John Williams
James Chapman Woods

Andrew Young